"Enthralling . . . Monroe has a knack for nosing a new story out of an old one, like a detective casting fresh eyes on a cold case."
—*The New York Times Book Review*

"Monroe maintains her implication—and her reader's—in what she describes, layering her chapters with personal anecdotes and alluding to a shared familiarity with the true-crime story's potent admixture of myth and intimacy, realness and simulacrum, chaos and clarity, violence and comfort."

—*Bookforum*

"In *Savage Appetites*, the pleasure comes from the way Monroe works backward, untangling the neat, tidy surface stories of her four subjects and embracing the nuance, messiness, and all-important context that an exploration into female desire requires. . . . The reader is left with the clues she's gathered and the insights she's made, to pick up and turn over, to solve or to obsess over—sort of like a crime scene."
—*The Texas Observer*

"Lively and well-turned."

—*Slate*

"[Monroe] has a unique ability to take a crime and go beyond the salacious facts and find the deeper cultural and political implications, without losing her ability to keep you reading with propulsive, what-happened-next prose. You can imagine a whole shelf of future books that pick up where Monroe leaves off, presenting a secret, feminist history of criminal justice in America."

—The Marshall Project

"Laser-sharp . . . Popular crime narratives, in order to gain their hypnotic force, exploit their audience's blind spots. In *Savage Appetites*, Monroe has her eyes wide open."

—*Los Angeles Review of Books*

"*Savage Appetites* is an elegant dissection. It picks apart the stories we tell ourselves in order to make violence legible or to clean up its aftermath or simply for our entertainment. It's a reminder that connecting the dots between events can obscure as much as it reveals."

—*The Nation*

"Monroe resists the need to sweep all of her material into a single, tidy narrative. Her prose—consistently lyrical and probing—does a lot of the work toward making it feel cohesive. . . . In allowing for messiness—narrative as well as moral—her book is a corrective to the genre it interrogates."

—*New Statesman*

"One of the most fascinating and intellectual approaches to true crime I've ever read."

—*Outside*

"*Savage Appetites* is required reading for those who understand that women aren't just reading true crime to protect ourselves—we're investigating cold cases, getting close to the families of victims, leveraging power to get men to embrace the validity of our 'hobbies,' and much more."

—CrimeReads

"An illuminating exploration rooted in a convincing thesis, and even the most dedicated true crime reader will find something new within it to enjoy."

—BuzzFeed

"Asks all the right questions, and even better, doesn't attempt to answer them (or at least, not completely) . . . Unsettling, brilliant, and impossible to put down!"

—Literary Hub

"Monroe's keen observations and probing journalism keep us from the satisfying feeling of closure that a good mystery novel or a true-crime documentary can provide. . . . Monroe does what true obsessives do: show us what is unresolved, what is unending, what might never be possible—and how important it is to try to fix it anyway."

—*The Lily*

"*Savage Appetites* is a chilling, compelling examination of the darkness in us all. This is obviously a book for true-crime fans, as well as anyone interested in human nature. A powerful, well-researched inquiry into why we find violent crime so fascinating, viewed though the stories of detective, victim, defender, and killer."

—Shelf Awareness

"This is a book sure to please fans of mystery and true crime. An insightful invitation to consider the contexts and causes of a gritty cultural obsession."
—*Kirkus Reviews*

"Monroe's writing is superb, and each woman's story is fascinating. . . . True crime aficionados will appreciate this spin on the genre."
—*Booklist*

"A provocative work best suited to readers with a strong interest in true crime and its historical roots . . . an original and bold contribution to the genre."
—*Library Journal*

"I read this book in a single day, but I know I'll be thinking about it for years to come—especially its keen appreciation for the mystery of what drives us through this world."
—Leslie Jamison, author of
The Empathy Exams and *The Recovering*

"*Savage Appetites*, Rachel Monroe's study on 'women, crime, and obsession,' can properly be described as brilliant. It informs, entertains, and leaves readers with new cultural perspectives that are long overdue. I'm now a Rachel Monroe fan, and after you read this book, you will be too."
—Jeff Guinn, author of *Manson: The Life and Times of Charles Manson* and *The Road to Jonestown: Jim Jones and Peoples Temple*

"This is like high-junk reading, both getting the information, snickering at the misinformation, stalking the stalkers, and really brooding on the possibility that the dead female body at the top of the film is feeding a female appetite for death and malfeasance and not yawn more jerk-off fodder for men. Our corpses, ourselves!"
—Eileen Myles, author of *Evolution*

"Rachel Monroe has long been one of my favorite writers at the intersection of crime and culture, and her first book, *Savage Appetites,* is the grand culmination of her reporting. It's a standout, formally inventive, and refreshing examination of the way we consume true crime, and the way it consumes us."
—Sarah Weinman, author of *The Real Lolita: The Kidnapping of Sally Horner and the Novel That Scandalized the World*

"I don't know how Rachel Monroe wrote a book so vivid and perceptive, but I couldn't put it down. . . . I'm not exaggerating when I say Monroe has written a new true-crime classic, one that both adds to and challenges the genre."
—Alice Bolin, author of *Dead Girls*

"Smart and seductive. In the tradition of Janet Malcolm, Rachel Monroe has turned our cultural hunger for crime stories back on itself, both evoking and interrogating the fascinations that grip us. I learned a great deal from this book, but what's more, I couldn't put it down."

—Alex Marzano-Lesnevich, author of
The Fact of a Body

"A deeply intelligent, intensely gripping work of metacrime. Rachel Monroe is a brilliant new journalist with a sparkly goth heart."

—Claire Vaye Watkins, author of
Gold Fame Citrus and *Battleborn*

"Rachel Monroe dissects the nature of [true-crime] obsession on both individual and societal levels in lucid and beautiful prose. You'll find this book as engrossing as any true-crime wormhole on the internet."

—Michelle Dean, author of *Sharp:
The Women Who Made an Art of Having an Opinion*

"A brilliant book, laced with a perspective that's long been missing from the world of true crime. Rachel Monroe holds up a mirror to our fascination with illicit tales—and her own—all while deftly unspooling four unforgettable stories from the other side. *Savage Appetites* is wholly unique and utterly riveting."

—Evan Ratliff, author of *The Mastermind*

"I loved this book. . . . *Savage Appetites* is a beautiful hybrid of a book that made me question my relationship to celebrity, media, and my own baser appetites."

—Claire Dederer, author of
Love and Trouble and *Poser*

"*Savage Appetites* is a marvel of original reportage and cultural criticism, and could not be more timely. Like a first responder to a crime scene, Rachel Monroe methodically investigates every inch of America's obsession with murder stories, unearthing more than a few discoveries and showing that what makes us tick now has been there all along."

—Kate Bolick, author of
Spinster: Making a Life of One's Own

SAVAGE APPETITES

TRUE STORIES OF WOMEN, CRIME, AND OBSESSION

RACHEL MONROE

SCRIBNER

NEW YORK   LONDON   TORONTO   SYDNEY   NEW DELHI

Scribner

An Imprint of Simon & Schuster, Inc.

1230 Avenue of the Americas

New York, NY 10020

First Scribner trade paperback edition July 2020

SCRIBNER and design are registered trademarks of The Gale Group, Inc.,
used under license by Simon & Schuster, Inc., the publisher of this work.

For information about special discounts for bulk purchases,
please contact Simon & Schuster Special Sales at 1-866-506-1949
or business@simonandschuster.com.

The Simon & Schuster Speakers Bureau can bring authors to your
live event. For more information or to book an event,
contact the Simon & Schuster Speakers Bureau at 1-866-248-3049
or visit our website at www.simonspeakers.com.

Interior design by Kyle Kabel

Manufactured in the United States of America

9   10   8

Library of Congress Cataloging-in-Publication Data is available.

ISBN 978-1-5011-8888-6
ISBN 978-1-5011-8889-3 (pbk)
ISBN 978-1-5011-8890-9 (ebook)

For my mother,
in gratitude for her dark mind and warm heart

it is finally as though that thing of monstrous interest
were happening in the sky
but the sun is setting and prevents you from seeing it

—John Ashbery

Contents

ALL CRIME ALL THE TIME

1

THE DETECTIVE

11

THE VICTIM

61

THE DEFENDER

121

THE KILLER

173

SCARY STORIES TO TELL IN THE DARK

231

Acknowledgments

237

Notes

239

Bibliography

255

SAVAGE APPETITES

ALL CRIME ALL THE TIME

Until a few years ago, Oxygen was a cable TV channel that targeted a young, female demographic with forgettable high-drama shows with names like *Last Squad Standing* and *Bad Girls Club*. According to network executives, the millennial women they were hoping to capture craved "freshness" and "authenticity," "high emotional stakes and optimism." It didn't take long for the executives to figure out that what young women actually wanted was more shows about murder. When the struggling network began airing a dedicated true crime block in 2015, viewership increased by 42 percent. In 2017, the network rebranded and adopted revised programming priorities: all crime, all the time.

Viewership skyrocketed; Oxygen had tapped into something big. For the past few years, as the US murder rate has approached historic lows, stories about murder have become culturally ascendant. The crime minded among us were inundated with content, whether our tastes tended toward high-end HBO documentaries interrogating the justice system or something more like Investigation Discovery's *Swamp Murders*. (Or, as was often the case, both. True crime tends to scramble traditional high/low categorizations.) Shops popped up on Etsy selling enamel pins of Ted Bundy's Volkswagen Beetle and iPhone cases depicting Jeffrey Dahmer's face. There were approximately a million new podcasts, and they all had something to *investigate*.

In 2018, Oxygen hosted its second annual fan convention—CrimeCon—in Nashville's Marriott Opryland hotel. The Opryland, as I was proudly told at check-in, was the second-biggest noncasino hotel in the world. You know that American tendency to equate bigness with luxury and plenitude with worth? The Opryland was that, in hotel form. There was lush indoor landscaping and fountains that erupted in elaborately choreographed spurts and infinite snack options you could charge to your room. You could eat a dinner at a steakhouse inside a replica of an antebellum mansion. For $10, you could ride a boat down the quarter-mile-long river that flowed through one of the hotel's atriums; the water, I was told, included a drop from every river in the world.

The week before CrimeCon, the Opryland had welcomed a group of cement salespeople, and the week after it would host a convention of international-supply-chain managers, but for these three days in May, it was full of young women wearing T-shirts that said things like BASICALLY A DETECTIVE and DNA OR IT DIDN'T HAPPEN and I'M JUST HERE TO ESTABLISH AN ALIBI.

On day one of CrimeCon, I found a seat in the ballroom among a couple thousand women and a smattering of men. The sound system blasted cheery pop music as the screens flanking the stage scrolled through a slideshow of crime-related images—mug shots and yellow police tape and close-ups of alarming, contextless headlines: "Man Accused of Stabbing Mother," "Deadly Stabbing Suspect Arrested," "Four People Shot."

Oxygen shows feature a stable of authoritative crime experts, mostly men with handsome-haggard faces and law enforcement experience. They're real people, but they always seem half in character, as if they were playing a beloved but slightly remote and overprotective father on a network drama. There seemed to be at least one of them on every true crime show, these inexplicably sexy cop-dads. One of them, former FBI profiler Jim Clemente, wearing a cowboy hat, strolled out onto the stage to a round of huge cheers. CrimeCon had officially begun.

"Crimes are driven by the *why*, the motive," Clemente said. "We need that *why* to solve most crimes. Because the *how* and the *why* gives you the *who*. We also use motives in daily life. Why eat a sandwich? Because you're hungry. But with crime, sometimes the motives are hidden. Why did she run away? Was it to escape coercive control? Why did he kill her? Was it jealousy? Or was it something more insidious?

"And why are *you* here? Do you love the genre? Do you want to solve a cold case?" Clemente's voice slowed and deepened; he was transitioning into serious mode. "Or you know or knew someone who got murdered? Or you yourself were a victim of a crime? I have a theory. You want to learn so you can protect those you love. It's a very altruistic goal." His voice changed again—I had a feeling these tonal shifts would get exhausting over the long weekend. *"Have fun,"* he bellowed. "And remember: hashtag CrimeCon on your posts!"

I should have felt at home at CrimeCon. For most of my postadolescent life, I've periodically sunk into what I've come to think of as a crime funk. I was the kind of gloomy child who filched her mother's *People* magazines to read not about the celebrities, but about the killers and kidnappers and suspicious overdoses. As I got older, my appetite for murder stories seemed to depend on how much turbulence was in my own life. The more sad or lost or angry I felt, the more I craved crime. I was a teenager storming with hormones when I pulled *Helter Skelter* off my parents' shelf and gave myself Manson Family nightmares, and a little older and a lot more depressed when I set out to read every single Manson Girl memoir. When I learned that the Columbine killers' journals were online, I read those, too.

In my crime funks, the perspectives I identified with shifted depending on what else was going on in my life. Sometimes I saw myself in the detective, the only one smart enough to put the pieces together; sometimes in the innocent victim, at the mercy of sinister forces much bigger than me; sometimes in the crusading defender, righting the wrongs of a flawed and corrupt system; sometimes, even, I saw myself in the killer.

That the true crime obsessives packing the hallways at CrimeCon were almost all women was, on its surface, perplexing. The vast majority of violent crimes are committed by men. Most murder victims are also male. Homicide detectives and criminal investigators: predominantly male. Attorneys in criminal cases are mostly men. Put simply, the world of violent crime is masculine, at least statistically.

But the consumers of crime stories are decidedly female. Women make up the majority of the readers of true crime books and the listeners of true crime podcasts. Television executives and writers, forensic scientists and activists and exonerees all agree: true crime is a genre that overwhelmingly appeals to women.

Women aren't just passively consuming these stories; they're also participating in them. Start reading through one of the many online sleuthing forums where amateurs speculate about unsolved crimes—and sometimes solve them—and you'll find that most of the posters are women. More than seven in ten students of forensic science, one of the fastest-growing college majors, are women. A few years ago, two undergraduates at the University of Pittsburgh founded a Cold Case Club so they could spend their extracurricular hours investigating murders; the group is, unsurprisingly, dominated by women.

Sometimes women's attraction to true crime is dismissed as trashy and voyeuristic (because women are vapid!). Sometimes it is unquestioningly celebrated as feminist (because if women like something, then it *must* be feminist!). And some argue that women read about serial killers to avoid becoming victims. This is the most flattering theory—and also, it seemed to me, the most incomplete. By presuming that women's dark thoughts were merely pragmatic, those thoughts are drained of their menace. True crime wasn't something we women at CrimeCon were consuming begrudgingly, for our own good. We found *pleasure* in these bleak accounts of kidnappings and assaults and torture chambers, and you could tell by how often we fell back on the language of appetite, of bingeing, of obsession. A different, more alarming hypothesis was the one I tended to prefer: perhaps we liked creepy stories because something creepy was in us.

The weekend at CrimeCon was a crime-y blur. I went to a panel on profiling, and a demonstration of a new DNA extraction technique by a forensic scientist who appears on Dr. Oz's *True Crime Tuesdays*. I was handed a card listing "11 Signs you may be DEALING WITH A PSYCHOPATH." (Number 9: lack of realistic long-term goals.) I browsed, but did not purchase, greeting cards featuring a birthday message from the Manson Girls ("charlie said to make sure you have a happy birthday. and we do everything charlie tells us to do"). I cried a little bit as three of the Golden State Killer's surviving victims celebrated the arrest of a suspect after more than thirty years. I listened to a ridiculously handsome former CIA agent claim that anyone who had been to a foreign country had been in a life-threatening situation. I was exhorted to sign up for an online course in how to "not be a victim," presented by Nancy Grace. A guy wearing a LOS ANGELES COUNTY CORONER hat tried to sell me a book about Ted Bundy, and when I said I wasn't interested, he offered me a book about the Zodiac Killer instead. He told me that he ran a small publishing house: "We used to do zombies and vampires, but that's going nowhere. It's all true crime now." Then he tried to sell me a book about a bank robber. I didn't hear a single story about the people who are disproportionately at risk of homicide: sex workers, the homeless, young men of color, trans women. Instead, there were more teaser-trailers for TV specials about murdered moms, or moms who murdered.

The whole hotel was encased in a glassy dome, and through the skylights I got the vague sense that weather was happening outside, but it didn't affect me. The Opryland reminded me of a Las Vegas casino: it was so relentlessly temperature controlled and pleasant, and so difficult to locate an exit, that any desire to go outside quickly withered away. Instead I charged ice cream sundaes to my room and gorged myself on crime. For the first time in my life I could have as much as I wanted, without any apologies or explanations. Everyone else at CrimeCon understood.

It was easy to make friends at CrimeCon; complete strangers were unusually open, even confessional. A woman who'd traveled to the conference from Texas likened true crime shows to an empathy roller coaster—you felt so bad for the victims, and for their families, and even sometimes for the perpetrator. In one of the hotel's many snack shops, I spotted one of CrimeCon's rare male attendees. I asked what had brought him here, and he nodded at his girlfriend over in the chocolate-bar section. He told me that they used to tour insane asylums, then they had a paranormal phase, and now they were into murder. Well, it was mostly her, he admitted. He was just along for the ride. I asked him if he had a theory to explain why the CrimeCon audience was so overwhelmingly female. "I mean, no offense for the stereotype," he said, "but I think you all like the drama."

I talked to a man in a button-down shirt who turned out to work for Oxygen in an audience-engagement capacity. If you look at the ratings for Investigation Discovery (Oxygen's true crime program-ming rival), he told me, they're the same at midnight as they are at 6:00 a.m. "People leave it on all night," he said. "They fall asleep to it. People tell me all the time that they find these shows soothing."

If so, it was a strange kind of comfort. Midway through day two at CrimeCon, sinister phrases had begun to rattle around in my head—*zip-tied to the dresser, scalp laceration, that was the last time anyone saw them*—although I'd heard so many horror stories that I couldn't remember which murder they belonged to. I wandered past a conference room where a woman was talking about the "cold-case epidemic," then a backdrop where I could've taken a selfie that looked like a mug shot. Somewhere Nancy Grace was recording a live podcast, but I wasn't in the mood for that. Nor was I in the mood for the Wine & Crime happy hour, or the virtual reality crime-scene-exploration game. I had the sense I was seeking something, though I wasn't sure exactly what.

In the middle of one of the exhibition halls was a long wall, with WHAT'S YOUR MOTIVE written at the top. Attendees had covered it with Post-its proclaiming their reasons for coming to CrimeCon:

- sick obsession
- so I can geek out this weekend on forensics :)
- my wife made me
- the patriarchy
- cuz I'm odd
- seek truth
- to be a nerd for a weekend
- murder is the new black!
- girls weekend
- true crime OBSESSED

- Fun!
- to not get killed
- Bitches #crimecon2018
- face my fears and celebrate justice
- exonerate the innocent
- Justice for JonBenet
- to catch the fucker and beat him at his own game
- girls trip #cupcakes

I stood in front of this Wall of Motives for a long time. It made for a strange stew, full of flavors that didn't seemingly go together: justice and rage, morbid curiosity and sisterhood, cupcakes and patriarchy battling, fear and revenge. But something about it drew me in. It was messy and honest. It was full of contradiction. I wanted to keep thinking about it.

For almost ten years now, I've been collecting stories of women who were drawn in by crimes that weren't theirs to claim—that is, crimes that didn't impact them directly, but to which they nevertheless felt a deep connection. Women who, like me, were susceptible to falling into a crime funk. This wasn't a conscious project; there was just something about these women that snagged my attention, something about their stories that I wanted to chew on for a while. Maybe learning more about them might help me figure out this larger phenomenon of women and crime. Maybe it would help me figure out myself.

These four women took things too far, at least according to conventional wisdom. They were immoderate and occasionally unwise. And they each paid a price: they lost jobs and alienated family members; one spent $150,000 on phone calls to prison; another is now incarcerated herself. But they also reinvented themselves, finding personal meaning through other people's tragedies. They used these murders as a way to live out other kinds of lives, ones that were otherwise unavailable to them.

These women lived in different eras and in different parts of the country. Their political leanings and class backgrounds were distinct. If you put them all in a room together, they wouldn't necessarily get along. They might even hate one another. And yet they all shared this same proclivity.

The more time I spent with their stories, the more I realized that there wasn't a simple, universal answer to why women were fascinated by true crime. Obsession was a recurring theme in their lives, but that obsession wasn't monolithic. It stemmed from different motivations, had different objects and different implications. Perhaps most significantly, each of the four women identified with a different archetypal crime figure: the objective, all-knowing detective; the wounded, wronged victim; the crusading defender, battling for justice; and even the dark, raging glamour of the killer.

In trying to learn more about these four women, I came to understand more about the world around me. Because it's not just individuals who find murders fascinating. Periodically, the culture at large will fixate on a certain crime or grant a murderer celebrity status. These collective obsessions are often dismissed as exploitative, sensationalistic, and distasteful. But the murder stories we tell, and the ways that we tell them, have a political and social impact and are worth taking seriously. Lessons are embedded within their gory details. When read closely, they can reveal the anxieties of the moment, tell us who's allowed to be a victim, and teach us what our monsters are supposed to look like.

Maybe you've had your own crime funks, spent time in the murky territory where murder and obsession coincide. You read a news story about some horrible event that took place several states away, and the questions start to worm their way into your brain: How do things like that happen, in what sort of world? What kind of person would do such a thing? So you engage in some late-night googling, and maybe you discover a message board with theories. You figure out the name that the murderer's ex-girlfriend is going by now and find her Facebook page. You click through her photos: there she is, fatter than in the news footage, smiling, holding a baby—hers? It's three in the morning and your computer screen illuminates your face with an unnatural glow. What is it, exactly, that you're looking for?

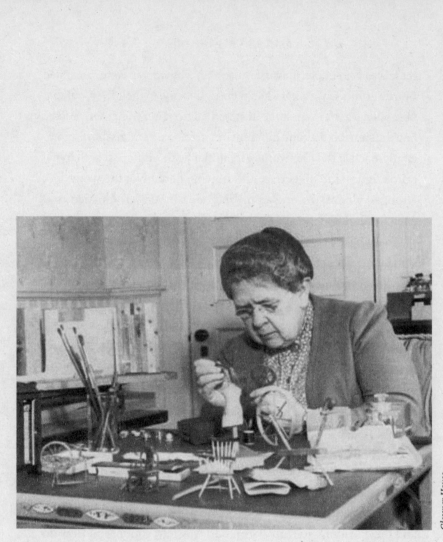

THE DETECTIVE

The bloodstains looked like the scattered fragments
of a mysterious pattern—a last message, a warning,
the writing on the wall.

—Klaus Mann

It's the day after Halloween in Boston, 1946. Outside, a chill is in
the air, a hint of the coming winter after a week of unseasonable
warmth. Inside a book-lined room on the third floor of a Harvard
Medical School building, a woman in a dark suit stands in front of a
group of men. She is in her late sixties, with gold-rimmed spectacles
perched low on her nose and waves of gray hair pulled back from
her stern, blocky face. She has an air of intense focus. She is talking
about death again.

She is lecturing a group of police officers, sturdy men in suits and
patterned ties. Thirty of them are arranged around a rectangular
table. Each has in front of him a thick binder stuffed with papers and
a crystal ashtray for his cigarette butts. Already this week they have
sat through experts lecturing on sex murder and infanticide. They
have stared at slides of burned bodies and drowned bodies. They have
discussed asphyxiation at length. *Fun* is maybe not the right word
for what they're up to, but it's not that far off, either. The men know
they're lucky to be here—these seminars always have a waiting list.

And, look, death happens—if anyone understands that, it's homicide detectives. *Someone* has to look at it closely.

In the 1940s, few women worked for police departments; those who did were largely relegated to clerical duties, or the women-and-children beat: runaways, prostitutes, fraudulent fortune-tellers. Detective work, particularly homicide investigation, was decidedly not a feminine space—and so, as discussions of dead bodies began to take up more and more of her time, the gray-haired lady at the front of the room often found herself the only woman in groups of men. That was fine with her. She was not particularly fond of women.

Decades ago, in a life that must feel as remote as the moon from this gritty world of crime scenes and blood-spatter analysis, her debutante announcement referred to her as "Miss Frances Glessner"; for her debut, she had a dress made out of white crepe de chine and wore three pink rosebuds in her hair. As a young society woman in turn-of-the-century Chicago, Miss Glessner did what was expected of her, dressing in tulle and going to balls and looking, her mother said, "as sweet as a peach." At nineteen, she was married to the son of a minor Confederate general and became Mrs. Frances Lee. At the wedding, her father offered the new couple a toast, praising his teenage daughter as a "sweet and lovely bride . . . whose joy is not in riches but in homemaking and the affection of husband and friends."

And almost half a century later, here she is, in the world she's grown to prefer, one of dispassionate discussions of putrefaction, where the precise hue of a strangled woman's face is more interesting than the color of her dress. Her family isn't pleased that she prefers late-night ride-alongs in police cars and the solemn urgency of crime scenes to your more typical old-lady hobbies—cookie baking, needlepoint. She's not the greatest grandmother. Her mind is often elsewhere, usually somewhere more gruesome.

Her favorite point of the week is the moment when she gets to introduce the police officers to her life's work: twenty dioramas built at the scale of one inch to one foot. They are intricately crafted down to the minutest detail: a dresser's drawers slide open, a miniature mousetrap snaps shut, an ashtray overflows with impossibly small hand-rolled cigarettes, a trashcan is stuffed with tiny trash.

Though there are dolls in these little rooms, Lee bristles when people call them dollhouses. They are something stranger and more serious than that. For one, they are intended as educational tools, not playthings. And for another, all the dolls are dead: purple in the face from strangulation, facedown on the stairs after a fall, suspended from a miniature noose in the attic. One model features a baby the size of a policeman's thumb, the pink-striped wallpaper behind his crib streaked with blood. Lee calls the models the Nutshell Studies of Unexplained Death, after a supposed policeman's credo: to convict the guilty, clear the innocent, and find the truth in a nutshell.

When I lived in Baltimore, a decade ago, I heard rumors of these little death dioramas secreted away in a government building downtown. An eccentric heiress's playhouses, full of dead dolls. I heard that the little figures inside the models were meticulously drowned and stabbed and strangled, and that their small murders had been done in the name of science. I heard that John Waters was a fan, and that David Byrne stopped by to see them when he was in town. I like things that are small and things that are macabre; those interests don't usually overlap.

One fresh April afternoon, I stepped into the imposing marble building that housed the office of Maryland's Chief Medical Examiner and took the elevator to the fourth floor. I walked down a long hallway, past a glass case displaying skulls of particular significance.

The ME's Office was set to relocate to a renovated building in the next few months; this one had an exhausted, overworked look, all scuffed floors and fluorescent lights. I remember thinking that a place that dealt so much with death should be more grand or reverent, or at least not so institutionally bleak—I suppose because I thought of death as aberrant and rare, something to be regarded with awe, from a great distance. But in this office, death was daily work.

From the acronymed police procedurals I watched religiously, I'd absorbed the idea that people who work in proximity to corpses were damaged in an attractive way, broody with haunted eyes and an air of tragedy. But Jerry Dziecichowicz, the ME's Office administrator and the Nutshells' caretaker, turned out to be a jolly, apple-cheeked man with a beautifully broad Baltimore accent. I stumbled over his last name, and he waved his hand as if it was no problem at all. "Everyone calls me Jerry D.," he said.

Of the twenty Nutshells that Frances Glessner Lee and her carpenter, Ralph Mosher, made in the 1940s and '50s, nineteen survive. Each depicts a dead body in a room; the spectator takes on the role of the investigator, who must determine whether the death was a homicide, an accident, or a suicide. The Nutshells were not puzzles to be solved, but rather tools to teach their intended audience—police investigators—to look more carefully and dispassionately. Ever the micromanager, Lee provided instructions for how to review her models:

It will simplify the examiner's work if he will first choose the point at which he enters the scene and, beginning at his left at the place, describe the premises in a clockwise direction back to the starting point, thence to the center of the scene and ending with the body and its immediate surroundings. He should look for and record indications of the social and financial status of the people involved in each model as well as anything that may illustrate their state of mind up to or at the time of demonstration.

Each Nutshell has crucial details hidden within it—a pinpoint-size bullet embedded in the rafters, love letters written in two different kinds of handwriting—that only reveal themselves after careful scrutiny. Lee wanted the Nutshells to represent a variety of circumstances. Some of her dead dolls are in posh parlors, others in rundown boardinghouse rooms; some are young women, others are old men. (Except for the occasional discoloration due to bruising or decomposition, though, they are all the same cream-bisque color—as if, in the deadly world of the Nutshells, only miniature white people meet tragic ends.)

Lee labored to get the details right, even those that weren't necessarily relevant to the investigation. In one Nutshell—a cozy, middle-class living room, with a woman's dead body sprawled on the stairs—newspaper pages are strewn on the floor. To create the paper, Lee took a full-size edition and photographically reduced it to a two-by-three-inch plate, which was then used to reprint a replica one-half inch wide. She sewed the pages together, then carefully tore the borders to mimic newsprint's jagged edges.

Miniatures are satisfying not because they are grand, but because they are *exact*. "It is the accuracy, the rightness, that is so rewarding," according to writer Alice Gregory. "It is a relief . . . to be in the presence of precision—and be allowed to like it." The Nutshells destabilize that sense of relief. The domestic is undergirded with malice. The housewife is dead at the foot of the stairs. The widow's face is a ghastly purple; her fluids leak out onto the lovely pink rug beneath her. The tiny frilly curtains are as daintily precise as the tiny noose. For one Nutshell scene involving potential arson, Lee and Mosher built a beautiful wooden cabin and filled it with furniture. Then they took a blowtorch to it.

In Baltimore, the Nutshells lived in a dim room at the end of a hall. Most of the models were embedded in the walls, visible through Plexiglass windows. A few were displayed on pillars. Each tragic tiny scene was presented with a dossier of key information: when the death was reported, the weather and time of sunrise/set, witnesses' statements. They read like little short stories, dramas in miniature: "It was really cold and I was surprised to find the door open. I put my head inside and called but no one answered so I went in to see if anything was wrong"; "I heard a sort of noise and went to see what it was, and found her lying on the ground below." ("It must not be overlooked that these statements may be true, mistaken, or intentionally false, or a combination of any two or all three of these," Lee's introduction warns. "The observer must therefore view each case with an entirely open mind.")

I moved slowly around the displays, feeling like a giant peering in at scenes of falls and hangings and shootings and stabbings, dolls dead in their beds, or in the closet, or on the pavement. The biggest and most elaborate Nutshell, known as the Three-Room Dwelling, sat in a clear case in the center of the room. From a certain angle, it looked like a classic dollhouse scene, an idealized depiction of family life. Three jugs of milk, the size of pencil erasers, sat on the front porch, neatly arranged next to a welcome mat. The kitchen was full of miniaturized homey details—cans of soup and tomato juice, a bread box, a toaster, a coffeepot, a box of Rice Krispies, a child's high chair, a toy rocking horse on a table.

But the Nutshells teach you to look for what's wrong, not for what's right. My gaze moved through the model, attuned to signs of disarray. A shotgun was discarded on the kitchen floor, and signs of trouble were evident in the further rooms—chairs turned over on their sides, blood on the wall by the telephone, a bloody boot print on the carpet, a pool of blood on the bedsheets. And, in the bedrooms, three dead dolls—mom, dad, and baby.

Is it strange to admit that something in me relaxed there, in the room with the Nutshells? I moved to the next scene (a bathtub drowning), and the next (the burned-out cabin). The Nutshells were tragedies at a scale I could handle. They dangled the promise of closure—if I looked long enough, and carefully enough, I could figure out what happened, and maybe even why.

I circled back to the three-room house. The husband doll was splayed on the bedroom floor, gore splattered carefully, almost *lovingly*, around him. I found myself wondering about who had killed him—not his murderer within the imaginary world of the Nutshells, but the woman who had dreamed him to life, then assigned him this ugly death. What kind of person would devote such scrupulous care—and so much money—to something so gruesome? And why? A bloom of curiosity unfurled inside me. It was an old feeling, and a pleasurable one. I had found myself a mystery.

This detective impulse first burbled up in me early, say around age eight. I'm not saying this makes me unique; maybe every kid who isn't skilled at sports has Sherlock Holmes daydreams. Think of all those tween sleuth books. Think of Scooby-Doo and his gang of meddling kids.

In retrospect, it makes sense. I wasn't good at being a child—"I wish that I was 10 or 9 or 11 or 12 or 13 or 14," I wrote in my journal at age seven. "I can't wait till I'm older. It's boring being young." Other kids seemed capable of a looseness, a self-forgetting, that I could never quite capture, particularly in public. I was too awkward, too much in my head. At recess, I sat by myself, watching my classmates play, constructing elaborate narratives explaining what I saw, and what I imagined I saw.

Detective stories make good reading material for misfits. They teach you that being overlooked can be an advantage, that when your perspective is slightly askew from the mainstream, you notice things that other people don't. If you imagine yourself as an investigator, you have an excuse to hover outside the social circle, watching its dynamics unfold. You're untouched and untouchable. Your weirdness becomes a kind of superpower.

Personally, I was always partial to Harriet the Spy, with her hoodies and her notebooks and her passion to know "everything in the world, everything, everything." Harriet was socially awkward, and a little mean. She was also brave, but in a secret way. Her adventures mostly involved putting herself into uncomfortable or dangerous positions where she could observe while remaining unobserved: an introvert's dream!

When she grew up, Harriet planned to figure out "everything about everybody" (including "medical charts if I can get them"). She'd have an office, with a sign on the door that said HARRIET THE SPY in gold letters, and she'd carry a gun and follow people around. It was a more appealing picture of adulthood than any other I'd heard. Maybe I'd be a spy, too. The menace of the world, with all its social risk, ebbed somewhat once I had permission to stand back and watch. I hoarded the thought; I knew right away that it was one of those ideas that would taste better if it was kept a secret. Maybe soon I, too, would know everything, everything.

Frances Glessner Lee grew up at a time when the whole world was crazy for detectives—and one detective in particular. In the 1890s, when Lee was a young girl, living in a mansion on Chicago's "Millionaire's Row," Sherlock Holmes was a pop culture sensation who helped establish the template of what a detective should be like: odd, brilliant, hyperrational. And male.

From the outside, the mansion where Lee spent most of her childhood looked like a fortress: huge blocks of rough granite interrupted by narrow windows. "Pathologically private," as one critic later described it. Inside, though, it radiated warmth and cultivation.

Frances—Fanny to her family—grew up surrounded by beautiful things: the hallucinatory gorgeousness of William Morris's floral wallpaper, busts of composers in the library. Her parents had a desk that was wide enough so that they could both read at the same time, facing each other. They had an egalitarian marriage, after a fashion, with Mr. Glessner ruling in the public realm and Mrs. Glessner in control of everything else. Mr. Glessner was a wealthy industrialist in the traditional nineteenth-century mode, a partner in an agricultural machinery company that eventually merged with other manufacturers to become International Harvester. Mrs. Glessner took her domestic responsibilities just as seriously, collecting books on the philosophy of interior decorating and founding a book club for the wives of University of Chicago professors. (Instead of reading the books themselves, the women would eat lunch on fine china as a pleasant-voiced young man read out loud to them.) Members of the Chicago Symphony came over for meals served in a dining room whose ceiling was covered with a thin layer of real gold.

Fanny was educated at home, in the classical mode; she became fluent in French, played the violin and the piano, and took dancing lessons. She was a strange child, with mercurial moods and an imagination that sometimes frightened her. (From her mother's diary, March 29, 1881: "Fanny called me in the night and said there was a wolf in the room. She called me again later, and said she was not sure whether it was a fox, a wolf, or a bear, but it was one of them.")

Homeschooling allowed Fanny and her brother, George, room to indulge their eccentric obsessions—I imagine their wood-paneled schoolroom as an early version of a Montessori classroom, full of projects and experiments. The Glessners spent summers at the Rocks, their estate in New Hampshire. They were the kind of family that brought their furniture maker on vacation with them; at the Rocks, he built Fanny a two-room log cabin of her own, a private domain with handcrafted furniture scaled down to child-size proportions.

Just as Fanny would later be infatuated with police procedure, her brother was fascinated by firemen. When George was a teenager, a local newspaper reported on the neighborhood's "auxiliary fire company . . . composed of four very enthusiastic and wealthy young men": George and three of his close friends. The boys' houses were linked up with the city fire department's emergency alert system, with "the wires running directly into the sleeping apartments of each lad." The boys telegraphed each other at all hours. "If a big fire occurs in the middle of the night, you can rest assured that [they] are in the thickest of it," the paper reported. "I do believe that if Chief Swenie ordered them to go up on a burning roof and direct a hose they would obey." Eventually George went away to college, but he didn't lose his appetite for disasters. He and his Harvard roommate—a flashy redhead named George Magrath—zipped around Boston on bicycles, watching buildings burn down.

Meanwhile, Frances was still back home in Chicago. She was curious and bright, eager to study medicine or nursing. Her grandfather suggested that the University of Chicago might be a good fit. Her father vetoed the idea; college was no place for a lady. So Frances wore her crepe de chine dresses and went to balls. By 1898, when she was twenty, she was married with a baby, her son, John. Two more children followed, Frances in 1903 and Martha in 1906.

"The marriage, instead of being a liberating influence for FGL, resulted in even tighter ties to her family's control," John recalled years later. "Benevolent and kindly as such control was, it was none-the-less control." Her parents had two twin town houses built one block away from the family fortress: one for Frances and her family, the other for George and his. Mr. Glessner supplemented his son-in-law's salary so his daughter could live in the luxury she was accustomed to. The Glessners were one of those families where it is difficult to tell the difference between closeness and claustrophobia, between care and control. Lee accepted her family's generosity, but she chafed at the conditions that came with it.

Just a few years after the wedding, her marriage began to show signs of strain. Neither Lee nor her husband were particularly good at adapting to others, her son explained later. "Also, she was probably spoiled by over-possessive parents. He was religious; she was not," John wrote. "His interests were almost completely indoors and intellectual, while hers also embraced the outdoors, and she had a creative urge coupled with high manual dexterity—the desire to make things—which he did not share."

Divorce was frowned upon in their social circle, so Lee's family sent her to their villa in Santa Barbara, along with a staff of five, to wait out the gossip cycle. As a divorcée, she was more dependent on her family than ever. For the next decade, as she raised her children, she remained closely entwined with her parents, dining at their house, accompanying them to the symphony, and vacationing with them at the Rocks. By now in her late twenties, she was retreading the emotional terrain of her youth: indulged but constrained; supported and both appreciative and resentful of that support.

Maybe it's natural that Lee eventually turned to making small things. Miniatures are a good hobby for the control freak or the obsessive. Their size demands fanatical tinkering, but because they're small and domestic, *cute* even, they can be mistaken as nonthreatening. Lee would eventually devote her time, money, and energy to murder *and* miniatures. But first it was just miniatures.

In 1912 at age thirty-four, she started her first small sculpture, a model of the Chicago Symphony Orchestra (which her parents had funded), for her mother's birthday. It took her two months to craft the ninety dolls representing the ninety musicians, each with a tiny musical instrument and a tiny score on his tiny music stand. Lee's mother traditionally sent the performers a carnation to wear during concerts, so Lee's miniature players had tiny flowers on their lapels, too. Her second sculpture was also musical: a model of a famed string quartet, another recipient of Glessner family patronage. This one took her two years. Getting it exact—not just close enough, but *exact*—was important. Lee took her teenage son, John, to see the quartet play, each of them sitting on opposite sides of the stage and making elaborate notes on each man's posture and dress—how the cellist's watch chain hung, where the violinist rested his feet.

Miniatures were something of a trend among wealthy women in the first decades of the twentieth century. In England, just after the conclusion of World War I, Queen Mary was given an elaborate three-foot-high dollhouse. It was an engineering marvel, as well as an aesthetic one, with toilets that flushed, sheets with tiny embroidered monograms, hot and cold running water, and a cellar stocked with bottles filled with thimblefuls of wine. Around the same time, in Dublin, Sir Nevile Wilkinson built his young daughter an Italian Renaissance–style dollhouse to "see if we can lure the fairies out to stay!" Called Titania's Palace, it featured three thousand pieces of miniature furniture and took fifteen years to complete. (In a show of dollhouse solidarity, Queen Mary donated a tiny china tea set to Titania's Palace's Royal Bedchamber.) The Colleen Moore House, built by an engineer father to cheer up his (adult) daughter, was completed in 1935 after seven years of work; it cost half a million dollars and is estimated to be worth about $7 million today. In permanent installation at Chicago's Museum of Science and Industry, it's an elaborate monument to fantasy and escapism, a palace suited to an imaginary world of princesses and fairies and infinite wealth. There are tiny glass slippers, a chandelier made out of real diamonds and emeralds, a postage-stamp-size painting by Walt Disney, a tiny pistol that fires even tinier silver bullets, and even, ostensibly, a piece of the true cross.

Around the same time, and just a few doors down from Frances Glessner Lee's town house on Prairie Avenue, another Chicago heiress was also obsessing over small furniture. Narcissa Niblack Thorne, who was friends with Lee—and whose family, like Lee's, had prevented her from attending college—spent decades on her meticulously crafted models. Like Lee's Nutshells, the Thorne Miniature Rooms were intended as teaching tools, not toys. They provided a kind of three-dimensional aesthetic edification, illustrating the best interior design across different geographies and eras: a Victorian English Drawing Room (featuring red satin curtains with gold fringe and inch-high portraits of Queen Victoria and Prince Albert); a nautical-themed, eighteenth-century Cape Cod living room (including a bottle containing a tiny clipper ship—a miniature of a miniature). The Thorne Rooms were visited by presidents and royalty; when they were featured in San Francisco's Golden Gate Exposition, they drew a million visitors. In the 1930s and '40s, as Lee was beginning to develop her Nutshells, Thorne was equally preoccupied, sometimes working ten-hour days, seven days a week, on her models. If she'd gotten paid for this work—and if she'd been a man—she might've been deemed a workaholic. Instead, people weren't sure what to call her. "It is certainly an exciting hobby," a reporter once told her. "Hobby?" Thorne replied. "It's a mania!"

There's something claustrophobic about imagining these adult women looming over their small, perfect models, fiddling. Just thinking about it makes me feel cramped. These palaces for fairies and princesses could be read as desperate attempts to create a refuge from the inhospitable realities of the normal-size world. Even Narcissa Thorne's miniatures, which are solidly grounded in the details of the actual past, have a sinister edge. Dollhouses are an almost too-literal example of these women's shrunken ambitions—of how, when you don't have control over the big decisions shaping your life, you narrow your focus to a world that's small enough for you to impose your will on it.

There's another spooky thing about these celebrated dollhouses— unlike the Nutshells, they're almost all uninhabited. There are no dolls in Colleen Moore's dollhouse, or in Titania's Palace. Only one of Narcissa Thorne's model rooms ever contained a human figure; she later claimed that its presence ruined the effect, and all her subsequent rooms were empty. It's as if these dollhouse creators felt that the only way to make a perfect domestic space was to eliminate all the people. Perhaps they were right. Human beings are unruly, troublesome. If you let them into the house, they might do something to disrupt the symmetry of the scene—such as murder their husbands or get their blood all over the pillowcases.

In 1910, a former preacher named Alice Wells was sworn in as a member of the Los Angeles Police Department and became widely known as the nation's first policewoman. Wells didn't wear a uniform or carry a gun, and she made it clear that her mission was nonthreatening: assisting vulnerable women and children through "applied Christianity." Her intrusion on the male world of police work was nonetheless deeply troubling to some. Newspapers treated Wells as a joke, printing caricatures that oozed gender panic, depicting her as "a bony, muscular, masculine person, grasping a revolver, dressed in anything but feminine apparel, hair drawn tightly into a hard little knot at the back of her head, huge unbecoming spectacles, small stiff round disfiguring hat."

Throughout the 1910s and '20s, as other women were spending fortunes on their dollhouses, a small but growing number of female officers were hired by municipal police departments. In 1913, the same year Frances Glessner Lee completed her orchestra model, her hometown of Chicago added ten white women to the police force. That brought the total number of policewomen in the entire United States to around forty. In 1918, the department hired its first black policewoman, Grace Wilson; New York City wouldn't have a black woman working in that capacity for another six years. These women were unarmed (the woman who headed up Detroit's first female police force said that her fellow policewomen "do not know what guns are" and "would not know what to do with them") and discouraged from using physical force. Most had backgrounds in nursing or social work.

Women found a place in early-twentieth-century police departments in part because the idea of what police were *for* was in flux. A hundred years later, we're accustomed to images of police as militarized soldiers in the never-ending war on crime. But in the early decades of the last century, policing was as much about promoting social welfare as preserving law and order. Female officers tended to runaways, enforced child-labor laws, and searched for missing children. In 1921, New York City established a Women's Precinct with a workroom, school, and hospital; it was intended to be a welcoming place "where a woman could seek information, advice or aid" from other women. But even as this kind of community caretaking was increasingly ceded to women, most higher-level roles within police departments, including homicide detective, still overwhelmingly went to men.

If Frances Glessner Lee couldn't attend college because it was unbecoming for a lady, then becoming a police officer was unthinkable. In any case, she didn't display a particularly avid interest in crime until the 1920s, when she was in her forties. At that time, she rekindled her friendship with George Magrath, her brother's college roommate and fellow fire watcher.

Lee had first met Magrath back when he was an ambitious college student; now he was one of the most recognizable figures in Boston. As the city's chief medical examiner, Magrath had a front-row seat to the city's most sensational crimes and accidents. After a storage tank ruptured, sending a flood of molasses coursing through the city's narrow streets at thirty-five miles per hour, it was Magrath who had to put on knee-high rubber boots and wade through the sticky streets of Boston's North End, cataloging the dead. He was so crucial to solving the Sacco and Vanzetti case that the governor personally invited him to witness the anarchists' execution. He testified at the circus-like murder trial of a flirty, notably bosomed housewife named Jessie Costello, who had "all the modest sex appeal of Lady Godiva plus clothing but minus horse," according to one local paper. Costello, who was accused of poisoning her firefighter husband, received as many as five hundred love letters a day; the bailiff brought her roses, and one juror requested permission to send her a box of candy. Even amid this heated atmosphere, Magrath managed to (briefly) steal the spotlight as the star medical witness.

Magrath wore bohemian clothes—tweed suits, floppy black ties, flat-brimmed hats, a pince-nez—and let his red hair grow long, making him look more like an artist than a doctor. He was a hearty, barrel-chested man, an Olympic-caliber rower, and a powerful singer.

One day, when he was a student at Harvard Medical School, he worked so late at Long Island Hospital that he missed the last boat to the mainland. "Student Magrath took off his clothes, tied them around his neck, swam to Spectacle Island, walked across it, swam to Thompson's Island, walked across it, then swam across the Fort Point Channel to South Boston," the *Boston Globe* reported. He then put his clothes back on and went to dissect a body. It was said that he ate only one meal a day, at midnight. It was said that he preferred his steak raw. It was said that he liked to testify in the afternoon, when the sunbeams streaming through the windows produced a more theatrical effect.

Lee wasn't just compelled by Magrath's charisma and bombast; she was also drawn in by his knowledge. Magrath was a professor of and evangelist for a field called legal medicine, a precursor to what we now know as forensic science, which deploys scientific and medical knowledge to solve crimes. Lee, who had once dreamed of being a nurse, had the misfortune of growing up in a family that believed she "shouldn't know anything about the human body," as she said later. Magrath was more than willing to serve as her mentor. He let her sit and watch while he conducted death investigations, and Lee soon became intimately familiar with the inner workings of the human form, and of what violence could do to it.

Lee and Magrath seemed to have found in each other an easy and decidedly nonromantic companionship. Magrath liked to tell stories—such as the one about the time the police urgently roused him from bed to examine a body that had washed up onshore, neglecting to mention that it was the body of a dog—and Lee liked to hear them. She grew so comfortable in the autopsy room that she had no problem eating her lunch in proximity to a corpse.

Midlife was an expansive time for Lee. Her children were grown, and the deaths of her parents and brother brought her a new level of both social and financial freedom. Spurred on by Magrath, Lee embarked on a campaign of self-education. Now that legal medicine was on her radar, she wanted to know everything about it. She began buying up rare books—including some that predated the printing press—and subscribing to trade publications such as the *National Coroners' Journal* and the *Journal of Medical Jurisprudence*. She purchased a photograph from President Garfield's autopsy, showing the hole where the assassin's bullet tunneled through his vertebrae. She bought, too, the poem that his assassin had scrawled in prison days before his execution. She even took a trip to Washington, DC, to meet FBI director J. Edgar Hoover and tour the FBI's brand-new crime lab. "She impressed me as being most intelligent, alert, and aggressive and I believe that she will apply herself to her plans very energetically," the head of the fingerprinting division wrote in an internal memo.

The more Lee learned, the more she saw opportunities for reform. Lee's mother had sponsored string quartets; her neighbor Narcissa Thorne had used her famous model rooms to raise money for the Architects Relief Fund. Spurred on by Magrath, Lee decided that her cause would be improving and professionalizing death investigation.

At first, her advocacy was limited to Magrath's pet project: getting rid of coroners. "If you want coroners condemned and thoroughly discredited," she sniffed in a letter to a friend, "all you have to do is let them talk in public." In the 1930s, if you dropped dead unexpectedly or your body was found in questionable circumstances, the person responsible for determining how you died was most likely the county coroner. Coroners were elected to their positions, and many had no legal or medical training. This system had made some sense when the United States was a fledgling country with a largely rural population—there just weren't enough trained specialists to handle all the dead bodies. But a few decades into the twentieth century, it was starting to seem backward and ineffective, even embarrassing. In 1933, a conference of pathologists gathered at Duke University to discuss the issue. "The system we are using in general is more or less a disgrace for a civilized country," one testified. Any improvements happened in "fits and starts," and generally only after something scandalous happened—such as the time a woman's body was taken to the morgue in Milwaukee, and the coroner had already started to cut into her before he realized that she was still alive. Inept coroners could torpedo murder investigations, overlooking crucial clues and diagnosing natural deaths as homicides or vice versa. The problem with coroners wasn't just their ignorance, but also their corruption. The pioneering investigative journalist Ida B. Wells traveled throughout the South, exposing how coroner's juries would rule that lynching deaths were accidents or committed by "parties unknown," even when a photograph of the lynch mob had just appeared in the local newspaper.

Lee and Magrath were part of a larger movement that advocated for replacing elected coroners with medical examiners who had specialized training in death investigation. Harvard was one of the only schools that taught men (because at this point they were all men) to navigate this tricky territory where medicine and the law overlapped.

In 1936, after Lee's father died and she came into the bulk of her inheritance, she donated a quarter of a million dollars—$4.5 million in today's money—to Harvard. Her bequest established a Department of Legal Medicine, the first of its kind in the country. University officials privately discussed their expectations that she'd leave the department four times as much in her will. Lee had always wanted to make a mark on the world; now she had a means to do so. Her money would go to pioneering a new field at the best university in the country. Anyone would be proud of this kind of legacy.

If Harvard had hoped that Lee would be a hands-off donor, just a sweet old lady looking for a place to park her money so it could be spent by experts who knew better than her, they had badly miscalculated. Lee had ambitious plans for the department she was funding. In the 1930s, Lee recalled decades later, "no one, including alas! my own self, knew exactly what Legal Medicine was supposed to mean." The definition she had in mind was expansive and went well beyond simply training medical students to perform autopsies. Other forensic methods—fingerprinting; ballistics analysis—were beginning to gain traction, but the field was dispersed and fragmented. As Lee saw it, the department should serve as a research hub for all kinds of cutting-edge crime-solving techniques that would make police work scientifically sound. Other countries had national forensic institutes; the United States would have the Harvard Department of Legal Medicine.

Lee offered suggestions for experiments, suggestions that sounded a lot more like commands: Someone in the department should make targets out of six-inch-square sheets of white blotting paper and shoot at them "from contact, and distances of 1-2-3-4-5-6-12-24 inches" to study the relative ballistic impact. Then they should repeat the entire experiment, but at greater distances, and with freshly killed pigs in place of paper targets. Then they should put clothing on the pigs and do it again, and then once more, with the pigs clad in heavier clothing. This experiment should be repeated with rifles, shotguns, and machine guns. "Also make shots through glass, through wood, et cetera, and show effects of ricochet shots, spent bullets, direct shots, and glancing shots," she went on. "Colored or color photographs of all the above, and painted wax models, should be included in this series. This is a demonstration of but one combination of weapon and ammunition and could be elaborated upon endlessly."

Endlessly! Lee's ambition—or her grandiosity, if you're feeling less generous—is remarkable: if only we had enough information, we could understand everything (everything!). Then a gunshot would not be a terrible force capable of ripping through and ruining a body, but rather a vector of information. Something to be studied, not feared.

By the time I hit middle school, being a detective seemed like a little kid's dream, as immature as wanting to be a ballerina or an astronaut. Fortunately, I had a new and more sophisticated word for my aspirations: forensics.

The summer after seventh grade, I toted Patricia Cornwell's fourth and fifth novels, *Cruel and Unusual* and *The Body Farm*, with me to summer camp, cramming them in my trunk alongside my Lisa Frank stationery and T-shirts with my name tag ironed into the collar. The novels starred Dr. Kay Scarpetta, the steely, wine-guzzling chief medical examiner of Virginia. Scarpetta was a version of a detective—she combed crime scenes, looking for clues—but her methods were driven by science. At the time she wrote her first Scarpetta novel, Cornwell said later, "the interior world of forensic science and medicine was a dark and chilly secret." Being let in on that secret was part of why I (and many others) loved the books; I was also happy to have found another prickly, sleuthing heroine. (Not everyone was a fan; certain reviewers complained about Scarpetta's "self-aggrandizement and interminable complaints" and described her as "an often annoying man hater.")

Cornwell set many of her books in Richmond, Virginia—our mutual hometown—and the mentions of familiar grocery stores and street names amid the accounts of rape and Munchausen's by proxy made the novels feel both frighteningly real and yet somehow also *cozy*. "I'm reading the Patricia Cornwell book," I wrote my mother that summer. "She talks about Woodberry Pharmacy and Carytown." I did not mention that the books had also just taught me what *autoerotic asphyxiation* meant.

Being twelve is strange. That was the same year my middle school class took a field trip to Washington, DC, where my classmates and I were let loose to visit the Smithsonian museum of our choice. My friend Mary and I were walking down some DC street, chattering about where we might be able to find a copy of a magazine with Leonardo DiCaprio, Mary's one true love, on the cover, when a businessman walking in the opposite direction gave her a long, appraising look. "Nice tits," he hissed as we walked past. He sounded, in that moment, as if he hated her. We both erupted in nervous giggles. I hadn't even gotten my period yet, and I felt covetous of, almost *angry at*, the bodies of my friends who had, in the archaic language of after-school specials, *become women*, but *tits* seemed like a dangerous thing to be in possession of. I was beginning to realize that I was on the cusp of coming into a terrible kind of power, a power that was also a vulnerability, and that being in the world would soon feel very different.

It wasn't just the businessman in the street that I found so disturbing; it was also my growing awareness of how many TV shows and movies featured abducted girls, stalked girls, murdered girls. The dead girl has long made for a reliable narrative engine, as cultural critic Alice Bolin has pointed out. *True Detective* magazine, arguably the first modern true crime franchise, sold 2 million copies a month in the 1940s in part by featuring imperiled women on its covers: women cowering, women bound and gagged, women with their eyes frozen wide with horror. (Not all endangered cover victims were created equal; *True Detective* preferred its victims white, attractive, and young.) Some readers identified with the shadowy figure looming in the background; certain serial killers, such as Dennis Rader (BTK) and Ted Bundy, have claimed at times that detective magazines and their tied-up ladies were sexually formative. Other consumers of crime stories identified with the woman bound by those ropes, the florid bloom of her panic. And some readers found their fear tinged with fascination and imagined another role for themselves.

If my childhood fantasy had involved seeing without being seen, I was coming to understand that as a young woman I wouldn't have the luxury of being invisible. Maybe that's why the Cornwell books were suddenly so appealing: They acknowledged the sexualized menace of the world, but also offered a way to navigate it. In the room with a corpse—a dead woman, naked, her neck purpled by ligature marks—Cornwell has Scarpetta peer closely at her skin, looking for fibers. In the face of paralyzing horror, she's active instead of passive. She's got a job to do.

When George Magrath retired as Boston's chief medical examiner, the city's reporters fell into a brief collective depression: "Murder Trials Won't Be the Same," the *Globe*'s headline sighed. Perhaps Harvard hoped that Lee would be less interested in meddling with legal medicine once her friend was out of the way. But if anything, Magrath's absence made Lee more committed to her cause.

Lee was rich, but not rich enough to fund the legal medicine department at the level she thought it deserved, so she found a sympathetic officer at the Rockefeller Foundation and convinced him to convince the foundation to give the legal medicine department money, too. "It is very heartening to find another enthusiast who speaks the same language," she wrote Alan Gregg after their first meeting. She also struck up a lively correspondence with Magrath's replacement, Alan Moritz. Their letters were an odd mix of the gory and the polite: Moritz wrote about the fauna of putrefaction and sent her copies of articles with such titles as "Semen and Seminal Stains"; she sent his family gifts of chocolate and ham. "As you know, this department is vitally interested in the development of better methods for the identification of burned, decomposed and mutilated bodies," Moritz wrote in one letter; "PS: The Moritz family are reveling in butter and are most grateful," in another.

Despite the friendly letters, strain was growing in their relationship. Lee wasn't pleased with the direction the legal medicine department was taking. She thought it wasn't doing *enough*—although, to be fair, it was impossible to do as much as Lee wanted. More important, she believed its focus on medical students was misplaced. Magrath had stressed to her that police officers were typically the first people to arrive at a crime scene. In those first, crucial moments, a case could be botched or on its way to being solved, depending on how the officers reacted. "Dr. Magrath always said: Start the training with the police. They're the most important," Lee recalled. She told friends that she hoped that Harvard could be convinced to "do as much for the police as it has for the businessman."

The problem as Lee saw it was that criminal investigation was anything but professionalized. Detectives worked based on hunches and assumptions; they did things the way they'd always been done. This ad hoc approach left room for bias and error to derail investigations—and bias and error were two things Lee found thoroughly unacceptable. But as it became increasingly clear that Harvard didn't share her enthusiasm for educating law enforcement, Lee realized she would have to find a way to do it herself.

By January 1944, she had come up with an idea: miniature crime scene models based on real cases, sprinkled with tiny clues that would reward careful, objective observation. That month, she wrote Moritz a letter that rushed on for three breathless pages. Her words crowded the page; she seemed to have forgotten that she was allowed to take paragraph breaks. Her "household is still in somewhat of a turmoil," she said in passing, but that wasn't what was on her mind. She had just started crafting the Nutshells, and she told Moritz about them with an excitement that teetered on the edge of mania:

> You will note from the above that I have in prospect, or completed, two hangings; two shootings; two assault with blunt weapon; one natural cause; one drowning; one found dead; one arson (I do not know yet how that gentleman was killed—am open to suggestions); and one poison. I need more traffic accidents . . . also another shooting or two, a stabbing, more poisonings, carbon monoxide, and a couple of puzzling Found Deads. . . . Would a couple of drownings be possible, or are drowned bodies too damaged and disfigured for representation? . . . Can we bring in some possible industrial accident? Can we do a couple of very good insurance problems?

She told Moritz that she was having the most difficulty with making sure the dolls' bodies looked realistic. "Are there any more or less standard proportions for the human figure available? Such as length of head as compared to length of torso (neck to hip or some such easily determined point) as compared to length of thigh, as compared to length of leg, knee-to-and-including foot. Also some comparative measurements of head; length, width from side to side, and thickness? Length of arms and breadth of shoulders, et cetera." She hoped to complete six models by May 1. She envisioned a full complement of forty-eight Nutshells; at a rate of five weeks per model, the work would occupy her for the next five or six years, she estimated, "provided hands, eyes and money hold out."

She wrote in closing, "Sorry to write you so many questions, but I do need the answers."

Lee was sixty-five when she wrote this letter, and fully aware that she didn't have all the time in the world. Within a few months, she would suffer two "rather sharp" heart attacks and be laid up with a broken leg. Despite her growing infirmity, she devoted herself to the Nutshells with a fanatical, even joyful intensity.

With the Nutshells, Lee believed she had found a way to train law enforcement to see differently. If a police officer interpreted her models only through the lens of his prejudices—say, presuming that the prostitute had died of a drug overdose, and that the lonely old woman killed herself—he risked overlooking the clues that would allow him to figure out what had truly happened.

Lee constructed the first models in her former playhouse at the Rocks; the three-quarters-size cabin must have seemed like an appropriate place to practice shrinking things down even further. When operations got too complex, she relocated to the property's four-story farmhouse, which she took to calling the Nutshell Laboratories. One room was given over to her carpenter, Ralph Mosher, who worked full-time on the Nutshells. Beyond it was a room dedicated to Lee's materials—doll-size furniture, fabrics cut from old dresses that had the right lived-in look—a collection that she guarded fiercely and allowed no one else to touch. She also had her own workshop, where she painted discoloration on dolls' faces and reupholstered tiny furniture so it matched the rest of a room's decor.

Lee based most of the Nutshells on crime scenes she had discussed with Magrath or Moritz, such as the one where a nursing student's body had been found by the side of the road in Concord, Massachusetts. The woman's unnaturally bent legs, Magrath had decided, indicated that the crime had likely happened elsewhere, and that the body had been in a contorted position—perhaps stuffed into a narrow space—when rigor mortis set in. Lee posed one of her dead dolls halfway in a bathtub, her legs awkwardly askew. A lazy or untrained detective might assume she'd gotten drunk, passed out in the tub, and drowned. But the odd angle of her legs was one indication of possible foul play.

As an observant and relentlessly critical person—her mind "worked with the accurate precision of a railroad watch," her friend Erle Stanley Gardner, author of the Perry Mason novels, once wrote. "I don't believe she has ever overlooked a detail in her life"—Lee had exceedingly high standards for the Nutshells. She was a fanatic about scale and texture. When she couldn't find the right kind of boot for one doll corpse, she enlisted an unfortunate Miss Simpson of the Harvard Purchasing Agent's Office to write a dozen letters to novelty manufacturers to find one for her; when nothing turned up, Miss Simpson resorted to making desperate inquiries to various Chambers of Commerce. For another doll—the woman drowned in the bathtub—Lee knitted tiny black knee-highs, using straight pins and a magnifying glass; the labor caused her so much eye strain that she could only complete one minute row at a time. It wasn't good enough to find an appropriately small coffeepot; it also had to be outfitted with a strainer and coffee grounds. "I found myself constantly tempted to add more clues and details and am afraid I may get them 'gadgety' in the process," she wrote to Moritz. "I hope you will watch over this and stop me when I go too far."

This obsessive attention to detail could seem fun killing, even punitive; certainly it sometimes drove the people who worked with her a little crazy. But isn't it also pleasurable to be this precise, to exert such complete control? Lee delighted in the Nutshells' exactitude, even embedding little jokes to amuse herself. "I wish you could see the latest model," she wrote to her son. "It's so cute."

By 1945, Lee (and Ralph Mosher) had ten Nutshells finished enough to put on display. Lee was immensely proud and invited her friends from the New Hampshire State Police over to show them off. The officers were impressed, not just by their craftsmanship, but also by the complexity of the cases Lee chose to depict. "Boy, she's a better detective than I am!" one officer remarked. The following year, Lee and Mosher made nearly a dozen more. Each Nutshell was carefully packed up and shipped to Harvard, where it was put on display to be studied by homicide detectives and admired by visitors.

If Lee had followed a typical career path, she'd most likely be retired at this point, but she'd never had a real job, so there wasn't anything to retire from. If anything, she was busier than ever in her sixties. In 1947, she invited thirty people to the Rocks to witness the autopsy of Bill Jones, a thirty-six-year-old gardener, who had died of a gunshot wound. It looked like a suicide, but a note pinned to Jones's body accused his archnemesis, Tom Smith, of having threatened Jones's life; the public autopsy was intended to determine what really happened. The corpse was, thankfully, made out of papier-mâché. "Gruesome details of the case bothered the guests not a whit when it came dinnertime, and all did full justice to a bountiful meal provided by Captain Lee—right in the same room with the 'corpse,'" the local newspaper reported.

At Harvard, Lee was increasingly treated as an oddity, a temperamental donor who needed to be indulged but not necessarily taken seriously. She had better luck with the cops. When she visited Richmond, Virginia, she cruised through the city with officers on patrol; when she wasn't in a squad car, she was listening in on a police scanner.

"How pleasant to hear units 15 and 57 called and to remember them and having driven with 15!" she wrote to the superintendent of the Virginia State Police. "Your disembodied voices are such constant companions that I feel as if you were all members of my family." The New Hampshire State Police appointed her as their first female police captain, a great (if largely ceremonial) honor. She'd been uneasy in her role as a daughter, as a wife, as a mother, but something in her softened around these police officers. It rankled her children and grandchildren, sometimes, how she lit up when these adult men in uniform called her "Mother."

Lee did eventually convince Harvard to host educational programs for law enforcement, not just medical students; the university agreed perhaps because she paid for the entire project. The biannual week-long homicide seminars introduced detectives from around the country to top forensic experts, who taught them about cutting-edge research and investigatory best practices. Lee's homicide seminars soon began to garner press attention, much of it focusing on Lee herself, and on the incongruity of her being an old lady who knew a lot about crime fighting. "Grandma: Sleuth at Sixty-Nine," read the headline of an article in *Picture Week* magazine, and "Grandma Knows Her Murders," in *Coronet*. There was a feature in the *Los Angeles Times*, and the *Saturday Evening Post* printed a picture of Lee, "whose zeal and generous purse have helped to free many an innocent person and convict many an unsuspected killer," using tweezers to make adjustments to one of the Nutshells. Most of these articles about her accomplishments made sure to mention (usually in the headline) that she was also a grandmother. Her gray hair was a kind of cover; it made her ambitions appear benign, even endearing. The woman who was prevented from going to college was now laden with honorary accolades. "If, as the Germans do, Captain Lee used all the various titles she holds throughout the country," *Yankee Magazine* wrote, "she would become Doctor Major Captain Mrs. Frances Glessner Lee."

At least one of these articles took her ambitions seriously, rather than dismissing them as a quirk: "Some day, innocent Americans will no longer go to jail for murder and manslaughter," *Coronet* predicted in 1949. "Homicides by the hundreds will no longer remain unrecognized. There will be no such thing as unexplained death. And Frances Glessner Lee will largely be responsible for all these victories in the war against crime."

I like to imagine Lee at this moment, the peak of her public success, confident in the lasting legacy of her Nutshells and her department and her homicide seminars. Every year, she spent an extravagant amount of money on a gala at the Ritz-Carlton for the policemen attending the seminars. Her son remarked on how she glowed at these dinners and seemed a whole decade younger than she was. I also like to imagine her guests, those small-town cops, most of whom had little experience with fine china and canapés, and the mix of discomfort and pride they must have felt when they received the engraved invitation summoning them for dinner at seven, and the smaller card notifying them of cocktails "at half after six o'clock." I like to imagine Lee greeting each man as he walked in the door, asking a hostess's genteel, engaged questions—Was he married? How did he become involved in police work? Did he enjoy it?—as waiters circulated with trays of hors d'oeuvres: foie gras, caviar, dainty miniature quiches lorraines.

A few minutes after seven, the maître d' and his assistant would pull back the curtains with a flourish to reveal a lavish dining room festooned with flowers. The policemen found their assigned places and settled into leather chairs. These evenings were always intensely managed; Lee arranged the flowers herself and decided who would sit where. The food was a New England version of fancy: salad, filet mignon, and boola-boola soup, a greenish local delicacy made of equal parts pea and turtle soup. A wine steward hovered in the background, topping off glasses; Lee commanded the Ritz's manager to treat her guests "like royalty." The food was served on a special set of gold-leaf china that the Ritz reserved for Lee. After dinner the policemen were treated to cigars and a postmeal nightcap. "One speaks of prices in a muted tone at the Ritz," a *Boston Globe* reporter wrote after one of Lee's dinners, before estimating that she spent about $30,000 (in 2019 dollars) for a fifty-five-person dinner party, over $7,000 of it on flowers.

On the days following the gala dinner, the police officers turned their attention to the Nutshells, which were the grand finale of every homicide seminar. For this part of the program at least, Lee was in charge. I like to imagine her authority in that room, with all those detectives listening intently to her words. Perhaps that authority allowed her to relax, to become an easier version of herself. Perhaps she finally felt satisfied as the burly men bent over her small models, the care she put into them rewarded with the care of their gaze.

Today, when forensic science is the focus of numerous police procedurals and when magazine articles about Frances Glessner Lee call her the "mother of forensics," her life can sound like a simple story of triumph: a self-trained amateur helps further a new area of scientific inquiry. But it wasn't that smooth, for Lee or for the field of forensic science.

In 1949, Lee's ally Alan Moritz left Harvard for a job in Cleveland, purportedly for health reasons—but the Rockefeller Foundation's Alan Gregg speculated in his diary that it was likely also because "Mrs. Lee's various interventions annoyed him." She'd also managed to alienate J. Edgar Hoover. After their initial congenial meeting in 1934, Lee had continued to pester Hoover for meetings and to offer unsolicited advice. When his assistants gave increasingly terse responses, Lee got irritated. Eventually, the FBI put a note in her file indicating that she was "somewhat antagonistic."

Looking back over the many letters between Lee and Harvard personnel, it's clear that the university didn't know what to do with her, this difficult woman who wouldn't stop thinking she had something valuable to contribute. After Moritz left the department, Lee tried to strike up a relationship with his replacement, a narrow, cleft-chinned man named Richard Ford, but Ford didn't have much time or patience for her. She had so many *suggestions*—for experiments, for classes, for more opportunities to showcase her beloved Nutshells, for more ways to assist police officers. It must've been exhausting for Ford, who just wanted to teach his classes, conduct his autopsies, and then go home.

The truth was that the department—"my Department," as Lee was fond of calling it—was struggling. It couldn't seem to attract enough students or get Harvard to take it seriously. Maybe Lee had a glimmer of where this would all lead. The schism between academia and policing would only grow wider. Soon enough, most forensic science work would take place in police crime labs. Seen as an applied science, the field would become a kind of neglected stepchild among the scientific disciplines. There would be little support for research, and little impetus to keep the field cutting edge. The utopian dream of using science to remove human error from crime investigation wouldn't work out as Lee had hoped; in fact, without scientific oversight or regulatory controls keeping it in check, faulty forensics would eventually be implicated in sending scores of innocent people to prison.

But before any of that happened, Lee and Ford got in an argument. It's unclear how it started, only that in its aftermath Lee felt disrespected and despairing. The only leverage she had, perhaps had ever had, was her money. She wrote her old friend Alan Gregg. It's a hard letter to read, with so much fury compressed into tight, genteel sentences: "I am now writing to tell you that in my opinion the Department is quite rapidly dying on its feet and that after another year of such a continued slump, I should have no further interest in giving it either my financial or moral support." She strongly suggested that the Rockefeller Foundation pull its funding from the department, too.

Considering that the Department of Legal Medicine was once Lee's most treasured project, her *legacy*, this was a shocking and massive betrayal. It's an example of how difficult Lee could be, how controlling and possessive, how quick to burn bridges.

In Gregg's reply, he pointed this out as gently as he could: Lee's attempts to undermine "her" department appeared "almost vindictive." He could think of only one solution that wouldn't result in "frustration" and "embitterment" on Lee's part. She would have to cede control entirely—give Harvard the money she'd promised, but with no strings attached. She would have to relinquish all ties to the department and let Harvard spend her money however it wanted. He reminded her of "what parental possessiveness did to you"; more than most, Lee should know that attempting to control something (or someone) resulted in resentment on all sides. "My experience has shown me that if you don't give freedom, you defeat your purpose," he wrote. "And Legal Medicine *is* important."

But relinquishing control was never something Lee was particularly good at. Within a few years, she let Harvard know that she'd written the Department of Legal Medicine out of her will entirely. The Rockefeller Foundation, the department's other main funding source, questioned whether legal medicine was a good investment after all: "It has been difficult to attract and to retain in the field able and qualified people because there is no recognition of forensic pathology as an entity and as a potential career," the foundation fretted in an internal report in 1955. Meanwhile, Richard Ford's position at Harvard was never made permanent, and he increasingly succumbed to alcoholism. In 1970, at age fifty-five, he shot himself in the head.

The experience with Harvard left Lee bitter. "This has been a lonely and rather terrifying life I have lived," she wrote in 1951, at age seventy-three. "Chief amongst the difficulties I have had to meet have been the facts that I never went to school, that I had no letters after my name, and that I was placed in the category of 'rich woman who didn't have enough to do.'" In the final years of her life, though she was disillusioned with Harvard, she was fonder than ever of her police officer friends. Their influence on her was so strong that after a lifetime as an atheist, she converted to Catholicism in her final years. Though her various medical issues made her "practically an invalid," she still made a point of attending the International Association of Chiefs of Police convention well into her seventies.

In 1962, at age eighty-three, Lee died at home in New Hampshire. There were two funerals: a small, nondenominational one for her family and a much larger service in a Catholic church attended by hundreds of law enforcement officers. People close to her reflected on her life with a mix of frustration and admiration. "Perhaps FGL should have been a man," her son wrote after her death, "at liberty to pursue a profession, required to earn a living, free from all the traditional shackles which restrained and infuriated her."

The Department of Legal Medicine, the institution that Lee once hoped would serve as the example and inspiration that would change the course of criminal investigation in America, endured a long period of decline. It officially shut down five years after Lee's death. The orphaned Nutshell Studies were packed up and sent to the Maryland Medical Examiner's Office, where the state medical examiner, a Harvard legal medicine graduate, agreed to take them in. One was lost in transit, and another was damaged beyond repair. To many people, they were just the remnants of an odd woman's odd hobby. For decades, Lee's dead dolls lived in that fluorescent-lit building in Baltimore. They were a complicated bequest, both an honor and a burden.

In her obsession with forensics, Frances Glessner Lee was about a half century too early. In the early 1990s, as the murder rate in the United States reached its highest-ever levels, everyone else caught up with her. It started with documentary shows such as HBO's *Autopsy Files* and the Learning Channel's *Medical Detectives*, which celebrated the work of forensic pathologists. The first of Cornwell's Scarpetta novels, which introduced thriller fans to the world of forensic investigation, was published in 1990; eventually, the series sold more than 100 million copies. By 2000, with the debut of *CSI* (soon to be followed by *CSI: Miami*, *CSI: NY*, and *CSI: Cyber*), crime scene investigation was officially a national obsession. The shows provided powerful—and increasingly outlandish—depictions of crime-solving science. On *CSI* episodes, the camera followed a bullet's path inside a body; computer programs summoned holographic reconstructions of crime scenes; facial-recognition software could put a name to a suspect's face in a crowd. At a time when crime felt out of control, this promise of ultimate transparency through scientific knowledge and technical prowess was deeply alluring.

Although the audience for crime procedurals was dispropor-tionately female, the people working in law enforcement were still overwhelmingly male, particularly in the detective ranks. In more recent decades, though, women who wanted to combat crime have found options that were slightly outside of or adjacent to traditional law enforcement—notably in the field of forensics. Forensic investi-gation offered a different style of crime fighting, one that prioritized careful, close observation over brute force. Eventually, a century after Lee was denied a college education by her father, the field she found so fascinating—now definitively referred to as forensics—became one of the few science careers where the vast majority of students were women.

That women are flocking to forensics has been explained in condescending ways, often with references to high heels: Female forensic scientists are drawn to the field by TV depictions of "intelligent women sampling bodily fluids in stilettos"; real forensic scientists, "unlike their counterparts on TV, [are] not wearing low-cut shirts or stiletto heels." "We leave the Prada stilettos at home when processing a crime scene," a forensic investigator told a reporter.

It's more likely that structural changes contributed to the influx of women in the field. In Washington, DC, crime scene investigators used to be drawn from the ranks of police officers—which meant they had to attend the law enforcement academy, carry a gun, and navigate their way through a culture that's still extremely misogynist. But when the city began to civilianize the work, handing it over to an independent agency starting in 2012—meaning that you could do crime scene work without having to be a cop—"the ratio of men to women changed drastically," Dr. Jenifer Smith, director of the District's Department of Forensic Sciences, told me. "It used to be ninety percent men. Now it's seventy percent women."

In 2012, the *Washington Post* spoke with a crime scene investigator named Emily Rancourt. Rancourt was in her early teens when Jeffrey Dahmer was found with severed heads in his freezer and a decomposing hand in his teakettle. She became preoccupied with the idea that a serial killer would come for her and her family. The fear had an odd magnetism—was it something she was afraid of, or something she was drawn to? In college, she began considering a career in forensics. Her mother was horrified; did her self-described "girly-girl" figure-skater daughter *really* want to work with dead bodies all day? To make sure she had the stomach for her chosen profession, Rancourt asked the county medical examiner to let her sit in on his next autopsy. He called her up the following morning at 6:00 a.m.; a body had just come in, a man who'd been decapitated in a car accident. Rancourt watched the whole process, helping weigh the man's brain and lungs and heart. After it was over, she told the medical examiner the experience had been "disturbing." He reassured her that her reaction was normal. "No," she told him. "I'm disturbed because I thought it was awesome."

The British sociologist Robin Williams coined a phrase for the seductive promise of shows such as *CSI*: "the forensic imaginary." It's the idea that "all . . . events are knowable and can be reconstructed from forensic evidence." In the daydream world of the forensic imaginary, the victim has always left a last message and the killer always reveals himself with a signature; every murder turns out to be a narrative that, with enough care or the right equipment, the detective can reconstruct. The forensic imaginary is rooted in an early principle of forensic science: that every touch leaves a trace. It promises that no action will remain a mystery to the true detective; with enough careful looking, the story of the crime will always reveal itself.

This helps explain why television programs about violent death can feel so strangely soothing: they teach us that even the most senseless crimes can be interpreted and, ultimately, explained. That fantasy of omniscience is not all that different from the appeal of a dollhouse. Small things awaken in us the "desire to possess the world more completely, to banish the unknown and the unseen," novelist Steven Millhauser wrote in his essay "The Fascination of the Miniature." The miniature universe and the forensic universe both promise a world of complete visibility, free from secrets, free from fear. A world in which it's possible to know everything, everything.

The forensic imaginary is a fantastical idea, one that resembles wizardry more than actual science. The reality, unfortunately, is not nearly so miraculous. As Frances Glessner Lee had feared more than half a century earlier, a gulf still yawns between police work and peer-reviewed science. Throughout the 1990s and even into the 2000s, only a handful of universities taught forensics; not until December 2017 did the first student graduate with a PhD in the subject. In the last decades of the twentieth century, all too often the expert witnesses who took the stand to testify about forensic evidence were police officers who had taken a weekend course in bloodstain-pattern analysis or coroners spouting unverified theories.

No single regulatory body keeps tabs on the field, which meant that fraudulent practitioners sometimes got away with giving false testimony for an alarmingly long time. A police chemist working at the West Virginia State Police crime lab was hugely popular with prosecutors for his ability to provide just the evidence they needed in tricky cases; when it turned out he'd been faking results throughout the 1980s, more than a hundred convictions were cast into doubt. Forensic experts who came up with "magic" results—such as the dentist-coroner in Mississippi who claimed he could use ultraviolet light to detect otherwise-invisible bite marks months after they had been inflicted, then definitively match those marks with a single suspect—got more business from investigators and prosecutors. Shoddy forensic science could be good business. (Up to a point, at least; that Mississippi coroner was eventually discredited, after his testimony was found to have resulted in numerous wrongful convictions.)

That kind of quackery was thankfully rare, but even forensic technicians with good intentions were plagued by confirmation bias and a reliance on techniques that didn't have a robust scientific foundation. Making matters worse, crime labs were typically operated by local or state law enforcement. This system had bias built into it, according to critics, since labs were incentivized to come up with findings that aligned with the preferred theories of police and prosecutors. (Sometimes quite literally—in certain states, crime labs are still offered financial incentives for convictions.) Law enforcement wasn't equipped (or inclined) to take a hard look at the techniques they relied on to identify culprits, and people who raised suspicions about questionable forensic methods, such as bite-mark or bloodstain-pattern analysis, are still sometimes decried as being soft on crime.

Lee had dreamed of a future where scientific advances would prevent innocent people from going to prison. Instead, we seemed to be living in an upside-down version of that world: in courtrooms, forensics had all the authority of science, but little of its rigor. In the most alarming cases, bad forensics were the *reason* innocent people got sent to prison. The extent to which this was happening didn't fully emerge until the late 1990s, along with advances in DNA profiling. In the two decades since, hundreds of people have been released from prison after DNA evidence exonerated them. In nearly half those cases, faulty forensics had contributed to the original conviction.

In 2009, the National Academy of Sciences released a scathing report about the "serious problems" facing forensics in the United States. Crime labs were understaffed, with "staggering" backlogs and erratically trained personnel; there were no uniform standards delineating who could credibly work as a forensic tech, no standard certification or degree that people calling themselves forensic professionals needed to have, and no mandatory boards or exams they needed to pass. Some jurisdictions did require certification, but the majority did not. The lack of gatekeeping and oversight posed "a continuing and serious threat to the quality and credibility of forensic science practice," the report's authors found.

The NAS report made it clear that we were living out the consequences of the problems Lee had identified nearly eighty years before: law enforcement that was too often seeing what it wanted to see; an academic community cut off from the messy realities of police work; and nothing to successfully bridge the gap between the two worlds. The report called for an independent institute to research, oversee, and regulate forensic science—a role that sounds uncannily similar to Lee's long-ago dreams for the Harvard legal medicine department. Under President Obama, some progress was made in that direction, including the formation of a committee that brought together scientists, prosecutors, defense attorneys, and other criminal justice stakeholders who didn't typically work together. But when President Trump was elected, forensic science reform was no longer a priority. "I don't think we should suggest that those proven scientific principles that we've been using for decades are somehow uncertain," then-senator Jeff Sessions said.

Why did it take so long for forensic science to begin to lose its shine? In part, it's because police and prosecutors were reluctant to question a useful tool or to cast doubt on past convictions. But many of the rest of us bought into the dream of forensics, too. It's reassuring to believe that an expert can walk into a bloody room and emerge with a story that neatly explains the horror that happened there. The forensic hero has a Sherlock Holmesian omniscience, bolstered by the authority of science. Who wouldn't find that seductive? Who wouldn't want to believe?

Yet there are so many ways that people can mess things up, so many ways our human tendencies toward bias, sloppiness, error, and fraud can get in the way. Ultimately, we're such bad detectives, at least by the standards of my young self. We haven't figured out how to see without being seen. We're far from all-powerful. We fail at omniscience. Even the best-trained, best-intentioned among us still move through a world teeming with so much that we don't, that we *can't*, know. Admitting this doesn't mean that forensic science is useless; only that it's not magic, and we shouldn't expect it to be. This is a less satisfying story perhaps, one that requires us to acknowledge our many limitations and blind spots, but it's a more honest one.

A few years ago, Susan Marks, a Minneapolis filmmaker, started making a documentary about Frances Glessner Lee and her contributions to forensic science. It was in some ways frustrating, she told me. So much material about Lee was out there, but the more Marks looked into it, the more she became aware of what was conspicuously absent—namely Lee's own papers, many of her letters, any journal she may have kept. Anything that would've given access to her inner life. None of that was in the archives. This seemed odd to Marks. Lee was a lively writer and a prolific correspondent. Surely there was more than what Marks had found in other people's archives. But when she asked Lee's family members, they were cagey, protective of their privacy. She was told that the materials she was looking for were lost or burned or never existed. Still, Marks couldn't let it go; she just had this *strong sense* that some key piece of evidence was missing. So who had it? And what might it reveal?

Marks didn't dwell on any of this in the film she eventually made, *Of Dolls and Murder*, but she did briefly mention that Lee's personal papers had never been found. That line resonated with viewers; soon Marks found herself with a small team of volunteer researchers trying to track down more information. She and her amateur detectives dug up enough new material that she made a second documentary, *Murder in a Nutshell.*

Marks and her cadre of ad hoc detectives were looking for some sort of clue, an incident in Lee's past that would explain why she was so repeatedly drawn to death. The answer, at least for fictional detectives, is often trauma. Mystery-solving women in crime procedurals and crime novels are often saddled with tragic, explanatory backstories. Olivia Benson, the steely-yet-vulnerable sex-murder investigator of *SVU*, was the daughter of a rape victim; in Patricia Cornwell's novels, Kay Scarpetta was scarred by the death of her father and was herself the victim of several near rapes. They were detectives who had been initiated into darkness against their will, by force. Now the darkness was inside them (or so the trope went). Their murder-adjacent careers were their attempt to prevent other women from suffering a similar fate—or, more darkly, a compulsive reenactment of a wound that could never heal. The subtext: if you were a woman who was inexorably drawn to murder stories, there had to be some terrible reason why. Even the villains in crime procedurals were usually assigned a motivation that, as improbable as it may be, attempted to address the yawning *why* at the core of every murder story. When *CSI* introduced a character inspired by the Nutshells—the Miniature Killer, who taunted the investigators throughout season six by leaving models of her murders at the crime scenes—the writers gave her a particularly baroque backstory with a dead mother and a ventriloquist father; a murderous psychosis triggered by the smell of bleach; and revenge fantasies based on a foster father's suicide. I didn't expect anything as extravagant as that had happened to Lee. But surely, there was something?

On the phone, Marks let me down as gently as possible. She told me that she had concluded that Lee's early life held no deep, dark secret, no revelatory trauma or formative violence. "It's not like fiction," Marks said. "We can't point to an inciting incident—that a crime happened to her, or to her family, or that there was some sort of romantic thing happening between her and Dr. Magrath. We want that. That's the kind of story our brains can handle. But I think we do her a disservice by thinking that something had to have *happened* to her."

A few years ago, researchers at West Virginia University asked female forensics students what drew them to the field. Most said they had an early interest in science; others talked about wanting to help people. Many cited another reason, too: a past experience of trauma. This fits with the broad cultural script that insists that women are interested in stories of violence because of their own history of violation—except that the women in the survey clarified that they weren't just talking about harm that had been done to them personally, but societal trauma, too. A lot of them mentioned 9/11. Pain doesn't have to be personal to be a motivating force. Which is another way of saying that of course something happened to Lee. Something has happened to all of us.

I was about to hang up, but Marks kept talking. Even though she knew that Lee's life wasn't some sort of puzzle to be solved, she told me that she still couldn't stop herself from looking for a solution. Figuring Lee out was like a project Marks couldn't put aside, even though it had absorbed more than a decade of her life. The gaps in the story drove her a little crazy. She was still looking for that one file folder, that box full of documents, that might decode the mystery of Lee's mind. "I'm still looking for these parts of her life," she said. "Those unanswered questions are what's fueling me."

A half century after her death, Lee was rediscovered. (Much of the credit should go to the photographer Corinne May Botz, whose book about the Nutshells introduced them to a wide audience for the first

time.) It made sense. Lee's story touched on a number of au cou-
rant themes: crime, forensics, forgotten women, outsider art. "The
dollhouses of death!" the internet articles clickbaited. "Dioramas
to die for!" By 2017, when all nineteen surviving Nutshells were put
on display at the Smithsonian's Renwick Gallery, which focuses on
"contemporary craft and decorative art," Lee—a woman who disliked
women, who insisted that her work was scientific—had been reclaimed
as a feminist, and as an artist. She would probably grumble about it,
but, alas, you can only exert so much control from beyond the grave.

For the Smithsonian exhibition, the Nutshells underwent an
extensive restoration, their first since they'd been sent to Baltimore
in the 1960s. Over several weeks, their tiny incandescent lightbulbs
were unscrewed from their tiny light fixtures and replaced with LED
equivalents; fake blood, which had oxidized to a deep purple, was
repainted the appropriate bright crimson. It was the first time that
this many of the models were available for public viewing. When I
visited the exhibit and saw all the people crowding around them,
theorizing about motives and looking for clues, I felt an unexpected
surge of territoriality that I immediately tried to stuff into the dark
closet at the back of my heart.

The Three-Room Dwelling occupied a prominent place in the
center of the exhibit. When I visited, a half dozen people were crowded
around it, frowning with clinical curiosity at the slaughtered doll family. "He could've been moved," a blond woman mused, considering
the bloody father splayed on the floor of the bedroom. Two old men
in matching fedoras and a younger woman in dark lipstick discussed
the peculiar bloodstain patterns on the kitchen floor. One of the men
spun a convoluted theory about how the milkman's wife—a character
he seemed to have invented based on absolutely no evidence—was
obviously the killer. "That's the problem with being a detective," the
blond woman said to me. "You get attached to your theory and then

you try to make it fit. I'm just looking for ways to make *him* guilty." She gave the dead doll-husband a dark look, as if she knew something about him that the rest of us did not.

This crew was so collegial in their speculation that I at first assumed they were part of the same group, but when I asked, they all laughed a bit nervously. No, they hadn't come here together; they didn't know each other at all. It was just that solving crimes was much more fun as a group activity.

I wandered on through the gallery, marveling at all the small dead women: one lying prone in a pink bathroom, her pink slippers arranged neatly on the carpet; another, drowned in the bathtub of a much seedier bathroom with peeling paint and an unraveling rug. A girl was dead in an empty house, a knife stuck in her stomach and her skirt shoved up; a woman had collapsed in a closet, her throat slit; and an old woman was hanging from a noose in the attic, love letters scattered at her feet. There were dead men, too—prone on a couch next to a dozen empty beer bottles, dead in a car in an orderly garage.

I had come alone, and I kept myself company by eavesdropping on other people's conversations. Although a handful of the Nutshell "solutions" have been made public, the Renwick chose to keep them all a mystery, and people were left to come up with their own theories, most of which seemed to involve some sort of romance gone wrong: *His wife kicked him out the night before, so he was sleeping on the floor, and then he got sick of it, so he came in with the shotgun; her drawers are open, so we think her boyfriend went through and took her cash.*

One Nutshell showed a woman lying on the floor of a placidly middle-class kitchen, a cake in the oven and peeled potatoes by the sink. The accompanying "police report" noted that she was discovered dead by her husband when he returned home from running some errands. A sign next to the model asked visitors to write their own theories or observations on Post-it notes and stick them on the wall.

Some people's notes were resolutely practical—"not suicide because why bake?"—but more seemed to be hoping for a solution that was as outlandish as a television plot twist: "knocked self out with ice cubes," "I think the husband killed her and used errands as an alliby," and one particularly knotty theory that required two Post-its to explain and involved a secret lover and a staged suicide.

On the train ride back south, I stared out the window. From the slight elevation of the railroad tracks, the backyards of northern Virginia, with their trampolines and tricycles, seemed out of scale, charmingly diminished. All that *looking* had left me in a strange state, spent but also exhilarated. Once again, the Nutshells had cast a peculiar spell over me; every object my eyes moved over seemed charged, vibrating with potential significance. I thought about how the detective's gaze—slow, hungry, attentive—is not so different from a caress.

You can find this same eager, almost fetishistic, devotion to detail on online forums for cold cases and unsolved mysteries. People (largely women) parse court documents and news reports, zeroing in on the smallest pieces of potential evidence—a mention of a blue truck; a witness's hazy memory of her assailant's thick calves—and following them down a rabbit hole. Michelle McNamara, who dedicated years of her life to attempting to identify the serial rapist/murderer she nicknamed the Golden State Killer, lingered in this heightened state of pleasure and compulsion, not always sure whether she was the predator or the prey. "The case dragged me under quickly. Curiosity turned to clawing hunger," she wrote in her memoir of investigating the case, *I'll Be Gone in the Dark*, which was published after her death. "I was on the hunt, absorbed by a click-fever that connected my propulsive tapping with a dopamine rush." She lost afternoons to tracking down former members of high school water polo teams because she had a hunch the perpetrator might've played.

She trawled the internet, searching for cuff links that resembled a pair stolen from a crime scene.

The fantasy is that all this speculation is productive, that it's building toward one glorious moment when everything clicks into place, when what used to look like disorder reveals itself as patterned, intelligible, *solved*.

But real life is messier than a network crime procedural. We know now that McNamara's theories mostly missed the mark, as did those of the Reddit detectives and professional investigators who also worked on the Golden State Killer case. Two years after McNamara's death, DNA evidence pinpointed a suspect, a former police officer named Joseph DeAngelo. He wasn't on anybody's radar. Which is not to say that McNamara's self-driven investigation was pointless. The sustained attention from her and others kept the crimes in the public eye and spurred law enforcement to follow up on old information. It mattered less what she saw than that she kept looking.

That first time I visited the Nutshells, Jerry D. had told me a story. He was trying to impress upon me how the models were not oddities or toys, but actual teaching tools so well crafted that they're still in use. The seminars for homicide investigators that Lee founded in the 1940s continue to this day, though at a much-reduced scale. (The group dinner now takes place at Ruth Chris Steak House instead of the Ritz, for example.) Their format hews close to the template Lee helped establish a half century ago: lectures on cutting-edge techniques followed by attempts to solve the Nutshells. The cops, all hardened veterans of homicide investigations, really get into it. They shine their flashlights into dark corners and break out their magnifying glasses to make sure they're not missing anything. Once,

Jerry D. told me, he caught a couple of cops sneaking into his office at night; they were so solution crazy that they were going to break into his filing cabinet to find the answers. These days he keeps the files padlocked. Just in case.

I bet this scene—cops driven wild by the complexity of the models—would please Lee more than all the documentaries and museum exhibits. She *did* enjoy being the one with all the answers. ("Since you and I have perpetrated these crimes ourselves we are in the unique position of being able to give complete descriptions of them even if there were no witnesses," she wrote to Alan Moritz. "Very much in the manner of the novelist who is able to tell the inmost thoughts of his characters.") Yet, Lee is dead and the models persist, with many of their mysteries still intact.

Lee's life, with all its frustrations and contradictions, is a warning against easy solutions. Her detective daydreams, like all fantasies of omniscience, were ultimately scuttled by reality. We're just too hemmed in by the prejudices of our times and the limitations of our minds. The detective inside each of us may wish for the world to be transparent, like a dollhouse cut open for our viewing pleasure—but if we're genuinely seeking truth, we must account for everything we can't see, our blind spots and biases, how much we willfully misunderstand, all the things we don't yet—and may never—comprehend.

My favorite Nutshell depicts a ramshackle wooden cabin cluttered with logging tools and discarded whiskey bottles. Wilby Jenks lies on the bed, completely swaddled with blankets. She has been dead for about two hours. The two lumberjacks she lived with are also at the scene, "very drunk," according to the case notes that Lee provided.

While the solutions to most of the other Nutshells are not publicly known, they exist—they're written down on a piece of paper in Jerry D.'s locked filing cabinet. Each death is classified as an accident, suicide, or murder. This model is different. The solution is a nonsolution: the cause of death will never be known. The doctor disturbed the crime scene. The county attorney didn't order an autopsy. The police chief wrote an incomplete report. Human fallibility has prevented the case from ever being concluded. A total of thirty-one errors were introduced into the crime scene by the officials themselves. You "solve" this Nutshell by enumerating each of those mistakes.

I think of this model as the key to them all. It's where the real detective lives. She looks—why not?—like a harmless old woman, bespectacled and stern. She peers at everything closely—too closely for her own comfort, perhaps. Even so, she abides in uncertainty, that shadowy realm, where she takes careful notes about all the things she doesn't yet understand.

THE VICTIM

The victim is every victim. She could be you or related
to you.

—President Ronald Reagan's
Task Force on Victims of Crime, 1982

In March 1990, a young woman named Alisa Statman moved into a
small bungalow in Beverly Hills. The little house sat off to the side
of a much larger ranch-style mansion; it looked like the kind of
place where the main house's owners might keep their less favored
guests, or perhaps stow a pool boy. The two buildings—the mansion
and its guesthouse—perched at the top of a winding street, Cielo
Drive. The guesthouse was snug, but its view of the city was private
and expansive. It was just right for a young woman starting out on
her own.

Statman was in her early twenties but seemed younger, according to people who knew her around this time, maybe because of her
girlish voice, maybe because she was so shy in company. She'd come
to California, angling for a career in Hollywood. In her first years in
Los Angeles, she found entry-level work on high-profile movies: as
a production assistant on *Dick Tracy*, as the second assistant director on *Free Willy*. In the evenings, after work, she drove the snaking
road above Benedict Canyon, through the wrought-iron gates, to her

small, temporary home. "I can't begin to explain it, but the moment you drove through the gates there was an overwhelming, peaceful easy feeling that was felt by all those who came to visit me," Statman told an interviewer years later. "And for me, that feeling outweighed the past atrocities."

You've probably heard about these atrocities. In July 1969, around the same time Statman was born, actress Sharon Tate moved into the main house at 10050 Cielo Drive, while her husband, director Roman Polanski, was in London shooting a film. Tate was eight months pregnant with the couple's first child; the baby's name, they'd decided, would be Paul. The Cielo Drive house had a pool and plenty of spare rooms for Sharon's friends to sleep over. A caretaker lived in the small guesthouse out back, far enough away that he didn't bother anyone. The house was made for movie stars; Cary Grant had lived there, and so had Henry Fonda. It was close enough to Hollywood to be convenient, but isolated enough—sitting at the top of its high hill at the end of a cul-de-sac, shielded by pine trees—to also feel secluded. That summer, in the final months of her pregnancy, Sharon had friends over and lounged by the pool. On July 20, she invited her parents, Doris and P.J., and her little sisters, Debbie and Patti, over. They sat in the living room and watched Neil Armstrong get his footprints all over the moon.

A few weeks later, on August 8, four followers of Charles Manson's—Tex Watson, Patricia Krenwinkel, Linda Kasabian, and Susan Atkins—pulled up outside the Cielo Drive house. They were carrying knives (Tex also had a gun) and dressed in black. Manson had instructed them to go to this house; he'd known its former occupant, a music producer. Maybe Manson wanted to attract attention away from Bobby Beausoleil, another Family member who'd recently been arrested for a different murder; maybe Manson wanted to send the producer, who had failed to give Manson the recording contract he coveted, a message. Or maybe he was just driven by a free-floating, drug-fueled malice. "You know what to do," he had told Watson earlier that evening. "Do something witchy," he commanded the women.

That night, Sharon had visitors: her ex, hairstylist-to-the-stars Jay Sebring; coffee company heiress Abigail Folger; and Folger's boyfriend, Holocaust survivor Woytek Frykowski. William Garretson, the property's teenage caretaker, was in the small guesthouse behind the mansion with an acquaintance named Steven Parent. Just after midnight, Watson, Krenwinkel, Kasabian, and Atkins arrived at the house, cut the phone lines, and scrambled over the fence. The first person they killed was Parent, who was in his car in the driveway, just about to leave. Sebring, Folger, and Frykowski were next. Sharon Tate was the last to die.

Garretson slept through the murders in the little guesthouse where Statman later lived. Faced with a gruesome crime scene the next day, the Los Angeles police immediately assumed that the caretaker was responsible. Cops knocked down the guesthouse door and found Garretson standing there, shirtless and sleepy eyed. A police detective shoved him against the wall and slapped handcuffs on him. "What's the matter?" Garretson kept saying. "What's the matter?" They marched him, barefoot, past the body of Abigail Folger, splayed on the front lawn. She was unrecognizable, so bloodied that he identified her as Winnie Chapman, the black housekeeper. In the news footage from that day, Garretson's curly hair sticks up from his head at crazy angles and his small mouth hangs open; he looks like a kid who's been caught up in something much too big for him.

After the murders, the Cielo house acquired its own dark celebrity. By the time Statman moved in, two decades later, the address had been changed to 10066 Cielo, an attempt to throw off the curious and morbid.

It's hard to know what to do with houses that have born witness to sensational crimes. Knocking them down seems like a futile attempt at repression, as if bulldozing a building could erase what happened there. Leave them up, though, and they risk becoming tourist attractions, drawing the kind of gawkers who cruise by slowly, looking at something banal—a high school gym, a brick apartment building, a two-story house in the suburbs—and picturing something horrific.

I've done it myself, taken a detour from I-25 on my way to visit family in Denver, compelled by a sudden impulse to have a look at Columbine High School. I had spent so much time reading about what happened there, thinking about it, even dreaming about it, that it seemed natural to pay it a visit while I was in the area. I had friends whose parents dragged them to Gettysburg and Yorktown; wasn't this just my own way of visiting a famous battlefield of the late twentieth century, of paying homage to its dead? I imagined myself sitting in my car in the parking lot, looking at the cafeteria, the library. I imagined myself crying. It was close to rush hour when I made it to Littleton, and as I sat in traffic, I began to feel ashamed of myself. I worried that I was treating this school as if it were some kind of roadside attraction: the biggest ball of twine, the giant cowboy boot, the site of the high school massacre. I turned around in a strip mall parking lot and got back on the highway. The line between honoring a tragedy and feeding off it was not as clear as I would've liked.

Perhaps the owner of the Cielo Drive property didn't have the money to knock down the house where Sharon Tate and her friends had died and build something new and untainted in its place. Or maybe, perversely, the structure's history was part of its appeal. Most people think of murders, especially highly publicized ones, as lowering property values. In many cases that's true; in California, sellers must disclose violent deaths that happened on the premises, under the assumption that a house's history of violence is not so different

from an insect infestation or a nearby nuclear waste dump. People
don't want to live with the bad vibes, or the ghosts. But sometimes a
famous crime has the opposite effect. "We bought this house because
of the historical value," proclaimed the woman who purchased the
Spanish-style home where the Manson Family killed Rosemary and
Leno LaBianca the day after the Cielo Drive murders, "just like Donald Trump bought the Ambassador Hotel knowing Robert Kennedy
died there."

The rich can buy up these infamous houses (or hotels); the rest of
us just cruise by slowly, murder on our minds. The point of imagining
yourself as a detective is to keep a safe distance from crime—but
sometimes what we want isn't distance or safety at all. Sometimes
what we want is to be close to the victim, to be let in on the secret of
what happened to her. To look at her house and weep. To imagine,
for a moment, that we are inside her pain.

Just before my senior year of college, a teenage girl went missing in
Richmond, Virginia, my hometown. Her name was Taylor Behl and
she was about to start her freshman year at Virginia Commonwealth
University. The last place she'd been seen was the Village Café, a late-
night restaurant downtown, the same place where my high school
friends and I used to sit for hours over milk shakes, testing the limits of
our curfews. The Richmond newspaper kept printing the same photo
of her over and over, Taylor looking at the camera straight on, her
dark eyes flashing. I liked her thick eyebrows and the big turquoise
ring she wore on her middle finger. She looked smart, but also playful.
I imagined that we could have been friends.

Two weeks after she disappeared, an off-duty cop discovered
her car parked in a residential area—an ominous clue, I thought, as

I followed the investigation from my dorm room across the country. Instead of doing the reading for my Victorian lit class, I scoured the internet for clues about Taylor. I found her Myspace page and then her LiveJournal. She wrote openly about her life, and the longer she was missing, the more each banal detail acquired a kind of tragic weight, such as how her favorite song was "Paint It Black," and that the top three things that scared her were: "Boys, Men, My dad."

Taylor's online confessions were mild, but they nonetheless seemed to make police officers and reporters, *older people*, nervous. It was 2005 and Facebook was a niche site open to only Ivy Leaguers; sharing your private feelings with an audience of strangers still seemed novel, even ominous. *People* magazine reported on Taylor's "secret life on the Internet." The *Washington Post* fretted about how she revealed "her moods, her crushes, her insecurities" to "a vast virtual community, a very public arena" in "a personal diary with no key."

Taylor's Myspace venting was useful for feeding the news cycle, at least. In the absence of a perpetrator, or any clear evidence of a crime, members of the media began to dissect her instead. Court TV reported, "Young Taylor did do a few things that put her at risk. . . . She was walking around in an urban area, presumably unescorted, at ten thirty at night. Finally, at least some of her new friends in Richmond were people who were very much involved in the local drug scene." MSNBC convened a panel, including one of Taylor's best friends, to parse her LiveJournal posts, which the station primly edited for language: "I'm so [blank] tired of everyone making decisions in my best interest. Don't I get a [blank, blank] say? No, sorry, not until you're 18."

"You know, she seems very dramatic," the host said. "She says in one blog, 'I know now that everyone is useless and really doesn't care.' Let me read that again: 'I know now that everyone is useless and really doesn't care.' It sounds like she was depressed."

Taylor's friend countered as best as a seventeen-year-old without media training could: "You know, when I was around her, she always seemed really happy, and fun and, like, loving. She would always just do the best things. Anytime you needed something, she would do it. So, I mean, I guess for the people she really cared about, she made a difference in their lives, you know? Like, she rules."

There were, of course, never any new posts on Taylor's Live-Journal, never any new photos added to her Myspace page. I kept coming back anyway, usually in moments of anxious procrastination. No other source provided the right mix of dread and distraction. The country was fumbling its way through a war and the president was always on TV saying stupid things, blinking his dumb, frightened eyes. I could not imagine a stupider president. In the evenings, my friends crowded around the TV in the dorm's common room to watch Tyra Banks give bony women startling haircuts. Taylor was right; everyone *was* useless. I'd scan some story about *Desperate House-wives*, or Abu Ghraib, and then go back to the LiveJournal—"Boys, Men, My dad"—letting the sadness of it wash over me. How her life had been truncated at this stupid juncture. How she didn't even get to pick her own last words. How maybe this was all of her there would ever be.

The day that Alisa Statman moved into the guesthouse, there was another visitor to Cielo Drive. Bill Nelson variously described himself as a researcher or an investigative journalist or an advocate for victims. Nelson was middle-aged and dressed like a high school math teacher: short-sleeved, collared shirts tucked into slacks, a belt worn straight across his broad belly, a gold wedding band glinting on his left hand. His voice was smooth and measured, and he regularly cited Scripture.

After years of trying, Nelson had finally talked his way into the main house at Cielo Drive, where the murders had taken place, and he walked through the hallways with the eager enthusiasm of a dedicated fan. "It was exciting!" he wrote afterward of his visit. "Wow!" He'd brought along his heavily annotated copies of the two best-known books about the Manson Family murders, Vincent Bugliosi's *Helter Skelter* and Ed Sanders's *The Family*, to refresh his memories of the details of the slaughter that night. There was the short hallway Susan Atkins had walked down to Sharon Tate's bedroom; there were the French doors he'd seen in the crime scene photographs, smeared with Abigail Folger's blood.

Nelson was particularly interested in the guesthouse, where William Garretson had supposedly slept through the murders of five people. Garretson's account was a point of contention for many conspiracy-minded Manson researchers, people who—like Nelson—believed that the full story of what happened that night in 1969 had never been told. But the guesthouse was not on Nelson's tour that day; the owner had just rented it out to Statman. In the self-published book he wrote a few years later, *Manson: Behind the Scenes*—an account as scrambled and self-serving as everything else Nelson wrote, it should be noted—he described watching the young woman lugging her boxes into the small bungalow. The mansion's owner must have noticed him watching. Bill Nelson was the kind of person you had to explicitly forbid from doing things; otherwise, once he got fixated on an idea, he'd overstep boundaries without a second thought—such as, say, scaring off the new tenant by babbling to her about a decades-old cult murder. The owner instructed him not to talk to her.

Nelson was not what you might think of as a typical Manson Family enthusiast, not one of those sad teenage groupies who pledged allegiance to Charlie. (Nelson would, however, gladly buy copies of Manson's letters and poems from those people.) It was the victims he was interested in, Nelson insisted. He wanted to bring justice to the victims. At the time, in the early 1990s, Nelson was a minor figure in the Los Angeles area's conservative political scene, the host of a weekly talk-radio show and publisher of a current-affairs newsletter aimed at Republican members of the California legislature. His real passion, though, was the small Manson-centric media empire he ran out of his Orange County home. As Pen Power Publications, he sold his self-published book, *Tex Watson: The Man, the Madness, the Manipulation*, and his self-produced video, *Sharon Tate: The Victim*, as well as VHS tapes of Watson's parole hearings ("The video that Tex Watson does not want you to see!"), for $19.95, plus $3.50 for shipping and handling.

It wasn't a bad business, all told. Twenty years after Charlie's "family" first made headlines, the crimes exerted a persistent magnetism. The August 1969 murders, popularly referred to as Tate-LaBianca, seemed to almost have *too much* meaning, to be too dense with symbolic portent. Joan Didion declared that they were the end of the sixties. That was an overstatement—Richard Nixon had already been elected president, a much clearer sign of the backlash against the counterculture—but even so, the murders were treated as if they marked some sort of limit or boundary. Once everyone knew what had happened, how a bunch of hippies had gone on a murder spree at the bidding of their elfin guru, it was difficult to spout the same easy lines about freedom and openness. Utopia, it began to seem, was right next to dystopia.

If you were the kind of person who wanted to think about what the sixties meant, you could easily lose yourself in the story of the

Manson Family. It had everything: movie stars and rock stars; satanism and sex; glamour and squalor and extreme violence. The case had a particular attraction for those with a conspiratorial bent. The people who died and the people who had killed them seemed so far apart on the surface, but if you looked closer, if you squinted a bit and let yourself make a few logical leaps, they started to seem connected by thin threads of chance or circumstance—or perhaps something more sinister. Had members of the Manson Family really gone skinny-dipping in the Cielo Drive pool months before the murders, as some of them later claimed? Did the LaBiancas' dog not bark because it was already familiar with the killers? How was it possible for William Garretson, tucked away in his little guesthouse, to have slept through the slaughter without hearing a thing?

In the internet era, if you find a crime funk creeping over you, you can lose a whole evening—or a whole week!—to Wikipedia and message boards, falling down a bottomless, blood-soaked rabbit hole with no end. In the early 1990s, though, the options for obsessing about crime were far more limited. Every few years *Hard Copy* or *A Current Affair* would do a Manson Family update, fifteen minutes that barely scratched the surface. There was *Helter Skelter*, of course, but any discerning reader could tell that Bugliosi had his own agenda; if you were halfway sensitive to bullshit, you knew he was reprising his role as a prosecutor and selling you a story. If you *really* wanted to know more about Tate-LaBianca, you had to do some work to get behind the official narrative. You had to explore unorthodox avenues. And you usually had to go through Bill Nelson.

Not long after his visit to Cielo Drive, according to the account in his book, Nelson received an order for the Tex Watson parole videotape. The name on the form—Alisa Statman—was unfamiliar to him, but the return address brought him up short: 10066 Cielo Drive. This Statman woman had enclosed a check with her order, and her phone number was printed right on it. She sounded shocked when Nelson called her up that evening; they ended up talking for an hour. The soft-voiced woman he came to know as Lisa had "a keen interest in the case and a real knowledge of the facts," Nelson wrote. (Notably, this origin story of Nelson's relationship with Statman, like much that would happen between them, is recalled differently by Statman.)

Lisa Statman's interest in the murder of Sharon Tate—when she began to care about it, and just how much it preoccupied her—is a key point of contention. Statman told me that when she decided to rent the Cielo Drive guesthouse, she knew nothing of the infamous house's history and had no interest in the Manson Family murders. "It was literally a fluke kind of thing," she said. "When you were looking for a place to live and you're young, you literally drive up and down the canyon roads, looking for FOR RENT signs." In her account, she initially befriended Bill Nelson out of interest in his purported Hollywood connections. However, two people who have known Statman over the years told me that she moved into the guesthouse specifically because of its connection to the crimes. At the end of the day, while Nelson is hardly a reliable narrator, he self-published his account of his relationship with Statman in 1997, well before much of the later drama unfolded, and I'm inclined to believe the broad outlines of the story he tells, if not always the more self-aggrandizing details.

By the end of their first conversation, according to Nelson, he had finagled an invitation to come see Statman at the guesthouse. Over the next few months, the unlikely pair—the middle-aged Republican and the young, ambitious woman—developed a wary friendship, founded on the mutual exchange of information about murders that had happened more than twenty years before. Nelson was indisputably an authority on the case; he'd been featured as an expert on *Geraldo* and *Hard Copy* and made regular appearances with Doris Tate, Sharon's mother, at victims' events. Over the years, he'd accumulated file cabinets full of information about Manson and his followers. But Statman had the guesthouse.

The owner of the mansion on Cielo Drive had banned Nelson from the main house over some drama about unauthorized video footage, so Statman was his only in. According to Nelson, she was careful to invite him over only when the owner was away. They ate pizza and drank Cokes; they admired the sunset views and listened to records. And they talked about the murders. Nelson grew to appreciate his new young friend. He was impressed by how closely she studied her rental home, parsing its layout with the careful eye of an investigator. Having lived there for a few months now, she told Nelson that she didn't buy William Garretson's story about having slept through that night. In between visits, Statman called Nelson up to chat—sometimes about Tate-LaBianca, sometimes just about her job. She brought him promotional swag from the Hollywood sets she worked on; Nelson thought it was particularly amusing to walk around Los Angeles wearing a baseball cap from a Shirley MacLaine movie that read THE BABE.

Nelson was useful to Statman in return. He loaned her some of his research materials—interview transcripts, files from the district attorney—so she could take them to work and make copies. One day he brought over the crime scene photographs.

These days, it's harder to avoid these images than to see them. Search for *Abigail Folger* and Google will helpfully provide you with five thumbnail images, three of a pretty dark-haired woman and two of a corpse. In the 1990s, though, few people had seen them. *Helter Skelter*'s cover may have loudly promised never-before-seen crime scene photos, but in the book's images of the carnage at Cielo Drive, the corpses were redacted, replaced with white cutouts in the vague shapes of bodies. In the immediate aftermath of the murders, a German magazine had offered $100,000 for the crime scene images, which no one managed to produce. But Nelson, with his wiles and connections, had got his hands on some copies. He sat next to Statman in his red van as she slowly thumbed through them. There was the thin cord around Sharon Tate's neck; there was the incongruous American flag draped over the couch; there was the living room disordered with blood. It took Statman nearly two hours. He wrote later that she was mostly quiet as she let the horror of the crimes wash over her, solemn, grieving, attentive.

September wore on, and the news about Taylor Behl dwindled. Many days when I scanned the Richmond newspaper online, there weren't any updates at all, just a void where more information should have been. That's how I remember it, at least; in reality, plenty of other awful stories were in the paper that month: about a deaf, mute, illiterate man who raped and strangled a sixteen-year-old girl; about a thirteen-year-old boy who was charged with murder in the death of a two-year-old; about a man killed over a motor-scooter dispute; about a man found dead in the front seat of a white Nissan, the city's sixty-fifth homicide of the year. But none of those stories wormed their way into my head the way Taylor's disappearance did.

The lack of new information perversely made me even more fascinated. I hadn't yet discovered the corners of the internet where people congregated on crime-themed message boards, collectively picking over the mundane details of unfamous murders. My fascination felt lonely. I couldn't imagine anyone else being interested—I couldn't imagine explaining to anyone else why *I* was so interested—so I kept it to myself. I had a particular appetite for mundane logistical facts about the night Taylor had gone missing: Where had she parked? What street had she been walking down? Where was she planning to meet up with her friends? The details were all so familiar; it wasn't that long ago that I had been seventeen in the same city and had made the rounds of the same coffee shops and all-night diners, the limited options available to you when you weren't twenty-one but you still wanted to stay out late. Something about these details made me shiver—for her, for me, for both of us? I wasn't sure.

Part of what I was looking for, I realized, was *overlap*, all the ways that she and I were similar. There was a troubling pleasure in thinking about how I could have been her, or she could have been me. As a teenager, I had had sketchy friends and not-great judgment; I had walked alone through the city at night; I had gotten too drunk and enjoyed doing things that scared me; I had a moody LiveJournal that, if read aloud on cable news, would certainly have made the TV host furrow her brow. There was, of course, one key difference between me and Taylor Behl: she was missing, and I was safe. But that might even have been part of what obsessed me about the case. It felt good, in a bad way, to think about my own proximity to violence. To imagine my life as a near miss.

Whether or not Statman's interest began before she moved to Cielo Drive, she was soon preoccupied by Sharon Tate and the terrible circumstances of her death. "The first time I ever met her, I was selling at the Rose Bowl flea market," one collector of Tate-LaBianca memorabilia told me. "I had this huge collection of Manson videos—back then you could get twenty-five dollars each for videos, and I had at least a hundred of them. She said she was going to buy everything I had, but she didn't end up buying anything."

Statman certainly wasn't alone in her fixation. Sharon Tate was a celebrity in life, but after her death her fame took on new dimensions. Her gravesite became a place of pilgrimage for so many people that her father, P.J., refused to visit it. He was so troubled by the strangers who flocked to mourn his daughter that he vowed that the family would have to bury him somewhere else when the time came.

The visitors who brought Sharon yellow roses, who stood, weeping, at her grave, surely meant to honor her, to show that she wasn't forgotten. Keeping her memory alive was a way to counterbalance the tragedy of her life, to protest the deep unfairness of what had been done to her.

Sharon isn't the only dead woman who attracts this kind of attention. You know the type: Like Sharon or Marilyn Monroe, or Lady Di or Laura Palmer, or Anna Nicole Smith, she should be a little sexy and a little sad. If possible, she should be white and blond. Her face should look good on a tattoo or a T-shirt. Dying tragically transforms her into an icon; she's more legendary, more ubiquitous, but she's also flattened. The more upsetting the circumstances of her end, the more beloved she'll be. Sex appeal and victimization, beauty and tragedy and celebrity: it makes for a potent mix. But is it that these women are loved because they're doomed? Or that they're doomed because they're sexy? Is it their doom that *makes* them sexy?

Even before Statman entered their lives, the surviving members of the Tate family were used to the strangers who fixated on Sharon and who seemed drawn to them as a way to get close to her. For instance, in the early 1990s, around the same time Statman moved to Cielo Drive, a plump, blond woman named Rosie Blanchard inexplicably began sending Doris Tate Mother's Day cards. Then, one August morning, P. J. Tate, Sharon's father, the gruff ex-military man everyone still called "the Colonel," answered the front door. Rosie was there, smiling. "Hi," she said cheerfully. "I'm your daughter Sharon."

P.J.' daughter Sharon had been dead for two decades of course. But Rosie was born in 1969, the year that Sharon Tate was killed, and had come to believe that this was no coincidence; clearly, she was Sharon reincarnated. She tried to explain this to P.J., but he slammed the door in her face before she could finish. Doris Tate did habitually talk to mediums and clairvoyants, convinced in some bone-deep way that she could still reach her eldest daughter, but this woman was definitely not the intermediary Doris had in mind.

Despite the family's attempts to rebuff her, Rosie kept popping up, buzzing at the margins of the family's life like an unslappable mosquito. She sent them holiday cards; she tracked down their home phone number and called repeatedly; she threatened to show up at parole hearings as a show of support for her "family." Fed up with the harassment, Patti Tate finally tracked Rosie down at her Burbank apartment. The room was bare and depressing. Rosie slept on a mattress on the floor, and a box fan moved hot air around the room. *You're not my sister reincarnated,* Patti told Rosie, and to her surprise, Rosie agreed. *There's something I've been wanting to tell you, but I haven't had the nerve,* the younger woman said. *I'm Sharon's baby! I'm your niece! I've been alive all this time!*

Eventually, Rosie faded from the Tate family's life for a couple of years. But she hadn't given up on her cause. Instead, she'd moved to Ohio and elaborated on her origin story. According to Rosie, on the night of the murders, the eight-months-pregnant Sharon delivered her baby—a girl—just before she died. Mysterious men in black suits spirited the infant away to an undisclosed location. That child grew up in New York as Rosie Blanchard, unaware until she was twenty-four years old that she was actually the daughter of one of the most famous murder victims in the world.

In Ohio, Rosie started calling herself Rosie Tate-Polanski. She also won her first, and only, convert: William Garretson, the young caretaker who had claimed to sleep through the murders in the guesthouse where Statman later lived. Viewed in a particular way, Garretson's life looked like a series of close calls, although you'd never describe him as lucky. He'd escaped Vietnam by dodging the draft and hitchhiking to LA, where he became the only survivor of that night at Cielo Drive. Then he'd endured an investigation by LAPD officers certain he'd slaughtered five people, including an interrogation where he was hooked up to a polygraph and asked repeatedly whether he had sex with men.

The murders and their aftermath seemed to have stunted Garretson in some vital, permanent way. By the time he was in his midforties, he was back in Ohio, working a series of dead-end jobs, and drinking more than he should. Then Rosie careened into his life. Within six months, they had moved in together. Soon, they announced their engagement.

On August 9, 2000, the thirty-first anniversary of Sharon's murder (and, supposedly, Rosie's birth), the couple threw a party in the conference room at the Best Western in Lancaster, Ohio. There were balloons and birthday cake and pictures of Sharon Tate tacked up on the walls. The only attendees, apart from Rosie and Garretson, were a reporter from the local paper and two journalism students. Someone asked the couple about their improbable relationship. "We both survived the same murder," Rosie explained. "And he was the only one who could empathize with my pain."

It's easier to understand why people might identify with the role of the detective, that heroic figure who masters crime through knowledge and understanding. But identifying with the victim—even for those of us who don't take it as far as Rosie Blanchard—is a more complicated proposition.

The victim is, in some ways, the central character of any true crime account—without her, there would be no story—but she also has the disadvantage of being dead. In many cases, though, hers is the only major role available to women. This is not a new phenomenon. In antiquity, notes the historian Mary Beard, women were allowed public speech only as victims or martyrs. Some of that old thinking still lives with us, baked into the bones of Western culture. So even as some victims are blamed or debased, others are afforded a kind of wounded authority, or an authority rooted in their wounds. Famous victims can speak for the rest of us. And we can use their tragedies to stand in for our personal cataclysms.

Lisa Statman and Bill Nelson talked about making a documentary about the Tate-LaBianca murders, maybe something for HBO, maybe for the twenty-fifth anniversary of the crimes. They agreed that it should combat the persistent publicity Charles Manson still got by instead focusing on the victims.

Statman suggested that Nelson visit retired LAPD cop Earl Deemer. Deemer had assisted with the murder investigations back in 1969, and rumors were floating around that he had a cache of Tate-LaBianca materials no one else had seen. Nelson tracked Deemer down—he was living in the desert a few hours outside LA— and drove out to visit him. The former detective was now in his seventies, slow moving from injuries, but still tall and handsome. At Nelson's request, Deemer produced the brown bag he'd stored in his attic for many years. Nelson started pawing through it. The bag was full of photographs and slides—crime scene images of the bodies, but also casual snapshots of Jay Sebring blow-drying Sharon's hair, Sharon in a negligee by the pool, Sharon frolicking naked in the snow. Nelson considered himself the premier Tate-LaBianca archivist, and there was stuff here even he'd never before seen. A treasure trove. When he got back to LA, he called Statman and told her what Deemer had. *I knew it,* she crowed. *And* you *didn't even want to visit him.* Nelson arranged another visit with Deemer; this time Statman would tag along, too.

On that second visit, Nelson peppered Deemer with questions—What had he seen? What did he remember?—while Statman picked through his collection. Some of the images were particularly painful to look at, the ones that showed the soon-to-be-murdered victims as achingly, vividly alive. There were Sharon, Jay, and Woytek, tan and dressed in bathing suits, lounging around the house where they'd all soon be killed. There was Sharon in a white bikini standing barefoot on the grass by the pool. She looked so lushly pregnant that the photos must've been taken in the last week of her life. Seeing these images, presumably the final ones ever taken of Sharon and her friends alive, in this old man's private archive felt like a violation; in later interviews, Statman recalled feeling a hot rush of anger rise through her, as if these were her own family photos that had been hoarded by a stranger. When Nelson and Deemer stepped out of the room, she slipped a few of the slides into her pocket.

During that long drive back to LA, she pulled them out to show Nelson. He was furious—she had betrayed his source!—but Statman didn't care. She was full of a righteous indignation. So much had already been taken from Sharon's family; her murder did not make her public property. The images belonged to, and with, the Tates, and Statman intended to do whatever it took to make that happen.

* * *

Murder is like an earthquake; the chaos of its aftermath reveals the fault lines between people. Which is to say, in the 1970s, that troubled, dystopian decade, twenty years before Lisa Statman entered their lives, the Tate family collapsed in on itself.

Debra was sixteen when her sister Sharon was killed. Debra had always been the misfit of the family, the redheaded middle child who kept a bat as a pet. *Non sei Debra, tu sei diavola!* the family's Italian priest used to joke. In the aftermath of her sister's murder, she refused to be brought low by grief; instead, she went a little wild. Patti was eleven, soft-spoken and shy. She'd later struggle to remember anything at all about that period of her life; when she tried to call it up, nothing was there but a big blank. A temperamental gulf already loomed between the sisters, and the loss of Sharon widened it.

Before Manson's arrest, P. J. Tate coped with his eldest daughter's death by attempting to solve the crime himself. For months, he dressed up like a hippie and cruised the Sunset Strip, hoping he'd overhear something incriminating. Nothing much came of his investigations, and he increasingly turned to alcohol. Doris Tate survived on pills for a while, sedatives that muted the pain of the tabloids that insinuated that Sharon was somehow responsible for her own death: "Live Freaky, Die Freaky," as one columnist declared. The trials of the various Manson Family members stretched into 1971, followed by seemingly endless appeals. The tabloids printed photos of those stupid girls lurking outside the courthouse in their culty robes, *X*'s carved into their foreheads, acting as if somehow Charles Manson were the real victim. In 1975, Manson Girl Squeaky Fromme, cloaked in a red nun's habit, pointed a gun at Gerald Ford while screaming about pollution. It seemed as though it would never end. Doris Tate sank into her grief. Then, slowly, she began to emerge.

It started when Doris began attending meetings of a new group called Parents of Murdered Children. POMC was founded in 1978 in

Cincinnati by a couple whose nineteen-year-old daughter, Lisa, was bludgeoned to death by her ex-boyfriend in Germany; he served only sixteen months for the crime. (In 1997 he killed another woman and was sentenced to death in 2002.) Charlotte Hullinger, Lisa's mother, was shattered by her daughter's murder. But just a few months after the funeral, Charlotte's friends and coworkers seemed nervous when she brought it up; she got the sense that they thought she should be over it by now. Her priest put her in touch with three parents who'd suffered similar losses, and they arranged to meet in person. "It began out of our personal need, and not out of any altruistic motives," Hullinger told *People* magazine three years later. By that time, there were seven chapters of POMC nationwide, with seventy-five members. The bereaved parents gathered in church basements and private homes, where they held hands and told their stories. Though the circumstances of the crimes that affected them were different, POMC members shared an understanding of the deep isolation of grief. "Violent death brings anger so intense most people can't stand it," Hullinger said. "We find that those who would normally be helpful, like people in the church, especially don't like these unacceptable emotions and will try to smooth them over with platitudes like 'It's God's will' and 'You've got to accept it.' I think the most helpful thing to say to all that is 'Baloney!' People have to be allowed their anger. Those feelings are there."

Doris was active in the Los Angeles chapter of the group and soon became its president. "It started out with maybe six people," mostly mothers, Debra Tate told me. "As time went on, the dads would start joining them because they would see the improvement in their wives and wanted to share in the healing." Doris hosted meetings in the Tate family house in Palos Verdes, an upscale coastal neighborhood in southwestern Los Angeles. Up to thirty bereaved family members packed into the living room to vent and weep and be with one another.

They lit tea candles and set them afloat in the family bathtub in honor of those they'd lost.

These POMC meetings were akin to the feminist consciousness-raising groups that had emerged in the 1960s and '70s, in which survivors of sexual assault and domestic abuse met to talk through their experiences with a supportive community. Survivors—not just of gender-based violence, but also Vietnam vets—found relief in groups where their stories were affirmed instead of undermined. "Trauma isolates; the group re-creates a sense of belonging. Trauma shames and stigmatizes; the group bears witness and affirms. Trauma degrades the victim; the group exalts her. Trauma de-humanizes the victim; the group restores her humanity," psychiatrist Judith Herman wrote in her landmark book, *Trauma and Recovery*. For too long, survivors had been told that what had been done to them conferred shame on *them*; this new era of finding your voice, of refusing to be silenced, felt like a corrective to a repressive and damaging past.

Inspired by the women's and antiwar movements, Herman and others began studying people who had been through terrible things. Much of what we now understand about the mechanisms of trauma—that survivors' accounts may be scattered and spotty because traumatic memories are fundamentally different from other recollections; that fragmentation and numbness aren't indications that a person's story is untrustworthy, but rather are adaptive responses, the brain and body attempting to protect against the overwhelm of violence; that there is no "normal" when it comes to recovery from trauma—stems largely from this era. Researchers were also realizing that the impact of violence on family members and friends, people who were adjacent to crimes but not themselves physically harmed, was much more diffuse and long-lasting than previously thought. "The body reacts to the shock the same way it does to major surgery," Hullinger told *People*. "But employers don't know what's happening. Teachers in schools don't." Dealing with traditional authorities—the police, the justice system—too often compounded the original violation.

The mounting number of grassroots victims' groups weren't content with just providing a supportive space; they also wanted to enact change. Activists founded rape crisis centers and encouraged police officers to learn how to handle trauma survivors appropriately. They lobbied for laws that would ensure victims were notified if their abusers were released from prison. "It was a time of excitement, it was a time of passion," said Janice Rench, an early advocate for victims of domestic violence. "We didn't have any plans, any books, but as we listened to the victims, we certainly got a sense of what was going to work and what wasn't. And so it was the victims themselves, I believe, that really started this field."

POMC soon became more than just a support group; it was part of a growing political movement calling for expanded legal rights for victims. POMC members who found their voices in meetings grew increasingly frustrated that they had no such voice in the justice system. In US criminal law, crimes are considered offenses against the state, not against an individual. (This stems from our legal system's roots in English common law, which considered the king to be the ultimate victim of all lawbreaking.) In practice, this meant that victims had no defined role within criminal proceedings. A victim might be called on to testify in court as a witness—which often meant she'd be subject to withering cross-examination—but otherwise, she had no official part to play. The rigid script of judicial proceedings provided her no space to say what had happened to her, to include as part of the official record what the physical, emotional, psychological, financial, spiritual, and practical impact of a crime had been. The crime was in some fundamental way not *about* her.

In response, the burgeoning victims' rights movement lobbied for victim impact statements to be incorporated during sentencing and at parole hearings. This idea is routine now—such statements are a part of the sentencing process in all fifty states and federal cases (as well as in Canada, the United Kingdom, and Australia)—but in the 1980s, it was revolutionary to suggest that the justice system should make space for people impacted by crime to stand up and say to the judge, to the defendant, to the world, "There's an emptiness I cannot manage to fill," or "You bought me a ticket to a planet where I lived by myself."

This growing focus on victims' stories was reflected in popular culture. The pulpy crime-focused books of the 1960s had tended to center on criminals, typically men who lived outside the bounds of polite society and preyed on strangers. These books aimed to excite their (putatively male) audience—"People are in need of the extra thrill. Drugs don't do it, adultery doesn't do it, sex doesn't do it any more. . . . [True crime] gives a fix on a lifestyle that most folks don't have access to," according to an editor of old-style true crime books, the kinds about homicidal carnies and cold-blooded hit men.

But in the 1980s and '90s, blockbuster true crime writers such as Ann Rule turned their attention to a different category of crimes, the kind that happened on placid suburban streets, in neat houses with neat lawns. The victims were typically women—preferably middle-class white women—and the villains were often their too-perfect husbands, men who hid their true intentions behind a facade of normality. If old-style true crime was powered by the libidinal thrill of vicarious deviance, the new kind ran on an engine of empathy. These books took a more sympathetic and lingering look at victims, inviting their largely female readership to view the crimes through the victims' eyes.

Rule and her ilk were tapping into something potent. While women are less likely to be murdered, they make up about half of all victims of violent crime—perhaps more, since many crimes that disproportionately affect women (intimate-partner violence, sexual assault) are underreported. Crimes against women are often committed by people close to them: around two-thirds of murdered women are killed by family members or intimate partners, while roughly 10 percent are killed by strangers. (For comparison's sake, about a third of male homicide victims are killed by people they don't know.)

Violence within families had long been considered a taboo subject, a private matter that was best dealt with internally. True crime books were a socially sanctioned way to learn about abusive and controlling behavior and its potentially dire consequences. (Another bestseller of the era, *The Gift of Fear: And Other Survival Signals That Protect Us from Violence*, promised to teach female readers "the ability to predict the harm others might do us and get out of its way.") Rule's books alone sold more than 20 million copies; clearly there was a market for media that acknowledged—or, more cynically, stoked—women's fears.

Doris Tate, a folksy, charming grandmother who baked cookies for people she liked and cursed out the ones she didn't, was a perfect figurehead for the nascent victims' rights movement. Her daughter was famous and beautiful, the victim of one of the most high-profile crimes of the century. Doris knew how to turn up her Texas accent, to sprinkle her conversation with down-home sayings: "Sometimes you just have to turn shit into ice cream." She called politicians "darlin'," and they found it difficult to say no to her. "Doris just steamrolled into a room," a fellow victims' rights activist told me. "There was no one else. You did what she told you to do." In the 1980s, as the victims' rights movement gained momentum, she became the first member of a victim's family to speak at a parole hearing in California; she was also the first person in the state to make a victim-impact statement: "What about my family?" she asked Tex Watson at his

1984 parole hearing. "When will [Sharon] come up for parole? When will I come up for parole? Can you tell me that?"

As society turned its attention to victims, victimhood became an increasingly contested space, with right and wrong ways to inhabit the role. In 1990, Suzan LaBerge used her victim-impact statement to argue for leniency on behalf of Watson, who had killed her mother, Rosemary LaBianca, the night after the murders at Cielo Drive. Watson had spent twenty years in prison, and LaBerge, a devout Christian, believed that he was sincerely repentant and deserved another chance. The whole thing made Doris Tate furious. Victim-impact statements were not supposed to be used to advocate for criminals, particularly not serial murderers such as Watson, she believed. Doris confronted LaBerge in the parking lot following the parole board hearing: *You know, your mother is probably rolling in her grave because of what you did today,* she told the younger woman. Then Doris went on TV to make sure everyone else understood. "If Suzan LaBerge were here in this room, what would you say?" an interviewer asked. "You dumb shit," Doris snapped. "That's what I'd probably say to her."

Now that she had a cause, Doris was inexhaustible. She appeared on talk shows and radio shows and lobbied politicians. By 1985, she was a board member of Citizens for Truth, Justice for Homicide Victims, the California Justice Committee, and Believe the Children. She founded the Coalition for Victims' Equal Rights and volunteered with the Victim Offender Reconciliation Group. She developed a strong distaste for Rose Bird, the first female chief justice of the California Supreme Court, who consistently overturned death penalty verdicts. In 1986, Doris went on *The Phil Donahue Show* to lobby against Bird. "One thing is certain," Doris told Donahue, working her drawl. "[The death penalty] will cut down on recidivism because the guy that goes to the gas chamber, well, my dear, he's one less we have to worry about." That November, voters overwhelmingly elected to oust Bird;

it was the first time a sitting chief justice had ever been removed in California. Over the next several years, California's Supreme Court upheld death sentences at one of the highest rates in the country.

Though Doris's activism gave her life new meaning, it also caused trouble at home. When she appeared on *Geraldo*, she offered up the family's address in Palos Verdes, encouraging grieving parents to write to her. She freely gave out their phone number, too, and victims called at all hours, interrupting family dinners and birthday parties. "Everyone in the world could call that house, and they did," Robin Olson, a friend of Patti Tate's, told me. The more engaged and active that Doris Tate became, the more disengaged her husband grew. When TV crews lugged their equipment into the house for yet another interview with Doris, P.J. would disappear upstairs, shutting the bedroom door firmly behind him. He didn't participate in Parents of Murdered Children meetings. "I love my dad," Debra told me, then heaved a sigh. "To a man like my father, a military man with a stiff backbone who's been trained by the military regime to not have feelings—he didn't want to have anything to do with it. He'd kind of make fun of it." His drinking intensified, and he was fine, or fine-ish, when he stuck to beer, but he grew volatile when he drank hard liquor. (Debra also told me that P.J. was physically abusive to both Sharon and Doris, which adds another dimension to Doris's activism on behalf of victimized women, and P.J.'s dismissal of it.)

Around this time Doris met Bill Nelson, the radio host and self-appointed Manson researcher who would later befriend Lisa Statman. Like Doris, Nelson was deeply disturbed at the idea of Tex Watson—a man he called "more dangerous than Manson"—getting out of prison, and he and Doris made common cause in preventing this from happening. When Doris Tate went to Stockholm as the US representative for the International Victims' Rights Conference in 1990, she brought Nelson along with her. Doris's daughters found

Nelson off-putting, but their mother tolerated him. Sure, he could be bombastic and arrogant, a smooth-voiced bully in the Rush Limbaugh mold, but he was also usefully tenacious. To build a case against Watson getting parole, Nelson tracked down Watson's high school classmates in Texas and probed the finances of his prison ministry, sniffing for fraud.

Nelson was particularly incensed that Watson had fathered four children in prison through conjugal visits, and that their mother received public assistance. Every time Watson's wife and kids moved, Nelson found out their new address. He lurked outside the prison with his telephoto lens and took photographs of the children on their way to visit their father. He sent endless letters to public officials: "If this is the year of family values and welfare reform, how can we let this go?" he demanded of the California attorney general. "That is unspeakable!" he wrote the governor. "It is financial!" (Nelson had no such problem with Manson Family member Susan Atkins, aka Sexy Sadie, with whom he exchanged friendly letters. Nelson visited Atkins in prison a few times and declared her to be "a very attractive mature forty-three-year-old women [sic] and still quite sexy.")

In 1990, Doris Tate agreed to an on-camera interview with Bill Nelson. They sat facing each other in a formal living room, surrounded by brocaded furniture and gilt-edged frames. In the video of the interview that Nelson later released on VHS, Doris is poised in neutral tones, her hair upswept; Nelson has traded his typical polo shirt for a suit and tie. It's impossible to watch this interview without becoming transfixed by Nelson's face as he talks to Doris about her dead daughter. His eyes are bright and eager; a persistent, inappropriate grin twitches the corners of his mouth. He looks—there's no other word for it—*excited*.

During the interview, Nelson corrects Doris about a minor fact related to the case. He has always had a pedant's fixation on details, been careful to get the proper nouns right—that Tex Watson drove a white-and-yellow 1959 Ford that night, that the firearm he had with him was a nine-shot .22-caliber Hi Standard Ned Buntline revolver. Doris reminds him that she hasn't read any of the books about Sharon's murder. Nelson smiles and says that he's read nineteen or twenty. He likes that she hasn't read them, he tells her. That way he can get her fresh reaction to things. "Let me read you something you've not read," he says.

"I haven't read any of it," Doris says again.

Nelson peers down his nose at a sheaf of papers and begins, " 'As Sharon pleaded for her life, sitting on the couch, Susan [Atkins] says, "It felt so good the first time I stabbed her. When she screamed at me, it did something to me, sent a rush through me. I stabbed her again. I just kept stabbing her until she stopped screaming. It was just like going into nothing." ' " He goes on and on; the recitation feels interminable. Doris sits quietly, her back straight; she must have realized that she wasn't there as an interviewee, but as a player in some perverse psychodrama concocted by Nelson. He goes on and on, talking about Sharon's innocence, talking about how it was violated. He describes Susan Atkins saying that seeing Sharon's blood spurting out felt like a sexual release. He finally looks up at Doris. "That's your daughter," he says unnecessarily.

Doris does what she can to steer the conversation back to policy issues. She talks about parole, about conjugal visits. But Nelson isn't finished: "Sharon was so delicate. She had sixteen stab wounds. . . . Are you aware that they intended to dismember the bodies? Did you know that?"

It's remarkable how stoic Doris remains during this onslaught, as Nelson obsessively circles back to those last twenty minutes Sharon was alive, as if her death were the central fact of her life, the thing that makes her worth thinking about. Or perhaps Doris's composure is not remarkable at all; the worst has already happened, and the whole tawdry aftermath—including this man's lingering fascination with her daughter's body and what was done to it—is just the long shadow cast by the original crime. Talking about stabbing is not as bad as stabbing. Even so, this conversation feels like a violation.

The word *victim* is rooted in the Latin *victima*, which means "sacrificial animal." This feels apt, but in an awful way. Because she's dead, the victim can become whatever people need her to be. Because she's dead, we can say anything we want about her, and she can't talk back. For some people, she is more valuable this way: holy, symbolic, silent.

Not long after this interview, Doris Tate severed her relationship with Bill Nelson. One of his many antagonists had let Doris know that Nelson had once been charged with felony counts of lewd and lascivious conduct with a child; the two girls in question had been twelve years old. He pleaded no contest to a misdemeanor charge, spent two years on probation, and registered as a sex offender.

At the beginning of October, the police found Taylor Behl's body in a shallow ditch in a rural area an hour east of Richmond. The next day, they announced that they had a suspect in custody. I read about all this online, the brutal story made more terrible by the terse factuality of the sentences: "Various reports are now saying the suspect Ben Fawley, 38, of Richmond has admitted to being with Behl on the night she died. According to local reports, Fawley . . . spoke with investigators and told them he accidentally choked her during an intimate encounter. The two were in her car in Mathews County when this occurred. Reports say that Fawley told the police that he panicked and dumped her body in a ravine."

When I saw Fawley's name, I sat up straight in my chair. I knew him by sight; we had lurked around the same coffee shop. I remembered him as slight, moody, vaguely goth. Narrow shouldered and a little pathetic. Every week he'd post a half dozen cryptic classified ads in the free alternative weekly, snarky little haiku that were always signed "Skulz." Making fun of him had been a low-key group activity among the coffee shop crowd. I mean, come on. *Skulz?* Really?

All the time I had been wondering about what happened to Taylor, turning over the mystery of her last hours in my head, he was sitting in his apartment, keeping the truth to himself. I had never before thought about the terrible *privacy* of murder—how something so awful could be done to you and the only person who would ever know what had happened was the person who did it. How you couldn't tell anyone what you'd been through because you'd be dead. How they got to own the story. How it was a kind of *evil* intimacy. It seemed unbearable.

In the next few days, Taylor's mom went on TV. She seemed to feel she had to defend her daughter against the story Fawley offered, and against the stark words in the newspaper: *intimate encounter, choked, ravine.* Taylor had met Fawley a few months earlier, when she'd come to Richmond for a college tour, her mom explained. He had a thing for younger girls; Taylor was drawn to damaged people. She let him take pictures of her. They exchanged a few flirty messages online. They slept together once, but Taylor later told friends she wasn't into it. Then, that day in September, just before school started, when she was new in town and hardly knew anyone, she agreed to meet up with him again.

Details from Fawley's jailhouse confession began to leak. His account was disjointed and difficult to believe. He claimed that he'd bound Taylor's legs and feet with duct tape and put a bag over her head. He claimed that the rough sex was at Taylor's instigation—although none of her previous boyfriends corroborated this interest, and Fawley was the one with a long, documented history of boundary-pushing fetishes. He claimed that she had teased him, that he "flipped out," and that he didn't remember what had happened next. He admitted that he'd "flipped out" with a girlfriend before; afterward, she'd told him that he'd tried to strangle her, but he had no memory of that, either.

I read about all this with mounting horror. For a month, I couldn't know enough about Taylor Behl. Now I suddenly felt as though I knew too much. Whatever dark pleasure I'd gotten, whatever distraction the story had given me, the spell was broken. I abruptly cut myself off from following the case. I barely registered when, a few months later, Ben Fawley pleaded guilty to second-degree murder—an Alford plea, meaning that he pleaded guilty but still maintained his innocence—and was sentenced to thirty years.

A few years before moving into Sharon's house, Statman became friendly with a young actress named Rebecca Schaeffer. Schaeffer was a rising star, building off a lead role on a CBS sitcom she'd landed as a teenager. Her fan mail included letters from an Arizona man named Robert John Bardo. It soon became clear that Bardo's interest in Schaeffer was excessive. He showed up at the Warner Bros. set, once with a giant stuffed bear and once with a knife; both times he was turned away by security. Statman met Schaeffer on the set of a film, *Scenes from the Class Struggle in Beverly Hills*, which included a scene of Schaeffer in bed with a man. This enraged Bardo; it proved that she was "another Hollywood whore," he explained later. Bardo got her home address from her DMV records, sent his sister an ominous letter—"I have an obsession with the unattainable. I have to eliminate [what] I cannot attain"—then headed to LA one more time. On July 18, he knocked on Schaeffer's door and spoke with her briefly;

she told him not to come back. An hour later, he returned. When she answered the door "with a cold look on her face," as Bardo described it, he shot her in the stomach, killing her.

Publicity over Schaeffer's murder inspired California lawmakers to enact one of the first antistalking laws in the country. Her friend's death shook Statman, too. On the film sets where she worked, she began gathering petition signatures in support of gun control. Around this time she also became aware of Doris Tate and her work on behalf of victims. Two years later, with the photographs of Sharon she had taken from Detective Deemer in her possession, Statman reached out to Doris's daughter (and Sharon's youngest sister) Patti.

Unlike her mother, Patti wasn't an activist; many of her acquaintances didn't even know about her famous sister, or her famous sister's famous murder. Patti had blocked out those awful weeks after Sharon's murder, which was convenient when she got married, at age twenty, to Don Ford, a six-foot-nine-inch NBA player with shaggy blond hair and a horseshoe mustache. Don didn't like to talk about, or even think about, what had happened to his wife's sister. He forbade Patti from discussing it, according to a couple of Patti's friends. It seemed to make him uncomfortable, as if something about having such a lurid story in the family were shameful. Or perhaps the silence was meant as a kindness, as if the best way to recover from tragedy was to create a nice life for yourself where murder wasn't allowed to intrude. There was only one photograph of Sharon on display in the Ford household, an eight-by-ten glossy in the garage, over the washing machine, mounted next to a picture of Patti. Everyone agreed that the sisters looked so similar it was spooky. They both had that same narrow nose and pretty smile, that same blond warmth.

Patti Tate became Patti Ford after her marriage. Among their friends, he was the famous one, the one with his name in the paper.

"When she first told me what her maiden name was, what her family history was, my first thought was 'Oh my God, I do not want to be friends with this person,'" her friend Robin Olson told me. "Especially the way my life was at that time." Robin and Patti were in their late twenties, stay-at-home moms with young children and handsome, athletic husbands. As Olson described it, their lives were like a film montage of upscale 1980s suburbia: tennis in the morning, drinks by the pool in the afternoon, a Jacuzzi in the backyard, cruise-ship vacations. "It was a really happy time, a fun time," Olson said. "We had a blast in those years, and Patti just wanted to fit in and be like everybody else. She didn't want to be related to that subject either."

During these years, Patti kept her distance from her mother's activism, her dogged attendance at parole hearings, her TV appearances and political speeches. "Mrs. Tate had a big personality," Olson said. "She was a pistol, very opinionated. Now, I really respect everything she did, but at the time, in my twenties, I was not a big fan of hers. She kept Patti under her thumb, sheltered her, told her what to do. She was a very domineering mom, very nosy. She wanted to know everything that was going on. She'd call me and pump me for information about Patti."

One thing Doris wanted to know about, which Patti was reluctant to discuss, was Patti's increasingly rocky marriage. Once Don's basketball career was over, the family faced financial struggles. Friends described failed businesses and real estate deals that didn't pan out. Patti wasn't exactly sure how bad things were—Don handled their finances and gave her a cash allowance every week—but she knew they owed the IRS money, and that they were overleveraged enough that, while they lived in gorgeous homes, they struggled to afford health insurance.

According to Debra Tate, Statman tried to get in touch with her first. A friend told Debra that he knew someone who was desperate to meet her, that her name was Lisa, and that she lived in the guest-house at Cielo Drive. Debra told me that she made it clear she had no interest in meeting this person: "It just screamed wackadoodle to me."

According to Statman, she never reached out to Debra. Instead, she got Patti's address from the voter rolls and sent her a letter that described the photographs. Statman wrote her phone number at the bottom of the page. About a week later, Statman spoke with Patti for the first time. "She called me in tears, saying she'd never seen [the photographs] and how grateful she was that she got to see them," Statman told me. The two women started talking regularly. Because Statman was in and out of town for her job, the first few months of their friendship happened entirely over the phone.

It was a difficult time for Patti, and not just because of her financial difficulties and crumbling marriage. In late 1991, doctors discovered a malignant tumor in her mother's brain. Doris was in her late sixties and still had plenty of work she wanted to get done, and Patti promised her mother that she would try to carry on her legacy. Within a few months, the fast-moving cancer had claimed Doris's ability to speak. Debra Tate moved into the Palos Verdes house to care for her mother, and Patti visited every weekend. Confined to a wheelchair, Doris balled up her fists, her face contorted in frustration at being forced into silence. She died less than a year after her diagnosis.

Patti's friend Robin Olson—who, it should be noted, has a long-standing feud with Lisa Statman—remembers Patti telling her about Lisa, her new friend who was living in the house where Sharon was murdered. (By this point, Statman had moved out of the Cielo Drive guesthouse and into the main house.) The situation creeped Olson out. As she recalls it, Statman invited Patti to come visit her at the Cielo house. Olson says that Patti begged her to come along;

they could tell their husbands they were going shopping in LA. The idea repulsed Olson, who was seven and a half months pregnant with her third child at the time: "I was like, you want to take me *this pregnant* to *Sharon's house*?" (Statman denies making this invitation.) Olson says she advised her friend to drop it, but something in Patti couldn't let it go. Shortly after this conversation, according to Olson, Patti drove down to Los Angeles by herself. Olson remembers talking to her friend a few days after this visit. *Oh, Robin, you were so wrong about Lisa,* Patti said. *She's just this young girl, an innocent person. She was so sweet, she wasn't scary at all.*

Olson and her family were busy making preparations to move back to the East Coast; she was heavily pregnant and distracted by her family responsibilities, maybe not paying as much attention to Patti as usual. Still, she did think it was slightly strange when, a few weeks later, Patti told her that the girl with the photos of Sharon had moved out of the Cielo Drive house and into the guesthouse behind Patti and Don's home in the foothills of Santa Barbara. "Immediately I was suspicious about that," Olson told me. "Because she was still working in LA, and why would anybody give themselves a three-hour commute?" But Patti didn't appear troubled by it, and Olson knew that her friend could use the money. Perhaps Patti would even benefit from having a companion close at hand, since Olson would soon be on the other side of the country. Patti was one of those people who always liked to have another person in the room with her. "I remember thinking, 'Maybe she'll be friends with this girl. She'll have someone there.' I remember having that one prayer-thought," Olson said.

Olson and her family moved to the Washington, DC, area in September. A few months later, Olson told me, she got a frantic phone call from Patti. Her family's financial picture was much worse than she'd thought. Their beautiful house was being foreclosed on, and she was leaving Don. She and the kids needed to find somewhere else to live within a week. A mother of three young children with no work experience to speak of, Patti had few options. She moved back into the Palos Verdes house with her father—and Statman came along with her. The women worked out an arrangement with P.J. where Patti and her kids stayed for free, while Statman paid a nominal rent—a few hundred dollars a month—to Patti, so she'd have some cash to spend. Soon P.J. moved out, too, leaving the two women and two kids (Patti's oldest daughter had opted to stay with her father) in the Tate family house.

"By 1993, Lisa had discontinued many of her long calls," Bill Nelson groused in his book. "She had obtained all the information she could from me." (Statman says she broke off contact with Nelson following the visit to Deemer.) After Doris's death, and as Statman grew closer to the surviving members of the Tate family, Nelson sensed he was being pushed out. He helped arrange an appearance for Patti on *Maury Povich*, but then he was pointedly not invited to come to the taping. When he watched the episode, he spotted Lisa Statman in the audience where he used to be.

For Patti, this period after her mother's death was a time of great change. She was getting used to the idea of going to parole hearings and inhabiting the spotlight. "Patti was terrified, quaking in her boots," Olson recalled. "She was this meek little housewife who was scared of everything, and now she was stepping into her mom's big shoes, going on TV—it was a huge transformation for her."

"You have to understand what a heroic thing this was for Patti," Statman told me. "Up until that point she hadn't read anything about Sharon's murder, she didn't know any of the details, she didn't *want* to know any of the details. . . . She had blocked so many of her memories with Sharon from her mind for self-preservation, so for her to take this on for her mother was a huge, huge thing."

Thankfully, Statman was there. Unlike Don, she encouraged Patti to connect with her past and tried to help her coax memories of Sharon out of the fog. Patti visited the DA's office to look at the crime scene photographs and evidence. She and Statman read P.J.'s files, sorting through the information he'd gleaned during his own undercover investigation. Statman also helped Patti begin writing her memoirs. "I did most of the writing," Statman told me. "We would just talk about where she wanted it to go, what she wanted in it, what her personal feelings were for each chapter."

To be a better witness, a more effective victim, Patti needed to connect with the family tragedy that she'd repressed for so long. Before one TV appearance, Debra Tate told me that Patti asked her to do her makeup so she looked more like Sharon, adding, "I thought it was a strange request, but Patti said it would help her channel Sharon. The story was that it would help her feel more passionate, to speak with conviction in her voice."

At Tex Watson's 1990 parole hearing, the one Bill Nelson videotaped and sold on his website, a member of the parole board asked Watson why he'd decided to have children in prison. "Things looked different" in the 1970s, Watson said. "We were on rehabilitation instead of punishment," and everyone, it seemed, was getting a parole date. Even someone such as him, a man convicted of multiple brutal murders, could hope to one day be released. "Then the tide started to turn in 1982. Things looked completely different."

Watson wasn't wrong. In the 1960s and '70s, California had been at the vanguard of a movement to grant inmates more rights and privileges, including the family visits that enabled him to father four children. Inmates could use their time in prison to study for a college degree or get vocational training. A progressive approach to crime was ascendant nationwide. The Supreme Court, led by Chief Justice Earl Warren, issued rulings that limited police power and expanded the rights of defendants—to be assigned a public defender, to hear their Miranda rights, to not have illegally obtained evidence used against them.

Then, in the 1980s, the pendulum began to swing in the opposite direction, with California, once again, leading the way. In 1982, Doris Tate had lobbied vigorously for Proposition 8, an amendment to the state constitution that came to be known as the Victims' Bill of Rights. When Proposition 8 passed handily that November, it "made some of the most fundamental changes ever seen in the handling of criminal cases in California and created, virtually overnight, significant rights for victims of crime," according to legal scholars J. Clark Kelso and Brigette Bass.

Proposition 8 was among the first laws of its kind in the nation, and other states soon followed suit. As became common in legislation associated with the label *victims' rights*, Proposition 8 didn't just provide benefits to crime victims; it also limited the rights of people accused or convicted of crimes. The new law put limits on plea bargains and the use of the insanity defense; eliminated the "limited capacity" defense; and instated sentence enhancements for "habitual criminals." Over the next decade, the victims' rights movement's grieving mothers and their heart-wrenching stories were mobilized to justify a number of tough-on-crime policies: mandatory minimum-sentencing guidelines; fifteen-year parole denials; three- (or even two-) strike laws for repeat offenders.

In the name of victims' rights, politicians passed laws that locked up more people, for longer stretches of time, and that made prison a more unpleasant place to be. California got rid of its family-visit program, the one that Doris Tate and Bill Nelson had so despised. Congress banned prisoners from receiving Pell Grants, effectively decimating higher-education programs for inmates. Research showed that prisoners who maintained family relationships or who got an education behind bars had lower rates of recidivism, but all that earnest talk of rehabilitation and social incentive proved no match for the simple, effective refrain of victims' advocates: Why should this criminal get to enjoy conjugal visits / college classes / conditional release when my daughter never will? "Sharon was sentenced to death without a fair trial or without a jury," as Doris Tate once told the parole board. "I was sentenced to life in prison without any possibility of parole. And I say to you, should Susan Atkins's sentence be any less?"

"We quickly grow used to the way things are," David Garland writes in *The Culture of Control: Crime and Social Order in Contemporary Society*, his account of recent upheavals in the criminal justice system. For people such as me who grew up in a country with more than 2 million of its citizens incarcerated, the United States' astronomical incarceration rates have a bleak normality. For as long as I've been alive, this has been the status quo. But Garland, an NYU sociologist who studies crime, argues that there is nothing normal about it—that the change in our understanding of criminal justice over the last decades of the twentieth century marks a dramatic departure from an earlier approach that had centered on reform and rehabilitation.

Starting in the mid-1970s, though, that language—and those goals—began to evaporate. Increasingly, and coinciding with the victims' right's movement's ascendance, they were replaced by talk of punishment and incapacitation in the name of maintaining social stability. Politicians, even the most ardent Democrats, proclaimed themselves to be gladiators in the war on crime, vying to outdo one another in toughness, leaning hard on the language of law and order. This radical ideological shift, and the policies that emerged from it, resulted in "the steepest and most sustained increase in the rate of imprisonment that has been recorded since the birth of the modern prison," Garland notes.

The underlying, unarticulated assumption of this political talk was that victims and criminals were two distinct categories of people with diametrically opposed interests. Victims were righteous innocents whose violation needed to be honored, and whose safety needed to be guaranteed; they were pitted against offenders—unrepentant, unredeemable figures who profited from a naively lenient system. The two sides were locked in a zero-sum game where any concessions made to criminal defendants were seen as a loss for victims, and where supporting victims became equated with being tough on crime.

If the victims' rights movement had limited its appeal to actual victims of violent crime, it would never have grown to be as large or as powerful as it did. The movement's genius—the thing that made it enough of a political force that we now have a federal Office for Victims of Crime, and that most states now have constitutional amendments enshrining victims' rights—was transforming who counted as a "victim." As Ronald Reagan said in his 1985 State of the Union address, "One does not have to be attacked to be a victim." Instead, the victims' rights movement created a strategic alliance between those who had been immediately affected by violent crime and people who had not been victimized, but still lived in heightened anxiety—those who felt, rightly or wrongly, that *something dangerous* might be coming for them.

Violent crime rates did indeed begin to track upward dramatically starting in the early 1960s—the murder rate doubled between then and 1990—but the culture was transforming, too. The shifting mores of the era, all the sex and drugs and rebellion, not to mention the impact of the civil rights movement, felt like social chaos to a large segment of the population. In a 1968 Gallup poll, 81 percent of Americans agreed that "law and order has broken down in this country," with the most commonly identified culprits being "Negroes who start riots" and "Communists." These were the people whom Nixon claimed as members of the silent majority. Later, as the victims' rights movement grew, it similarly appealed to nonvictims who nonetheless felt threatened by a changing society and increasing crime. The movement's calls for a new, stricter approach to criminal justice tapped into broader political trends and certain segments of the public's desire to turn back the clock on the social and judicial reforms of the fifties and sixties. These reactionary currents were expressed economically, too, as politicians did their best to dismantle the social safety net. A neat, punitive logic was at work here: if the state wasn't doing much to make Americans feel secure, it could, at least, lock people up.

Some victims' rights advocates pointed out that victimization transcended race, gender, age, and class. Victims could be black, white, Latino, Asian, young, old, famous, poor, or wealthy; violent crime touched all demographic categories. But certain victims' stories were invoked much more frequently than others. Ronald Reagan's Task Force on Victims of Crime report opens with a lengthy, harrowing fictional account that begins by encouraging the reader to imagine herself as the victim: "You are a 50-year-old woman living alone." The whole story is told in the second person, and it feels like a choose-your-own-adventure story without any choices. First, "you" are abused by a criminal, then "you" are abused by an unfeeling and foolishly lenient justice system.

The Task Force report's story has no racial identifiers, but there didn't need to be any; this narrative already had a clear racialized subtext. The victims the movement leaned the hardest on, the ones whose stories were told and retold by politicians and the press, were overwhelmingly white women. The implicit narrative that "we" lived in a society spinning out of control, in which innocent victims—that was always the phrase, *innocent victims*—were menaced by hardened criminals tapped into preexisting racist anxieties. Politicians could just say "thugs" or "career criminals" or "superpredators": they could invoke, as Reagan did, "the stark, staring face—a face that belongs to a frightening reality of our time: the face of a human predator"; and let the listener imagine for herself what that face might look like. This story line was woefully limited and incomplete: during the heyday of the victims' rights movement—and still today—the people who were actually the most likely to be harmed by violent crime were young black men from low-income neighborhoods.

Studies of victimization find over and over again how similar victims and perpetrators are, but in the new rhetoric of victimhood, the world was divided up more neatly. A community of actual and potential victims, "us," was pitted against actual and potential offenders, "them," a division along lines that were far from arbitrary. "This struggle between victims and offenders, between good and evil, had a familiar ring to it," law professor Markus Dubber has written, in that "it reflected and barely concealed long-standing socioeconomic divisions within American society." Not just socioeconomic divisions, but racial ones, too. The criminal was the "other," and the victim was "us."

By the mid-1990s, the victims' rights movement—now a coalition of crime victims, prosecutors, prison officials, and conservative politicians—was one of the most powerful lobbying forces in the state of California. Nationwide, a new and distinctly populist current dominated national criminal justice discourse, one that disregarded experts and instead "claim[ed] the authority of 'the people,' of common sense," Garland writes. This new penal populism explicitly identified with the symbolic figure of the victim—"symbolic" because of the growing disjunction between actual victims of violent crime and "the victim" as invoked in stump speeches and on cable TV. Crime rates were no longer on the rise—quite the opposite was true. But that commonsense idea that the public, *us*, the innocent (potential) victims, were in constant danger persisted.

The collective feeling of being threatened did not have much to do with statistical threat levels; the crime rate has dropped precipitously since its peak in the early 1990s and is now half what it was then. But when Gallup conducts its annual poll about how people *feel* about crime, the answer is almost always the same: a significant majority believe that crime is increasing, even as the trend consistently runs in the opposite direction. This effect is particularly pronounced among women, who are much more likely than men to report that they feel crime is up in the area where they live.

Crime isn't worse, but it *feels* worse. Something feels worse, at least. It's not so hard to imagine how such a thing might happen. How, if your world felt as if it were changing underneath your feet, if your life felt precarious and out of your control, and then you heard a good story that explained why that was, a story that placed the blame on a clearly defined bad guy, and then you kept hearing that story over and over, it might indeed begin to seem true.

In the 1990s, as the victims' rights movement gained momentum and Patti Tate accustomed herself to her newly public role as spokeswoman, Lisa Statman was a near-constant presence in her life.

The tenor of their eight-year relationship—to what extent they were variously friends, roommates, lovers, and/or collaborators—is contested. Statman says that she and Patti were romantic life partners for many years, and that they hid their relationship because they both worried that being out would bring Patti negative media attention. Debra Tate doesn't believe this. "My sister was asexual," she told me. "[Sex] was something she did, but she wasn't really into it." Three of Patti's close friends told me variations of the same thing—that they never saw any indication of a romantic relationship between the women while Patti was alive, and that they were shocked when Statman started claiming one after Patti's death. I found myself resisting this narrative, perhaps because homophobia is its own kind of bullying, and because the inside of anyone else's relationship is like a strange private chamber. It seems presumptuous to claim to know what goes on inside it.

Whatever the precise quality of their intimacy, Patti and Statman indisputably lived together for years and were close. "She was a wonderful, genuine person," an old friend told me. "[Statman] was a good friend to Patti and very supportive of her." When Statman got hired to work on the Mel Gibson movie *Maverick*, she arranged for Patti to get a temporary gig on set. When Statman worked as first AD on the TV series *High Incident*—a show about street cops fighting the war on drugs "one criminal at a time"—she got Patti hired as a permanent extra. Statman started working on *Ally McBeal*, and Patti did, too. Statman claimed Patti as a domestic partner, which meant that Patti could finally get health insurance for herself and her kids. Statman also helped write Patti's speeches for press conferences and parole hearings, matching her own words to the Tate family pain; when Patti faced her sister's killers at parole board meetings, Statman waited right outside the door. Some of what Statman's detractors see as evidence of sneakiness and duplicity could be chalked up to the difficulty of negotiating a world built on heterosexist assumptions, such as how, after Patti was diagnosed with breast cancer in 1997, at age forty, Statman lied to hospital staff, claiming that she was Patti's stepsister in order to be able to visit her. But some of Patti's old friends felt concerned about the relationship and worried that Patti was becoming increasingly isolated.

Soon, Patti's condition worsened. She had a tracheostomy tube put in, and she moved into Statman's bedroom. Her friends saw and heard even less of her. Several old friends told me that they felt as though Statman was keeping Patti away from them. In her final months, few people had any idea how sick she was. In June 2000, Robin Olson learned of her friend's death via a newscast on CNN.

After Patti was buried next to Sharon and Doris in Los Angeles's Holy Cross Cemetery, Statman stayed in the Palos Verdes house to raise Patti's two teenage kids. A year after Patti's death, Statman lobbied for a law that would've allowed non-family members to speak at parole hearings. Susan Fisher, who was then head of the Doris Tate Crime Victims Bureau, a victims' rights lobbying group, got wind of the proposal and found the idea troubling. "You know, I'm the sister of a murder victim," Fisher told me. "I would not want someone who is not related to me to have a legal right to speak in a parole hearing. I have a real strong reaction to that." Fisher said she and Debra Tate met with the state legislator who'd previously met with Statman and talked him out of taking the bill forward. (In 2008, California voters approved Marsy's Law, which allows victims' families to appoint representatives to speak at parole hearings.)

Eventually, Statman purchased the Palos Verdes house—where Patti and Debra grew up, where Sharon would come to visit her parents for Sunday dinner—from P.J. The house was full of Tate family memorabilia, boxes of old notes and photographs, all the miscellaneous detritus a family acquires over fifty years. Statman used some of that material in a book she published in 2012, *Restless Souls: The Sharon Tate Family's Account of Stardom, the Manson Murders, and a Crusade for Justice.* The story is told in an amalgam of voices, cobbled together from Doris, Patti, and P.J.'s stalled-out memoir drafts, family correspondence, and parole-hearing transcripts. The book includes stories from Doris's role in the heady early days of the victims' rights movement. It also features a long, lingering treatment of the murders at Cielo Drive, one that stretches out over eleven pages and vividly imagines the play-by-play of Sharon Tate's final moments: "Sharon writhes from his grip. As she twists away, his knife shot out a lick just below her rib cage. Her heart batters as she scrambles on her hands and knees. She reaches for the end table, grappling for leverage, but her blood-slicked fingers slip across the wood surface."

Several of Patti's friends told me that the book upset them. The sections written in Patti's voice didn't sound like her to them; the book felt like an act of failed ventriloquism, a version of their friend's voice that they didn't recognize.

Patti's daughter Brie contributed an afterword for the book, but Statman handled almost all the promotion. She appeared on TV, first to promote the book and then as a general-purpose Tate-LaBianca talking head. On the forty-fifth anniversary of the murders, or whenever Charles Manson did something scandalous, Statman would pop up on CNN or CBS or *Nancy Grace*, billed as "Sharon Tate's family friend," or the author of a book "which tells the story of Manson's crimes from the Tate family perspective." This kind of thing drove Robin Olson crazy. "You would think her last name is friggin Tate," she told me. "She slipped into those shoes. She feels as if it happened to her."

The book also displeased Sharon's sister Debra. While billed as an account of "the Sharon Tate family," Debra is mentioned a mere handful of times, and only in passing. The injustice of this consumed Debra for a few years. She'd already lost Sharon, lost her mother, lost Patti, lost her father, lost the family house; now she was being written out of her own family story. It felt to her as though the Tate legacy, with all its pain and complication, was being taken over by an interloper. Worse, an interloper whose interest in Sharon's death, Debra believed, was disproportionate, verging on fetishistic. "She wants to wallow in it," Debra told me, her voice dripping with disgust. "Like a pig."

Four years after *Restless Souls*, Debra published her own book about Sharon, *Sharon Tate: Recollection*. Once you know the backstory, it reads like an intentional rebuke to Statman's book. *Recollection* addresses Sharon's death only obliquely—"In 1969 my sister was involved in an event that changed the country in ways that still resonate," Debra writes—and instead features quotes and anecdotes from Sharon's famous friends about how kind she was, and how funny. But mostly it's a book of pictures: teenage Sharon with a pageant tiara (Queen of the Tri-City Autorama), and straddling a US Army missile in *Stars and Stripes* magazine; grown-up Sharon in a short skirt and tall boots; wide-eyed with a fringe of fake eyelashes; practicing karate with Bruce Lee. The Sharon of *Recollection* feels a little unreal—perfect looking, perfectly kind, perfectly good-hearted. "It's difficult to describe her character," the book quotes Roman Polanski as saying. "She was just utterly good. . . . She never had a bad temper, she was never moody. She enjoyed being a wife." When I read this, my first thought was cynical: *That's the kind of comment you can only make about a wife who died young.*

A few years ago, I was walking to the farmers' market in Lexington, Kentucky, when I came across a small memorial that was, its stone base proclaimed, "dedicated to all innocent victims of crime." There was that word again, *innocent*. It made me think of Bill Nelson's quest to disabuse the world of the pernicious rumor that Sharon Tate and her friends had been high—on weed, on MDMA, on whatever—the night they were murdered. As if their doing drugs would have made their deaths less tragic, as if a victim who wasn't perfect was somehow less of a victim.

In the political rhetoric of the 1980s and '90s, the idea that only certain victims counted was less subtext than text. Reagan's Task Force report focused on the victims it deemed worthy: "the innocent victim and all law-abiding citizens"; "the innocent, the honest and the helpless." This implied that certain people impacted by crime were excluded from the charmed circle of victimhood: the sex worker who got beat up by a client, perhaps, or the drug dealer who was shot by a rival, or the prisoner raped by his cellmate. Perhaps even just a black teenager wearing a hoodie, walking down the sidewalk. *He was no angel,* the newspapers would feel compelled to remind their readers. Or, *She had a checkered past.*

Insisting that victims be *innocent* dramatically limits who stands to benefit from policies that claim to support victims' rights. New Jersey's Victims of Crime Compensation Office has denied funds earmarked to cover therapy or funeral costs to victims whom it judges to be somehow unworthy or complicit in their victimization—for getting into a car with a drunk driver; for having been convicted of an entirely different crime years earlier.

Even more distressing, rhetoric around protecting victims has been enlisted to enact policies that make the most at risk even more vulnerable. While the prominent narratives of the victims' rights movement told of serial predators attacking women in their suburban homes or molesters preying on children, most of the people who got caught up in the "tough-on-crime" policies championed by victims' advocates were nonviolent drug offenders, the vast majority of them black. The effects of these policies have been devastating. As legal scholar Michelle Alexander outlines in *The New Jim Crow*, her best-selling account of the War on Drugs and its impact on the criminal justice system, more black men are currently under correctional control in the United States than were enslaved in 1850.

Since 1980, when the victims' rights movement took off, higher-education spending in California has decreased by 13 percent, while investment in prisons has grown 436 percent; the state now spends far more money on prisons than it does on colleges and universities. Meanwhile, violent crime rates held relatively steady between 1973 and 1993, then dropped precipitously over the next two decades. But, as Alexander writes, "by locking millions of people out of the mainstream legal economy, by making it difficult or impossible for people to find housing or feed themselves, and by destroying familial bonds by warehousing millions for minor crimes, we make crime more—not less—likely in the most vulnerable communities."

A few weeks before Christmas, I met Debra Tate for coffee in the sprawling suburban fringe at the eastern edges of Los Angeles County. The ceiling was strung with blinking lights, and TV monitors broadcast silent, looped news footage of the foothills on fire. The atmosphere felt distinctly Californian, equal parts festive and apocalyptic.

Debra has her mother's frankness and a youthful, easy laugh. She moves gingerly. Seventeen years ago, when she was working as a mail carrier, she opened a mailbox and was flattened by a homemade explosive someone had hidden inside; last year she was diagnosed with cancer, just like her mother and sister before her. "I say it's because I'm fighting the devil," she said. "So things keep getting thrown in my path."

Some of Debra's charisma stems from how confidently she seems to divide the world into good and bad. She told me that she sometimes wishes that all the murderers and sexual predators could just be shipped off to a tropical island somewhere. If they killed or molested one another, fine; they had been sent there for a reason, after all. We talked about Lisa Statman, who was "evil," Debra said, and "like a cancer growing in my family." Patti's been dead for almost two decades now; Statman is still in the Palos Verdes house and still making TV appearances where she speaks for the Tate family. (Years after Patti's death, Statman married a retired detective and forensic science expert named Karen Smith, who also shows up on crime TV programs.) "It was so hurtful and hateful what was going on that I just wanted not to live," Debra told me. "This is all sick stuff, really sick stuff. But that saved my life a few times. I knew I couldn't pull the trigger of the shotgun that was in my mouth because I knew that if I did that, she would win."

The news cycle that fall was consumed with stories about men and their bad behavior, and since we had been talking about sexual predators, I asked Debra about Roman Polanski. Passing judgment turned out to be more complicated when it was someone she knew. In the years after Sharon's death, she said, Roman had been incredibly kind to her. When he was in town, he'd stay at the Playboy Mansion, and she'd visit him there. "No funny business or hanky-panky," she assured me; they mostly just talked about Sharon. Their friendship was interrupted in 1977, when Polanski arranged a photo shoot with a thirteen-year-old girl, Samantha Geimer. He got her to take her clothes off, gave her champagne and part of a quaalude, and then he raped her. Afraid that the case's judge would make an example out of him, he fled to France and has never since returned to the United States.

Debra sighed and said, "Roman did what he did. He has never said he didn't, ever ever ever. And was he wrong for doing it? Absolutely. But in France that's the way things happen every day of the week. So to him it wasn't . . . he didn't stop to think. And he should have.

We all need to pay attention to the laws of the place we're in. And he didn't. And therefore he's a bad, bad boy. But he knows that. And he did make restitution—he did everything, plus more. And they're still using this as a political ploy, and it really makes me sick." (Geimer herself is an example of how complex victims can be, and how they rarely fit the simple story lines that are created for them. She maintains that Polanski's assault on her was deeply harmful, but that the DA's office's focus on the lurid details of the case, and its insistence on pursuing it for decades against her wishes, has been more of a violation than the original rape. She has publicly forgiven Polanski and now directs much of her ire at the prosecutor's office, which has refused to drop the case, which she believes should be terminated.)

Debra has lived in California for nearly all of her life, but she was feeling as though maybe it was finally time to get out. It was partly because of the fires, the mudslides, the inescapable end-of-the-world feeling, but also because of how the state has been reconsidering its approach to criminal justice. Those tough-on-crime decades nearly bankrupted California. In 2009, the state's prisons were so underfunded and overcrowded that the Supreme Court declared the situation cruel and unusual, and therefore unconstitutional, and mandated that forty thousand prisoners be released over the next few years. Seven years later, California voters overwhelmingly approved a ballot initiative that walked back many of the policies enacted in the 1980s and '90s. The new law's most prominent supporter was Governor Jerry Brown, who had been a vocal advocate for mandatory-minimum sentences three decades earlier. "What we did, what I did—we didn't fully grasp the consequences," Brown said. "We just didn't know, and I say it's an error that should be corrected." Recently, state prisons began allowing family visits for lifers again.

Debra despaired of these policy changes. If what had happened in

1969 hadn't happened, maybe she would have enjoyed a quiet life in the desert, spending her days communing with horses and chickens, ignoring the sand fleas of politics. But having her life wrenched apart by violence at an early age meant that she couldn't *not* take crime personally. She couldn't *not* be involved. Over the years, she's counseled other victims, particularly those affected by high-profile cases. (She got close with Ron Goldman's family during the O. J. Simpson trial.) This new trend toward leniency felt like a slap in the face to her. "I don't like sitting in judgment of other people. But I do know that there should be an obligation to protect the greater good, and to protect the innocent. That's what society is, we're the innocents that these other people are preying upon. And it's unacceptable," she told me. She was leaning forward; she seemed to want to make sure I understood. "Because what they're doing breaks you *forever.*"

For a while, it seemed as though the country as a whole would once again follow California's lead and move away from punitive penal politics. The new commonsense approach to criminal justice was bipartisan and evidence based, the newspaper editorial writers assured me. Then, on a moonless night in the summer of 2016, I was driving alone through West Texas. Outside the night air was chilly, but inside my truck I felt cozy and safe. I imagined how I would appear to someone looking down at me from a great height: a small, swift point of light moving through a large and silent desert. I had a long way to go before I would be home.

My antenna picked up only one radio station, which was broadcasting live Donald Trump's keynote speech from the Republican National Convention. For a little while, his words fuzzed in and out, but by the time he got around to talking about crime, the signal was clear and strong. "I have a message for all of you: the crime and violence that today afflicts our nation will soon, *and I mean very soon*, come to an end," Trump bellowed. "Beginning on January twentieth of 2017, safety will be restored." I switched off the radio and drove in silence. The speech lingered in the car—not so much Trump's words but the effect they produced, a kind of emotional afterimage of keyed-up anxiety. I switched the radio back on. "The first task for our new administration will be to liberate our citizens from the crime and terrorism and lawlessness that threatens our community." I switched it off again. Trump's speech, one of the longest in convention history, lasted the rest of my drive home. I would listen as long as I could stand it, then drive in troubled silence, then turn it back on to catch the next piece of ugly rhetoric—the equivalent of watching a horror movie dismemberment through a screen of fingers. But I didn't need to hear all the words to get the gist: *You are afraid,* Trump was saying, *and you are right to be afraid. Things are bad, they're out of control. You are in danger. And anyone who tells you otherwise is not to be trusted—they're a fool or a dupe, possibly even an enemy.* The next time I switched the radio on, I didn't hear Trump's voice at all—instead it was just the white noise of the crowd, roaring in agreement.

Stories of victimhood short-circuit logic and rationality; they target us in a place that's more deep and vital. At its best, this impulse can inspire empathy for people who have endured something unthinkable and provoke us to take action to prevent such misery from happening again. Feeling someone else's suffering as if it is our own can encourage us to make the world a more just place.

But the danger of a politics of empathy is that our own biases are built-in, from the foundation up. Pain that looks more like our pain is easier to imagine as real, as *painful*. This isn't always a matter of active cruelty; often it happens in the parts of the brain not subject to conscious control. In *Against Empathy*, psychologist Paul Bloom discusses a European study that used male soccer fans as its subjects: "The fan would receive a shock on the back of his hand and then watch another man receive the same shock. When the other man was described as a fan of the subject's team, the empathic neural response—the overlap in self-other pain—was strong. But when the man was described as a fan of the opposing team, it wasn't." It takes so little for us to shut ourselves off from someone else's suffering—all he has to do is be wearing the wrong team's jersey. Human beings are such good othering machines, so talented at dividing up the world into who matters and who doesn't.

Shortly after Ben Fawley was arrested, a reporter from the Richmond newspaper attended a community meeting. He asked the people present if they could name any of the city's murder victims from that year, who numbered seventy-one. "Taylor Behl!" dozens of people enthusiastically piped up. Behl had been killed in a neighboring county, the reporter pointed out. Maybe someone knew the name of any other victim? Even just a first name, or a last name? Did anyone want to hazard a guess? The room was silent; Taylor's death was the only one that had made a lasting impression.

Just a few years later, two other college-age women went missing in Virginia. Both were last seen in Charlottesville, home of the University of Virginia. November 2012: Sage Smith told a friend she was going "to go meet a man" and never came home. September 2014: Hannah Graham vanished from Charlottesville's Downtown Mall. Their cases were unrelated and differed in many of their particulars, but they became twinned in the public imagination as a stark reminder of inequity. Sage Smith was a poor, black trans woman; Hannah Graham was a white UVA sophomore. The Charlottesville police pursued both cases seriously—but the police, the media, and the community all clearly took Graham's disappearance more to heart. "Only a very small fraction of our community has taken interest in Sage," a Charlottesville detective told reporter Emma Eisenberg. In contrast, Graham inspired the most intense and extensive search in Virginia's history, a $100,000 reward, and a press conference in which the town's police chief wept openly.

"I think, I felt as if I were in the shoes of [Hannah's] parents, as a dad having a fifteen-year-old girl who is growing up too quickly," the police chief said after the press conference. "I'm a human being and I can't always control how I react to things." Had he cried about Sage? someone asked. No, he admitted. No, he had not.

Reading old newspaper articles about Taylor Behl, I was struck by how she had gone missing on September 5, 2005, shortly after Hurricane Katrina made landfall. The day her disappearance was reported was the same day the US Army Corps of Engineers finally repaired the levee breach and began to pump water out of New Orleans, revealing hundreds of drowned bodies in attics, in nursing homes, on street corners. It was the week that Secretary of Homeland Security Michael Chertoff declared the storm to be "probably the worst catastrophe, or set of catastrophes," to ever hit the United States. Katrina was another disaster I watched from a distance, its horror mediated through screens. Nearly two thousand people died throughout the Gulf Coast, and I don't know a single one of their names. Despite (or perhaps because of) the scale of the tragedy, Katrina didn't impress itself on my mind with anything like the intensity of Taylor Behl's murder.

In Bloom's book, he repeatedly compares empathy to a spotlight: "It makes visible the suffering of others, makes their troubles real, salient, and concrete. From the gloom, something is seen." But a spotlight is a limited instrument. It illuminates, but only narrowly. Its light is so bright that you can forget how much it leaves in the dark.

*   *   *

I eventually reached Lisa Statman on the phone; by the end of our hour-long conversation, it was clear she was frustrated with me and concerned with how I would evaluate the negative things about her I was hearing. "The most important thing to remember in all of this are the victims," she said. "Whatever you choose to write, especially if you choose to write about me in a negative way, just remember that that impacts their memory. Because if I am this crazy person that infiltrated Patti and P.J. and Doris and was able to worm my way into this family under these false pretenses, it takes away from the dignity of their memory. Because it makes them seem like idiots. And it makes them seem vulnerable, and it makes them seem stupid. So you can say what you want, but just remember, everything you say—it's the victims that it impacts."

Meanwhile, Robin Olson was forwarding me emails from a handwriting analyst who concluded that Statman's signature displayed what graphologists apparently call "the felon's claw": "This woman is unstable, devious, grasping and probably charming," he summarized. "High level PSYCHOPATH!" Olson wrote. Debra Tate passed along a message from Roman Polanski, who said that he was "stupefied" to learn that Statman had opened up Sharon's grave without his permission, to place Patti's ashes inside. Statman told me that Debra was hoarding P.J.'s ashes "as some type of revenge." Everyone was accusing everyone else of forging documents, of lying, of profiting from Sharon's death, of disgracing the Tate family name.

It got messy for a little while, navigating all that grief. One night when I couldn't sleep, I found myself silently apologizing to Sharon. *Sorry, Sharon,* my brain said to itself. *Sorry about the drama. Sorry about your family. Sorry about everything.* I imagined her in some parallel universe where she'd been allowed to live. She would be plump and happy and wearing a caftan. She would be somebody's grandmother. Parallel-universe Sharon smiled at me indulgently: *Sorry about what? I've led a beautiful life.* But that was not the universe that I was inhabiting.

I tried to bully myself to sleep, but that worked as well as it always did, which was not at all. Eventually I gave in and let the dead and the living make their strange nightly parade through my head. I thought about Abigail Folger on the front lawn of 10050 Cielo Drive gasping, *I'm already dead,* as some hippie girl stabbed her, and Woytek Frykowski, who had survived the Holocaust only to be murdered in Beverly Hills, and Jay Sebring, bleeding all over his striped pajama pants. I thought about Sharon. I thought about poor, bespectacled Steven Parent, and about barefoot William Garretson, whose life was unraveled by the screams he couldn't, or refused to, hear. I thought about Rosie Blanchard, who felt her own pain vibrating at the same frequency as Sharon Tate's, and I thought about Doris and Debra and Patti and P.J., and the public and private life of the Tate family pain. I thought about Lisa Statman moving into a dead woman's house, and I thought about creepy Bill Nelson and his telephoto lens. I thought about Tex Watson's wife and her toddler daughter and the prairie dresses they wore to prison visits, before Doris Tate pushed to get those visits banned. I thought about all the other mothers and daughters and wives and sons and fathers and friends of those in prison, about their millions of visits, and the visits they were denied. I thought about Suzan LaBerge's dedication to forgiveness—naive? holy? insane?—and I thought about her murdered mother and her murdered stepfather, and I thought about the gravestone of poor unborn Paul Tate. I thought about the Cielo Drive house, razed to the ground after Statman moved out in 1994, and I thought about the scavengers who came that night, to salvage scraps for their collections. I thought about the neighborhoods hollowed out by the drug war, and the scientists who now say that grief is not just individual but communal. I thought about how trauma gets passed around communities like a disease, and how it gets passed on inside a family like the worst kind of inheritance. I thought about just how many victims there are in this story, and how if you started to count them, you might never stop.

THE DEFENDER

When you have to decide to do something, always do
what will cost you the most.

—Simone Weil

Lorri Davis first saw Damien Echols on a movie screen. It was March
1996, and she was attending the New Directors / New Films festival
at the Museum of Modern Art in New York City. The documentary
she watched that day, *Paradise Lost: The Child Murders at Robin Hood
Hills*, was about a terrible crime she'd never before heard of, three
eight-year-old boys—"Boy Scouts," everyone kept calling them, as
if to underscore their innocence—found dead in the woods in West
Memphis, Arkansas. The film opened with footage from a police video.
Men in uniform crouched on a pipe bridge over a drainage ditch full
of muddy water, peering at two kid-size bikes. As the camera moved
through the woodsy crime scene, it lingered on an awful image—three
pale bodies, each bent at an unnatural angle. Stevie Branch, Christopher Byers, and Michael Moore. They'd been discovered submerged
in the ditch, naked and hog-tied. One boy's skull had been smashed
in; another had an ugly wound where his penis once was.

Lorri was thirty-two, a landscape architect who spent her days
thinking about the gradations of rich people's backyards, figuring out
the optimal placement for Oscar de la Renta's pool. This kind of human
horror wasn't something she typically indulged in; she preferred

French films, where most of the violence was emotional. But having grown up in West Virginia, Lorri was uncomfortably familiar with the world the documentary depicted: the fear stirring the community, the churchy judgment, the hunger to assign blame.

Twelve minutes into the film, Lorri saw him, the teenager who was accused of committing the terrible murders. Damien Echols. He was eighteen years old, a high school dropout, a Wiccan. The prosecution's theory was that he was the mastermind of a local satanic cult, and that he and two friends—Jason Baldwin and Jessie Misskelley Jr.—had killed the boys as part of some sinister ritual. The baffled teenagers denied committing the murders (and being members of a cult). All three were put on trial, but the film lingered on Damien. Other people in the movie said his name with a kind of hushed, horrified awe.

He didn't look evil to Lorri; he looked way in over his head, this Damien Echols. He was baby faced and doughy from prison food, pale from lack of sunlight. His black hair was cut in an unflattering style, a hasty jailhouse trim given to him by his public defender. His mouth twitched when he was nervous. He made a terrible advocate for himself, playing into the local mythology: Damien, the neighborhood weirdo, the trench coat-wearer, the putative murderer. "I knew from when I was real small that people were gonna know who I was—I always had that feeling. I just never knew how they were gonna learn," he told the camera with a kind of bashful bravado, pressing his plump lips together. "I kinda enjoy it because now even after I die people are going to remember me forever. They're going to talk about me for years. . . . It'll be sorta like I'm the West Memphis bogeyman. Little kids'll be looking under their bed before they go to bed—*Damien might be under there.*"

Someone more cowardly, or more strategic, might have made a play to seem chastened or at least less interested in the occult, but Damien was thoroughly, disastrously himself. From the back of a cop car, he flipped off the local news reporters. On the stand, he said that he had never read any books by Aleister Crowley, described by the prosecutor as "a noted author in the field of satanic worship," but added that he would have if he'd come across any. He was intelligent and strange and, Lorri thought, clearly innocent. He was so obviously trying to be brave. He was so obviously terrified.

When the movie ended and Lorri walked out onto the hectic midtown sidewalk, it was dark. That night she had a hard time sleeping, and the next night, too. Her appetite vanished. That whole week was "one of the strangest . . . I've ever experienced," she wrote later: it was as though the story she'd seen in the documentary had infected her. She thought about the last scene, after the jury had announced the guilty verdict, when two men in suits helped Damien into a bulletproof vest, then led him through a jeering crowd. "You're gonna fry, Damien," someone shouted. Lorri thought about the title card that had flashed on the screen at the end of the film: "Damien Echols has been sentenced to death." The injustice of it seemed so huge and inescapable that it was impossible that the world should go on as usual. Yet it did.

In the weeks after she watched the documentary for the first time, Lorri went to the New York Public Library and scrolled through the microfiche to find newspaper articles about the trial. She couldn't find any indication that the case was being appealed, that the legal system was going to remedy this massive wrong. At work, she put on headphones and listened to Kate Bush and Counting Crows as she tinkered with the estates of wealthy people. She tried not to think about Damien, because when she thought about Damien, she cried. Here she was, free and single in the most exciting city in America, at liberty to do whatever she wanted, able to eat doughnuts for dinner if she wanted to, and meanwhile Damien was moldering away on death row. What was that even like for him? She couldn't imagine; she'd never visited a prison or been close to anyone who'd served time. To be so taken over by a stranger's problems felt peculiar. She was consumed with the desire to somehow be of *use*, but how much help could she be from so far away, without any applicable skills or knowledge?

Lorri had grown up in a fundamentalist Baptist family in suburban West Virginia. Her parents were high school sweethearts, "conservative as all get-out," she said later. Both of her sisters were elected homecoming queen. Lorri was the odd one, the kind of kid who brought her pet chameleon to school on picture day so they could pose together. In high school, she was well liked—she had great hair, a big bright smile, and an air of palpable kindness—and she found friends across many social groups, from the popular kids to the disaffected weirdos who hung out in the smoking pit. Even so, she felt strange, misaligned somehow, as if she and her classmates weren't exactly speaking the same language. She liked to creep out of her house in the middle of the night and take long walks through the sleeping neighborhood, looking at strangers' windows, imagining the mysteries of their lives. Her parents didn't know what to make of her, this sensitive, dreamy, questioning child. One time, a relative called her "a kite without a string." As if she was just drifting, without anything to ground her.

When she was older and living in New York—another decision her family found difficult to comprehend—she would sometimes follow strangers who snagged her fancy, à la Sophie Calle. She liked daring herself to follow an impulse wherever it took her; once, she ended up on a train to upstate New York. She didn't choose her strangers because they were particularly beautiful or glamorous; what drew her in, she wrote later, was "something else, something striking—or dark, or 'off.'"

She had other ways of immersing herself in the enchantment of the world—watching movies, for instance. She watched *so* many movies, and she preferred to be in the first row, where the sensory experience was maximally overwhelming. But this documentary about the murdered children, and the town's panic, and the teenagers railroaded for the crimes, created a different kind of disorientation, one that didn't dissipate after she walked out of the movie theater. It was as if she were possessed. She couldn't get it out of her head. She kept thinking about the misfit kids from her high school, the ones who hung out in the smoking pit. She kept thinking about Damien, his obvious intelligence, how invested he was in appearing strong, and how his vulnerability shone through nonetheless. How desperately he needed someone to help him. How it was unclear if anyone would.

It wasn't as though she had some huge emptiness in her life, some psychic gulf that needed filling. She loved her job, she loved traveling. She loved her Brooklyn apartment and her Brooklyn world. In some ways, her life was like a cheery sitcom version of a young woman's life in the city. Her best friend even lived in the apartment upstairs. And yet. "I was also very— I was wanting more," she told me more than two decades later. "My whole life I knew that I did not want a mundane life. But I didn't know what that was." Those sleepless weeks after she learned about Damien's case, she began to wonder: Was this the big thing she had been looking for all along?

For a few weeks in my late twenties I would wake up feeling guilty, as if I had just spent hours being harangued by a superior dreamworld version of myself. Dream-me was vocally disappointed with the way that actual-me conducted my life. I was a writer in the least glamorous sense of the word, churning out cheery content for financial institutions in order to fund what felt like my real vocation, meandering literary journalism about sad people and the sad things that happened to them. None of it had much of an effect on the world (or made me much money). Maybe, I started thinking, I should try to be a lawyer. But everyone I knew who'd gone that route had haunted eyes and alarming student loan balances. *Don't go to law school,* they all rasped in the same urgent tones. *Whatever you do, don't go to law school.*

And yet. The more I spent my days immersed in the kind of writing that felt frivolous, either because it was ("Ten tips for a stress-free retirement!") or because barely anyone would read it, the easier it was to idealize the law. Its selfless defense of the desperate. (Because of course I imagined myself as one of those noble, lowly paid, virtuous lawyers.) Its arcane, solid vocabulary. How it made things in the world *happen.*

When I moved to rural Texas in 2012, I began volunteering with a nearby federal public defender. Mostly, I was just looking for an excuse to hang out with Liz Rogers, the office's highest-ranking attorney. I'd heard about Liz soon after I arrived in town; she was something of a local legend. All the tall girls in the tri-county area, myself included, swooned over her. She was taller than all of us—six feet two inches I'd guess—with a steel-gray bob and a smoky rasp of a voice. Liz was a certified quail naturalist, the latest hardy descendant of one of the first white families to settle in the harsh terrain that was now Big Bend National Park. Her grandmother had tracked mountain lions on horseback—riding sidesaddle because she was a lady. Liz had met Sandra Day O'Connor. Liz was dating a cowboy—a real one, not some billionaire faker from Dallas who liked to play dress-up on the weekend. At parties, Liz was always calling you over to introduce you to someone because she was at every party and knew everyone and seemed to sincerely believe that the world would run more smoothly if we all knew everyone, too.

As a federal public defender, Liz had spent her career defending the indigent. She spoke Spanish fluently, albeit with the exact same ranchland drawl that she had in English. At the small office in Alpine,

Texas, Liz met with clients and had long cajoling phone conversations as I sorted photocopies into the appropriate folders. I felt like a small, unpaid cog in a vast and important machine. It wasn't a bad feeling. One day I was putting papers in their proper places when I realized that a chant was playing on a loop in the background of my brain: *I'm helping, I'm helping, I'm helping.*

The *Paradise Lost* documentary that Lorri watched that day at MoMA suggested that the case against Damien and his two friends was part of an unsettling episode in American history that had begun a few decades earlier: the Satanic Panic.

It kicked off in 1973, when a British Columbia psychotherapist named Lawrence Pazder started seeing a twenty-seven-year-old patient named Michelle. For the first four years of their work together, the therapy followed a routine course—discussions of Michelle's violent, alcoholic father; her erratic mother; and her three miscarriages. But then something changed. Michelle had a dream in which a nest of spiders erupted out of her hand and woke up with a sense of a dark secret she wasn't able to articulate. Her therapy with Pazder intensified. Instead of sitting on a chair, Michelle would lie down on the couch and try to find her way into the hidden chambers of her brain. Once, she screamed for twenty minutes straight. Pazder held her as she regressed to her five-year-old self; their therapy sessions now sometimes lasted as long as six hours. Speaking as her child self, Michelle slowly began to recount memories of the satanic cult her parents had joined and the tortures they'd inflicted on her. The abuse that Michelle recalled was operatic in its cruelty. She had been locked in a cage, been raped, been rubbed with the blood of murdered babies. She remembered a satanic operating room, where a satanic doctor surgically attached horns and a tail to her body. She remembered being the central figure in an elaborate eighty-one-day ritual that succeeded in summoning Satan from the bowels of hell.

In 1980, Michelle and Pazder cowrote a book detailing their therapeutic journey, *Michelle Remembers*. It featured an enthusiastic blurb from the Catholic bishop of British Columbia, and a slightly warier one from the pope himself. (The book neglected to mention that, during their work together, Michelle and Pazder had divorced their spouses and married each other.) As one of the first accounts to claim that a growing satanic threat was menacing America, it was used as a training document for police officers, prosecutors, and social workers. *Michelle Remembers* became a bestseller, and soon other satanic-cult memoirs followed. Lauren Stratford's book *Satan's Underground*, which recounted her lurid experiences as a satanic sex slave / baby breeder, was typical of the genre. An earlier account, *The Satan Seller*, was one of the few occult-survivor memoirs written by a man, Mike Warnke, who billed himself as a "Former Satanist High Priest, Now America's Number 1 Christian Comedian."

The books sold so well that television soon picked up on the story line. In 1989, Michelle and Stratford appeared on *Oprah*. Stratford "was part of a group of young women and children forced to surrender their bodies into some of the most evil rituals imaginable. Her own child was used in a human sacrifice," Oprah told the camera, without a hint of doubt in her voice. Stratford also showed up on Geraldo Rivera's notorious two-hour special *Devil Worship: Exposing Satan's Underground*. Viewer-discretion disclaimers scrolled across the screen as Geraldo, his eyes serious and sincere, pleaded with his audience to make sure their children weren't watching—the stories were just too depraved, too awful.

In his special, Rivera quickly and confusingly showcased dozens of examples of ostensibly satanic activity: alienated teenage boys who'd killed their friends while high, pentagram graffiti scrawled on abandoned buildings, metalheads in mosh pits, children's drawings of murdered babies. The program culminated with a segment on Lauren Stratford and other self-identified baby breeders. "There is no longer any doubt" about human sacrifice being practiced in America, Rivera told his audience. "The ideal sacrifice, we are told, requires babies. And there are those in satanic sects who tell of babies being bred for sacrifice." Stratford was calm as she explained the gruesome process that she claimed to have endured: "It is most common for the heart to be taken from the child and offered to Satan," she said. A decade later, when tastes had shifted, Stratford would pop up again as Laura Grabowski, a (fake) Holocaust survivor who claimed she had been experimented on by Josef Mengele.

Satanic abuse stories drew big audiences because they were salacious. But they were also the right kind of salacious for their time. After the Manson murders and Jonestown suicides, it was not such a stretch to imagine that seemingly normal people could behave in aberrant, even homicidal ways, particularly if they were in thrall to a malevolent leader. In addition, growing awareness of physical and sexual violence against women led to similarly frank discussions about child abuse, itself vastly underreported. By the eighties, with Ronald Reagan as president and evangelical Christianity an ascendant political force, the culture was primed for particular stories of violation. Abuse was more palatable when it was presented as horrific, elaborately organized, and explicitly anti-Christian. These threads—anxiety about cults, growing awareness of abuse, the spread of therapeutic culture and its emphasis on trauma, plus the rise of the religious right—all contributed to a strange national obsession with satanic cults that peaked in the mid-to-late 1980s.

"Not a single state is unaffected" by satanic crime, 20/20 reported in 1985. "We think there's a widespread problem here that you deserve, that you *need*, to know about," Geraldo warned his viewers. "These ritualistic crimes are everywhere—and yet in most communities they are either overlooked or underreported." One often-repeated statistic claimed that cultists in the United States sacrificed fifty thousand innocent victims per year. If this seemed ludicrous—at the peak of violent crime in the United States, around twenty-five thousand people were killed annually—well, that was just proof of how sneaky these satanists were, and how powerfully well connected. (The going theory was that the satanists had their own breeding program for creating sacrificial infants, whose lives—and deaths—never became part of the public record.) "We are seeing in the streets the sign of Armageddon," said Dale Griffis—an ex-cop from Ohio who had reinvented himself as an occult expert—to a roomful of Virginia police officers.

Eight percent of Richmond, my hometown, was "involved in Satanic worship at some level," according to Patricia Pulling, founder of Bothered About Dungeons and Dragons (BADD). That estimate, she noted, was conservative. Around this same time a cop came into my second-grade class to solemnly warn us about the roaming drug gangs in our local malls, bent on dosing suburban elementary school kids with LSD. Who knew what else they were capable of, he told us. Even then I remember wondering why anyone in his or her right mind would give away drugs for free. But that question had an easy, all-purpose answer: *evil*. Plenty of people scoffed at accounts of satanism, but their doubt just made the believers more sure. Nothing makes people more righteous than feeling they are in possession of a truth that others don't want to hear.

In 1992, a year before the three children were murdered in West Memphis, a local juvenile officer, Jerry Driver, attended a seminar on satanic ritual crime in Little Rock. The occult-crime lecture circuit had become something of a cottage industry, with cops and social workers racking up continuing-education hours by learning about cults and human sacrifice; it was certainly more entertaining than

sitting through another thirty-hour workshop on Professionalism in
the Workplace. This particular class was led by the same Dale Griffis
who had recently lectured in Virginia. Driver had attended a few
such seminars before, in Texas and Tennessee, but learning about
the occult from Griffis was a particular honor.

Griffis, a lanky man with long, drooping earlobes, was an early
convert to the cause. He had been working as a cop in Ohio in the
early 1980s when he first became attuned to the growing satanic
menace. He became fixated on the hidden world of occult crime, and
on informing the public about the danger. Griffis got in trouble with
his boss for running up large phone bills at the police station, talking
at length about cults with fellow cops across the country. In 1985,
Griffis saw a red thread dangling from a pine tree—red thread being
a telltale sign of a satanic ritual location—and convinced the county
sheriff to excavate five hundred square feet of parkland, claiming that
as many as seventy-five human sacrifices might be found. (Nothing
was there.) Shortly afterward, Griffis left the force to do satanic con-
sulting full-time. He photocopied pamphlets of occult symbols and
distributed them at the lectures he gave across the nation. He went on
20/20 and sounded the alarm to a television audience of millions: "We
have kids being killed. We have people missing in America—our own
MIAs right here. We have cattle being killed," he intoned solemnly.
"We have all types of perversion going on, and it's affecting America."

After the Little Rock class was over, Jerry Driver asked Griffis
about some of the things Driver had noticed on his patrols in the West
Memphis area: pentagrams spray-painted on concrete pillars, dead
dogs that may or may not have been ritually sacrificed, teenagers
who wore black trench coats and seemed troubled. Griffis agreed that
these were indeed evidence of a ritually abusive sacrificial cult, and
that there was a good possibility "that children and animals would
be sacrificed" in the near future. Driver started driving around town

on nights when there was a full moon, a one-man task force aimed at intercepting satanic crime.

Driver was particularly focused on one local teenager, a black-haired high school dropout named Damien Echols. Echols, many people in the small town agreed, was *different*. He wore black and collected animal bones. In a county where a quarter of the population lived below the poverty line, his family was worse off than most. He spent his childhood in a clapboard shack with no running water, heating, or air-conditioning. He suffered from terrible headaches and breathing problems, particularly when crop dusters swung low over the fields surrounding the house.

As a teenager, Damien was sensitive and intelligent, given to dark moods and intense fixations. When he was fifteen, he started attending Catholic services, drawn to their ornate rituals. In a town dominated by evangelical Christianity, this in itself was rebellious. When Damien's stepfather adopted him, Damien changed his first name—on his birth certificate, he was Michael—to honor Saint Damien, a nineteenth-century priest who treated lepers in Hawaii. (Once Damien was on trial for murder, local gossips spread the rumor his name was an homage to the demon child from *The Omen*.) A girlfriend introduced him to Wicca, which suited him even more than Catholicism. Finally, here was a way to tap into all the unseen mystery and power that churned right below the surface of the visible world. He began writing down spells in his journal: "*Improving the memory* if the heart, eye or brain of a lapwing or black plover be hanged upon a mans necke, It is profitable against forgetfullness and sharpeneth a mans understanding."

Damien could also be volatile, angry, difficult to deal with. He didn't always seem to realize that he could come across as arrogant or strange, or perhaps he just didn't care. Depression came on him hugely, and his moods sometimes frightened his parents. After his Wiccan girlfriend broke up with him, he unraveled further. The ex-girlfriend's mother reported him to the police for harassing her daughter and threatening to kill a male friend of hers. By the early 1990s, he'd done two stints in a psychiatric hospital. But the person he seemed most likely to be a threat to was himself.

Throughout 1992 and into 1993, Damien became something of an obsession for juvenile officer Jerry Driver. After all those seminars, Driver knew to be on the lookout for satanists, and Damien looked the part, "like one of the slasher-movie-type guys—boots, coat, long, stringy black hair," as Driver put it later. Damien wore his fingernails long and filed them into sharp points—"talons," Driver called them. After one incident—a fairly pathetic attempt to run away with his girlfriend that resulted in charges of burglary and sexual misconduct— Damien's mom gave Driver permission to search her son's room, and Driver seized Damien's journal as evidence. There was plenty in there to make a man attuned to the dangers of the occult sit up straighter in his chair: not just spells, but also doodles of upside-down crosses, pentagrams, spooky horned figures in cloaks, and bad poetry about sacrifice and blood and pain. And then one afternoon, Driver would later testify, he saw Damien and two other teenagers walking down the street wearing long black jackets and carrying "staffs." The satanic situation in West Memphis seemed to be heading, Driver said later, "toward some sort of crescendo."

Driver's subordinate was present on the May afternoon when the three boys' pale bodies were lifted from the drainage ditch. "Looks like Damien has finally killed someone," he reportedly said.

The next day, detectives interviewed Damien Echols for the first time, and they continued to question him over subsequent weeks. He had a decent alibi for the day of the murders, but that didn't dissuade them. They took notes on his belief in a female god and his love of Stephen King books. They asked him what he thought the killer's motivation was. "Thrill kill," he told them. "Damien feels that sex is boring," his interviewers noted. "Damien considers himself to be very intelligent. Damien wants to be a writer of scary books or poems at some time." Investigators also interviewed Damien's best friend, a sweet, slight artistic kid named Jason Baldwin.

On June 4, a month after the boys' bodies were found—another full-moon night—Damien and Jason were celebrating Jason's successful completion of the tenth grade by watching bad horror movies. *Leprechaun* was on when someone began pounding on the door of Damien's family's trailer. "We thought it was a game," Jason said later. "But it was the police." Jason protested as his best friend was placed in handcuffs: *I know him, he doesn't do drugs, he hasn't done anything wrong.* "Are you Jason Baldwin?" one of the officers asked. "You're under arrest, too." Damien and Jason would soon learn that earlier that day Jessie Misskelley Jr., a teenager from the trailer park with an IQ that classified him as having an intellectual disability, had confessed to involvement with the murders after a prolonged (and mostly unrecorded) interrogation. He had also implicated the two of them. Damien and Jason were only vaguely acquainted with Jessie, but now they were being painted as key members of the same secret, evil club.

The next morning, the West Memphis police held a press conference to announce the arrests. Someone asked Detective Gary Gitchell how confident he was in his case, on a scale of one to ten. "Eleven," Gitchell said emphatically.

Gitchell would come to regret being so public and so certain about the three teenagers' guilt. Looked at closely, the case against Damien, Jason, and Jessie was tissue-paper thin, largely based on Jessie's highly questionable confession, which he soon retracted. No solid physical evidence tied the three teenagers to the crimes, and no credible evidence suggested they had ever met or interacted with the victims. There was no clear motive. To help with that last bit, Dale

Griffis, cult expert, traveled to Arkansas to testify about the murders' satanic trappings. Sure, they didn't look occult on the surface, but consider that the victims were killed near water, and a few days after an occult holiday, and on the night of a full moon. Three was a significant number to satanists, and there were three victims. They were eight years old, and eight was a "witches' number," Griffis told the jury. Stevie Branch had been wounded on the left side of his head: "The right side is related to those things synonymous with Christianity," Griffis testified, "while the left side is that of the practitioners of the satanic occult." For anyone hoping to spot evil in the world, Griffis also helpfully noted that occultists tended to wear black nail polish, black shirts, and "black dungarees," and that they preferred art with the theme of "necromancy, or love of death."

In 1994, when Damien, Jason, and Jessie went on trial, the Satanic Panic was on its way out. The McMartin Preschool trial, during which seven California teachers were charged with more than two hundred counts of molestation and conspiracy, had concluded after seven years with no convictions; at the time, it was the longest and most expensive court proceeding in US history. The FBI released a comprehensive report about ritual abuse of children in the United States, concluding that it didn't exist. All those breeder babies, the tens of thousands of satanic sacrifices, the subterranean covens made up of political elites—none of it was real. After years of looking into the subject, Special Agent Kenneth Lanning was unable to find a single substantiated case of satanic ritual abuse in the United States. In 1995, even Geraldo apologized for having been "terribly wrong" about the satanic threat, and for the "many innocent people who were convicted and went to prison as a result."

But in Arkansas in 1994, enough people still believed in the satanic menace that Jason Baldwin and Jessie Misskelley Jr. were sentenced to life in prison, and Damien Echols was sent to death row.

*   *   *

Lorri Davis agonized over the first letter she wrote to Damien, in April 1996, a couple of weeks after she'd seen him in the documentary. She didn't want to seem like a tragedy groupie. In the documentary she'd seen how many cameras he'd had pointed at him during the trial, how the media had treated him like a zoo animal, a specimen to be gawked at. At one moment in the film, Damien was in the courtroom cradling his infant son, Seth, who'd been born while his father was in custody. It was his first time holding the baby, and he had a shy, proud, weirded-out look on his face. The journalists ate it up. "Change his diaper for us, Damien!" one called out. That was exactly the kind of monster Lorri didn't want to be.

The letter she finally sent was full of apologies and disclaimers: she was sorry for intruding, and she assured him he didn't have to write her back if he didn't want to. A few days after that, before he'd even had a chance to reply, she sent another note. She asked about his appeals, about his "girlfriend (wife?)," about what his days in prison were like. "I hope it doesn't freak you out to have someone that you don't even know mooning over you so much," she wrote. "It kind of freaks me out that this is happening to me. I cry about it a lot . . . since I have become 'acquainted' with you, it's difficult because I think about your situation all the time."

Damien's first letter to Lorri arrived while her parents were visiting her in Brooklyn for the first (and only) time. She didn't want to read it in front of them, so she slipped it in her pocket and carried it around with her all day, comforted by its presence. She waited until she was finally alone that night to open it. Damien's response was more casual than her letter had been—though it did mention that he was no longer in a relationship with the mother of his child.

The early letters between Damien and Lorri, some of which were published in a book called *Yours for Eternity*, veer between cautious reticence and frank intimacy. They're the correspondence of two intense people trying to not let their intensity show too much, for fear of scaring the other person off. "Damien," Lorri wrote in one of those first letters, "I promise I'm not a weirdo."

Fortunately, they were both fine with intensity—craved it, even. They began writing each other with increasing frequency, every few days, every other day, every day. They asked each other first-date questions: *What did you do as a child, when is your birthday, what is your family like?* They discovered similarities in their backgrounds, such as how they'd both chafed against the small-mindedness of the South and the hypocrisies of their church-going neighbors. Because they couldn't meet in person, they tried to explain themselves to each other in writing: what they cared about, what made them angry, who they were in the world. "Damien, if you could study anything, what would it be?" Lorri wrote on May 1, 1996. "Are you obsessive (unlike me—haha)? I'm incredibly so. As if you couldn't surmise—but I think it's a trait worth having—I just have to watch it sometimes—the combination of being obsessive and extremely emotional can wreak havoc on everyday life."

Getting to know someone through letters, with all their slow, romantic materiality, was deliciously old-fashioned. Lorri started kissing her envelopes before she put them in the mailbox. She hid secret messages underneath the stamps. It felt almost magical, how easily an envelope could travel from Arkansas's death row to her row house in Brooklyn, as if the judicial and physical obstacles between her and Damien didn't exist at all. Sometimes, though, all she could think about was those obstacles. She lost five pounds worrying over him, she wrote to Damien. Her friends thought she was nuts. Was she nuts?

Sometime in early May, after only a few weeks of writing back and forth, their salutations switched—it wasn't "Dear Lorri," "Dear

Damien," anymore; it was "Dearest." This friendship, relationship, whatever it was, was making it harder for Lorri to stay engaged in her workaday world. She was writing letters almost every day, and the life she lived in those letters felt more real, more vital, than her job, her apartment, her New York friends. That spring and into the summer, the correspondence became more intimate and revealing. Lorri mailed boxes of books by her favorite authors—Julio Cortázar, Mikhail Bulgakov, J. D. Salinger—to Arkansas. Damien read them all, even if they weren't particularly to his taste (he still preferred Stephen King), because he wanted to better understand how Lorri's brain operated. It was difficult to go gift shopping on death row, but Damien scrounged up trinkets and scraps from around the prison to send back to her: a spoon, a packet of "breakfast drink," a red pen, a strawberry candy, a prison-issued shirt with his inmate number stenciled on it.

They wrote about their shared childhood habit of walking through the streets alone in the middle of the night, watching people through windows, observing the world but feeling not quite *of* it. They discovered that they were both attuned to the inexplicable charmed feeling that can settle on you without warning when the light is right, when some mysterious energy electrifies the air—those moments that seem somehow set apart, elevated from mundane life. Damien had a word for it, *magick*. They planned little private rituals of their own, synchronized to the full moon. They speculated about whether they'd known each other in a past life. "I know this is real—nothing in my life has been quite so real," Lorri wrote in May. And "sometimes, every once in a while, I feel like I am you."

That June, *Paradise Lost: The Child Murders at Robin Hood Hills* was released on HBO—Lorri had seen a prescreening—and the case received a flurry of publicity. It was mentioned on *Good Morning America* and written up in the *New York Times*. Damien started getting dozens of letters a day, the vast majority of them supportive. Once he heard a stranger dedicate a song to him on the radio. After a few years of stagnation and despair, the case had a new and encouraging sense of momentum. "I know I'll be leaving here soon," Damien wrote Lorri on June 18, 1996. "I can feel a path opening before me."

In early July, Lorri and Damien spoke on the phone for the first time. At the end of the month, she flew to Little Rock to visit him in person. She arrived in Arkansas late on Thursday evening, too nervous to eat, and spent a sleepless night in a cheap motel. Their three-hour visit the next day was a whirlwind of emotion. Even with a thick pane of glass between them, Lorri felt Damien's presence palpably. They spent a lot of the time just looking at each other. Damien wrote her a letter the next day:

> Isn't it so wonderful to be completely overpowered by these feelings and emotions, even if they do also bring pain? To feel it so strongly that it destroys any hope of rational thought, action, or feeling? I love it. It's impossible to not be completely swept away, devoured. Nothing else could even come close to it. This is what I have been looking for my entire life, but I never even knew what I was looking for. All I knew was that I had a huge hole in me, a sense of emptiness that nothing ever filled, but now I have a sense of being complete, the hole is gone, the emptiness is gone, the pain is gone. . . . This is why I am here, this is what was meant to be.

They were now writing each other constantly—sometimes as many as six letters per day. If it hadn't been clear to Lorri before, it was now: this man, and his case, were her future.

In 1998, Lorri left behind her New York life and moved south— first to New Orleans and eventually to Little Rock—so she could visit Damien more regularly. Her friends were puzzled, but she was so committed that it didn't even feel like a choice. She got a job with the local parks department and settled into a very different kind of life. It was difficult to get good coffee in Arkansas, but there were benefits, too: huge old trees, kind people. Every Friday, she visited the prison for the permitted three hours. Surcharges and fees meant that each fifteen-minute collect call from Damien cost twenty-five dollars, so she tried to be disciplined about speaking with him on the phone between visits—but sometimes they'd talk for hours, interrupted every quarter hour by a robotic voice telling them their time was up, that he would have to hang up and call again. She daydreamed about the life they'd share once Damien was exonerated, fantasizing about the mundane pleasures of cohabitation, like how she would send him to the store with a grocery list and make him buy her tampons. "When we are married," she wrote in one letter, "we can have a joint bank account!"

Meanwhile, the appeals process moved sluggishly forward. Damien's court-appointed lawyers assured him that this was all to be expected. There was a template for how these things were handled, and you just had to follow it. Now that she was nearby, Lorri started attending Damien's hearings. She kept to the back of the courtroom. Increasingly, the case drew crowds of haters and supporters and groupies and rubberneckers, and she didn't want them to know who she was. At first just being there, breathing the same air as Damien, felt like enough. Once, a kind bailiff looked the other way while Damien briefly pressed her hand to his lips. It was the first time they had touched.

The law does what it can to remain remote, with its judges' robes and imposing courthouses (OBEDIENCE TO THE LAW IS LIBERTY reads the inscription on the stone building where Damien, Jason, and Jessie had their first pretrial hearings); all that Latin, all those arcane rules. But in the early 1990s, that closed world was beginning to crack open. In 1991, Court TV began airing live coverage of high-profile trials; now, instead of waiting for the thirty-second highlight reel on the evening news, you could watch every single minute of courtroom action and stick around after the jury was dismissed for the day to hear expert commentary and analysis. "It's natural drama, there's a beginning, middle, and end, and people want to know what happens," the network's founder, the attorney-entrepreneur Steven Brill, told the *New York Observer*.

Even in the splashiest trials, court proceedings are often tedious. Court TV made this procedural drone visible, yet it drew viewers anyway, millions of them. The audience wasn't tuning in for highly orchestrated thrills; that was something they could get elsewhere. Long trials, in all their florid boredom, provided a different kind of drama, at a different pace. The genius of Court TV, and of cable television in general, was making programming more addictive even as it was less satisfying minute by minute. Even in the channel's early years, the language of obsession and compulsion predominated: *Entertainment Weekly* published "Confessions of a Court TV Addict"; "If Court TV were any more addictive, it would be illegal," the channel proclaimed in its own advertisements. Viewers would leave Court TV on all day, unable to click away, the hum of objections sustained and overruled providing the background sound track to their days.

Watching Court TV could feel like peeking behind the curtain, witnessing a less mediated version of reality. If you appreciated human drama but were sick of the manufactured hysterics of daytime talk shows, you now had another option. "There's no Vicki or Montel or Sally or Geraldo mugging for the Nielsen families and telling us what to think," an *Entertainment Weekly* article about the new channel noted. "There's just a judge, a jury, and a solemn promise to provide us some answers with a verdict." The more court coverage people watched, the more they felt qualified to pick it all apart, to critique the legal strategy, question the credibility of witnesses, and poke holes in the investigation. Viewers got comfortable with the weighty law phrases—*voir dire*, *habeas corpus*, *due process*. The channel was like an engine of demystification, making legal processes visible to a wide audience. Running commentary by anointed experts such as Nancy Grace encouraged viewers to pick sides, and to feel less like spectators and more like participants in the unfolding courtroom drama.

And then there was the internet. In 1994, two Canadians, Paul Bernardo and Karla Homolka, were put on trial for a series of brutal rape-murders in Canada, a spree that started with the killing of Karla's teenage sister. The presiding judge issued a media gag order, assuming that the crimes were so sensational that any publicity would make it difficult for the two to get a fair trial.

Because it was 1994, the ban on media coverage worked for a little while. US newspapers and television still covered the trial—they weren't subject to the ban—but Canadian stations blocked their reports. Travelers crossing from Buffalo, New York, into Canada were only allowed to bring one copy of the *New York Times* across the border; any additional newspapers would be confiscated so they couldn't be sold as contraband. When *Wired* covered the media ban in its April 1994 issue, copies of the magazine were pulled from Canadian shelves.

Canadian true crime enthusiasts resented the ban, or maybe they just saw it as a challenge. Someone created a Usenet newsgroup—something of a cross between a message board and an email digest—called alt.fan.karla-homolka and began posting daily trial details and articles copied wholesale from US papers. When the Mounties shut down that newsgroup, others popped up—alt.pub-ban; alt.pub-ban.homolka—which were banned in turn. The whole thing was like a doomed game of Whac-A-Mole. (One poster suggested a solution: "Take the discussion to rec.sport.hockey. You silly Canadians would never ban that group.") Eventually, the juicy details from the trial were cross-posted on alt.true-crime, a group so huge that it was basically impossible to shut down. By the time Homolka pled guilty, an estimated quarter of the Canadian population knew the banned information. Subverting the publicity ban was a minor incident, a game of outsmarting the authorities, but it was also a taste of the future. "As the infosphere grows to encompass the planet, the question is no longer whether certain information is too sensitive to be made public," Anita Susan Brenner and B. Metson wrote in *Wired*. "The real question becomes whether it is even possible to keep certain information out of cyberspace."

Damien began calling Lorri his wife as early as 1996, the year that they met. The word felt natural coming out of his mouth. A few years into their relationship, he and Lorri were thoroughly, floridly devoted to each other. The lows were torture, but the highs were extremely high.

In between the weekly prison visits and the long nightly phone calls, Lorri had to figure out how to live her life. In the years before she met Damien, she had loved to travel; she'd visited Greece, Turkey, and Morocco. But now, leaving home was half torture—partly because it made communicating with Damien more difficult, but also partly because of how guilty she felt being at loose in the world while he was still on death row. "I love being out of society," she wrote Damien in 1998. "It's as if I want to have our situations as similar as possible—I mean only go out when I have to—otherwise I am here—completely here for you."

Lorri's self-imposed isolation in Little Rock concerned some of the people who were close to her. Once, when her parents were visiting, Lorri's mother turned and gave her the saddest look. *I'm so sorry you're alone,* she said. Lorri stumbled to explain that it wasn't like that at all—that she and Damien were so close that she was *never* alone. "Having Damien in my life was like having him live inside me, that's how close we were," she wrote later.

In 1999, Damien began the slow process of petitioning the prison to allow a wedding. "You will be my wife, you beautiful little animal," he wrote to Lorri. That winter, Damien and Lorri were married in a Buddhist ceremony on the prison grounds in front of six friends and witnesses. That afternoon, the party for the rest of their friends and supporters was bittersweet since the groom was back at the prison, alone in a cell on death row.

In 1996, three friends in their twenties saw a screener of *Paradise Lost* and, like Lorri Davis, couldn't get the story out of their heads. "I was *changed* by it," Kathy Bakken told me. "I felt like a different person after I saw it." Though they lived in Los Angeles, Bakken and her friend Burk Sauls were from the South, while the third member of their group, Grove Pashley, had grown up in Utah. The case touched a nerve for Bakken; it was frighteningly easy to imagine how the small-mindedness she remembered from her youth could swerve into something much more dire. One day you're the local freak; the next you're on death row. But what to do with that feeling? The friends had backgrounds in advertising and design, so they created their own little marketing campaign, distributing flyers protesting the convictions of the men they called the West Memphis Three. "There was nobody—seriously, *nobody*—who cared about the case at that point. And it was like—I guess *we* have to do it," Bakken said. The case continued to gnaw at her and her friends. "There was nobody to talk to about it," she said. "There was nothing on the internet. You couldn't tweet about it or post on Facebook. The newsgroups were the only outlet." Slowly, the three friends began to rally attention to the case online. One day, a college student messaged them and offered to build a stand-alone website dedicated to the West Memphis Three. "We were like, 'Great! What's a website?'" Bakken said.

The founders of wm3.org were early to a trend that would grow along with the internet: strangers congregating online to talk about crime. Often it started in a similar manner: a person watched a documentary or saw a short news clip about a case, and the story left them with a kind of mental . . . itchiness, let's call it. Even if there were an arrest and a verdict, they sensed that *more* was there, a story underlying the official narrative, one that was messier and more complicated and more true. Maybe they thought the stated motives didn't make sense, or that crucial evidence had been overlooked. Maybe they thought that innocent people had been convicted, or that guilty people had gone free. Maybe they didn't trust the cops to do a fair investigation or thought the media had unfairly taken sides, or that the DA was corrupt. Maybe they just wanted to make up their own mind. And so they went online.

What set these internet communities apart from those focused on fantasy baseball or recipes was the idea that they could make a difference. Eventually, the world of online criminal justice advocacy would take a number of different forms, with some factions focusing on solving cold cases, others on finding new angles on old conspiracies or putting names to unidentified bodies or working to get elusive serial killers arrested. Ultimately, thousands of these crime-centric groups would congregate on Facebook and message boards and Reddit forums. Many posters took on the persona of the righteous defender, the person who did the hard work that institutions couldn't—or wouldn't—do. If the detective knew everything and the victim felt everything, the defender was the one who fixed everything.

In 1996, the idea of amateurs using the internet to plug the gaps of a flawed criminal justice system was still novel and untested. Even so, shortly after the launch of wm3.org, the site found an audience. Strangers volunteered to add to the growing archive of information about the case. Within a year, it "had become the most extensive resource of its kind on the Internet relating to a single case," according to journalist Mara Leveritt. "It was all the more unique for having been created and funded entirely through the efforts of lay volunteers."

The site's founders immersed themselves in the case. They took trips to Arkansas, where they visited three different prisons to see the three convicted men. They walked through the woods where the boys' bodies were found. They started attending hearings and getting to know the defense attorneys.

From early on, the founders tried to include as much primary-source information on the site as possible, relying on locals to scan and upload documents that were only available in West Memphis. "We figured the more people saw, the more they would see this was all a sham," Bakken said. They posted trial transcripts, police files, and court documents—even, briefly, a dozen gut-wrenching crime scene photographs, until one of the victim's mothers furiously demanded that they be removed from the site. They posted updates on upcoming hearings and encouraged readers to email Arkansas governor Mike Huckabee (critically) and to write to Damien, Jason, and Jessie (supportively).

Damien, the most charismatic, most misunderstood, and most imperiled of the three, drew the most attention, followed by soft-spoken, principled Jason. Jessie was sometimes blamed for the whole debacle—his confession had been the key piece of evidence against Damien and Jason—and received the least support. The leaders of wm3.org were increasingly aware that they couldn't control what happened with the information they put out into the world, but they did their best to steer people in a constructive direction. "I think their favorite letters are the ones that don't come across as 'too sad,' and ones that don't dwell on the case, or how much the person can relate to Damien's 'strangeness,' Wicca, Witchcraft, Satanism or how screwy the justice system is," Sauls wrote on wm3.org. "They certainly know more about that than we do!"

The site drew a small but dedicated group of fans, who skewed slightly (though not overwhelmingly) female. Within a couple of years, wm3.org was racking up a thousand or so daily hits and selling T-shirts and wristbands to supporters across the country. In the late 1990s all the cool kids had a pet cause—"Free Tibet!" "Free Mumia!"—and "Free the West Memphis Three" fit right in. "People would say, 'I was just like Damien'—we heard that so many times," Bakken said. "'Nobody understood me, I was the freak in school.' People took it really personally, like it could've happened to them. Not just goths, not just musicians, but anyone who felt out of their element, a stranger in their own town."

In some ways, the more information they amassed, the more mystified the website founders felt: If the West Memphis Three hadn't killed those boys, then who did? "We just wanted to know what happened," Bakken said. "We wanted a way to interpret the evidence we had to create a scenario that would solve the mystery of what happened." They also realized that finding out who had killed Stevie, Michael, and Christopher would be a surefire way of getting the West Memphis Three released. To that end, Bakken read books about forensics and crime investigation and took online courses in profiling. At the end of one of the classes, she contacted the teacher, an Alaska-based criminologist named Brent Turvey, and gave him some information about the case. Turvey reviewed the evidence and agreed that the police had gotten it all wrong. He drew up his own profile of the killer. According to Turvey, the culprit was likely a macho guy, with a history of petty crime, and an explosive temper. He was probably unemployed, in a troubled marriage, drove a truck, and had a collection of knives and firearms.

Turvey's profile of the killer didn't sound anything like the convicted men. Instead, it bore a near-exact resemblance to the person many West Memphis Three supporters already suspected of having committed the murders: victim Chris Byer's adoptive father, John Mark Byers. Along with Damien, Byers—whom most people knew as Mark—had been a central figure in the *Paradise Lost* documentary. Six foot six and lean, with a long face, a bulging forehead, and an odd way of speaking, Byers was the kind of spotlight-hogging, self-mythologizing figure that documentarians dream of. When the camera was trained on him, he gave furious, extended speeches about the violence he wished to enact on the West Memphis Three, but his emotion never seemed to reach his eyes.

Turvey also zeroed in on a piece of forensic evidence that he thought the medical examiner might have overlooked: bite marks on one of the boys' faces. "Bite marks can be as unique as fingerprints," he wrote. "It can reveal to an examiner who committed the act." John Mark Byers had recently had his teeth pulled and now wore a full set of dentures. Byers claimed this was because of a medical issue, but to case watchers it seemed fishy. There was also the fact that Byers's wife and Chris's mother, Melissa, died of a drug overdose in 1996. From one angle, it was just part of the compounding tragedy of the boys' murders; from another it was highly suspicious.

In 2000, six years after the West Memphis Three were initially convicted, the *Paradise Lost* filmmakers revisited the case in a second documentary that focused in part on wm3.org and the online activists bringing national attention to the case. Whereas the first documentary hadn't taken a clear stance, this one was less circumspect. Not only did it make an overt argument in favor of the West Memphis Three's innocence, it was also a two-hour indictment of John Mark Byers.

Several of the victims' families had participated in the first *Paradise Lost* film, but this time only one parent agreed to be interviewed— Byers. After his son's murder and his wife's overdose, his other son had gone to live with his grandparents; Byers was alone and spiraling out of control. Years later, Byers admitted that he agreed to participate partly because he wanted to tell his side of the story, but also partly out of sheer loneliness. When the cameras were on, Byers was just as much of a showman as ever, and the filmmakers were just as eager to enable him. They lingered on his various arrests for bad checks and drug dealing and domestic violence. They accompanied him to the woods where his son's body had been discovered and filmed Byers, wearing overalls and a cowboy hat, as he macheted his way through the underbrush. The camera kept close to him as he staged a symbolic funeral for Damien, Jason, and Jessie next to the drainage ditch: "You wanna worship the devil? I'm gonna give you a farewell party," he crowed as he stooped to light a fire. His voice grew wild as the flames caught and crackled: "What do you think? You ready to die? Fire for fire, death for death, live through *this* fire, you animal! Oh, it ain't hot enough for you? Burn, go to hell, *burn*! . . . stomp on your grave, I *stomp* on your grave!"

Damien was interviewed again, too, but this time he was in control of his image. With his neatly trimmed hair and wire-rimmed glasses, he looked like a guy who hung out in coffee shops. The film included one note of caution, from West Memphis police inspector Gary Gitchell: "Are we accusing Mark Byers because he's got a ponytail and he's a big guy and he's kind of . . . boisterous?" But this was easy enough to dismiss, considering that Gitchell hadn't shown Damien, Jason, and Jessie anywhere near the same consideration.

The night the documentary was set to air on HBO, the wm3.org founders gathered in Sauls's downtown loft to watch. When the website URL flashed across the TV screen, so many people tried to access the site that the server promptly crashed. The next morning, they woke up to thousands of emails each. "It had really broken wide. It was a real *thing*," Lisa Fancher, the owner of a punk rock record label who had become a fourth leader of wm3.org, told me. But intermingled with the satisfaction of recognition was a nagging feeling of discomfort at the film's overt focus on Byers. "I would call [the second documentary] . . . deeply flawed," Fancher said. "I was bummed. Privately, we found him a very credible suspect, but I would never ever, ever say that somebody did it. Casting doubt on someone when you don't know—it isn't cool."

Sure enough, the reviews of the new documentary latched onto this story line. The *Village Voice* called Byers "the massive bastard offspring of John Brown and Leatherface"; according to *LA Weekly*, he was a "belligerent, mullet-headed oaf"; and *Entertainment Weekly* saw him as "the tall, creepy, angry, sunken-eyed, hellfire-Christian . . . [who] may have been the killer." If Damien Echols, with his black trench coat and collection of animal skulls, made an ideal bogeyman to one segment of the population, Byers was the other half's nightmare.

On wm3.org, moderators tried to rein in commenters who brazenly declared that Byers was a child murderer, but plenty of damage had already been done. From behind a screen, it was easy enough to forget that these crimes involved real people whose lives were impacted by idle speculation. Theorizing about murders and how they might have happened was part of the pleasure of engaging in a true crime community. But building a theory off the back of someone's off-putting behavior and criminal history was also alarmingly easy. Advocacy could quickly devolve into vigilantism. If Byers was guilty of murdering three children, then, sure, he deserved to have his life ruined. But if he wasn't?

The odd thing was, when the cameras were off, John Mark Byers was surprisingly friendly to the West Memphis Three's supporters. "When they weren't shooting [the documentary], he was just the nicest guy," Bakken recalled. "You almost hated yourself for liking him." During one key hearing, Byers and the wm3.org crowd stayed at the same hotel. On her way downstairs one evening, Bakken spotted Byers slumped in the lobby by himself. "It struck me how sad it was, if he didn't do it ... and at that point you really don't *want* it to be him. He's just a gentleman, so nice, not at all what you see on camera. You got to know him and he's not the scary monster he was in the movies."

Lorri found it surreal to watch her incarcerated husband become a low-level misfit heartthrob. Not that the attention seemed to be doing much good. The West Memphis Three were still stuck in the cycle of appeals. Though their plight was more widely known and they had more supporters, sometimes it felt as though the case was stalled out and that energy had nowhere to go.

During the heady tumult of Lorri's first few years with Damien, it had seemed as though the power of their love, the unexpected gift of it, might be enough to save him. But time ticked by and he was no closer to release. Dealing with the legal proceedings demoralized Damien; he hardly kept track of the various motions and appeals that were being made in his name. The public defenders and pro bono attorneys working the case had other priorities. It was increasingly clear to Lorri that if the case was going to progress, someone would have to take charge of it. And if not her, then who?

Deciding to play a bigger part in Damien's legal defense was not an entirely comfortable step for Lorri. It would mean being forceful and argumentative. It would mean asking people for money. It would mean going up against men in positions of power who would've greatly preferred that she sit down and keep her mouth shut. None of this came naturally to Lorri. Her most marked quality was her softness, an old friend of hers explained to me, which made her seem as if she had come from some other, gentler world.

Advocacy can be fraught for women. Although most law school students are now women, the vast majority of trial lawyers—particularly those who take on high-profile speaking roles—are still men. In part, this is because when women do occupy prominent places in the court-room, they open themselves up to intense scrutiny. Criminal trials are performative, and women's performances are judged in part on how well they conform to gender stereotypes. Lara Bazelon, who worked as a deputy federal public defender, pointed out that when the men she worked with wore the standard courtroom uniform of a dark suit and tie, their physicality was treated as unremarkable. But a female attorney's appearance was never neutral; her hair, her shoes, her makeup, her voice were always subject to critique. Women's behavior in the courtroom is similarly circumscribed by gender bias. When male attorneys express impatience, indignation, or anger, juries interpret these as their being "tough zealous advocates," one study found; when female attorneys do, they are deemed unpleasant or irrational. But there's peril in the other direction, too; a female attorney who presents as too overtly feminine risks being dismissed as weak. As the Stanford law professor Deborah L. Rhode has noted, women in the courtroom face a "double standard and a double bind." There are pitfalls in every direction; women face criticism for being "too 'soft' or too 'strident,' too 'aggressive' or 'not aggressive enough.'"

Despite the tightrope they have to walk, plenty of women still take on advocacy roles, both within the legal profession and outside it. Women are disproportionately represented among indigent-defense programs and other vocations that require an affinity for the underdog. I've always thought of this as an unexpected side benefit of sexism—how the experience of being dismissed or ignored, of interacting with systems that don't prioritize you, can make you alert to injustice that exists elsewhere in the world.

Similarly, I know I'm not the only woman who draws satisfaction from true crime stories that expose the corruption and errors of people in positions of authority—narratives such as that of the West Memphis Three. The shadow side to this, however, is something such as the Satanic Panic, a narrative that was largely advanced by women. The role of the defender, the one who knows the *real* truth buried under the official version, can tip into unsupported righteousness frighteningly quickly.

In 2000, Lorri learned that Pearl Jam lead singer Eddie Vedder had seen *Paradise Lost* and felt so moved that he planned to convene a team of legal and forensic experts in Seattle to brainstorm new approaches to the case. Lorri was pointedly not invited; Vedder's assistant and right-hand woman, Nicole Vandenberg, told Lorri that family members weren't welcome at the meeting. "Nicole is now one of my best friends," Lorri told me, "but back then she didn't know me from a bar of soap. But I remember being adamant: 'Sorry, I'm coming. You don't have to fly me up there or put me up. But I'm going to be there.' I had to do that over and over again, to get people to hear me. Because I would be dismissed. When you hear that this woman married this guy on death row—there was always skepticism in the beginning."

In Seattle, Lorri sat around a conference table with a half dozen legal experts as they parsed the case in detail. A lot of lawyerly grandstanding and ego, a lot of very *male* energy, was in the room. Not necessarily in a bad way. "I have to say, it was very productive," Lorri said. "I felt very empowered after that. We put together a plan. And it felt that we were finally moving."

But even when the legal system was moving, it was still incredibly slow and bogged down by procedure. Even highly regarded attorneys could be a letdown; Lorri says a lawyer spent $200,000 that she'd raised without his filing a crucial appeal on Damien's behalf. President Bill Clinton had recently signed into law a strict new limit on state prisoners' ability to file in federal court—part of his tough-on-crime stance—and if the proper paperwork wasn't in place by a certain deadline, the window would close and Damien would lose his shot at any sort of federal appeal. Lorri found herself with three months to raise another $200,000 to hire another lawyer who could ensure the appeal was filed on time. Begging for money did not come easily to her, but she did it anyway. When donations were short, she made up the difference with a nearly $50,000 loan.

These were the sorts of things that were keeping Lorri up at night in the early 2000s: habeas petitions, filing deadlines, Rule 37. She and Damien had been so naive early on, when he'd done a numerological analysis and concluded that he'd be free by the time he was twenty-three. Now he was thirty and still on death row. Damien did what he could to keep his head together, meditating as many as six hours a day, running in place in his cell until his feet bled. In Little Rock, Lorri lived a similarly monastic life. She ate kale and did an hour of yoga every day; she hardly left the house except to go to work and visit Damien. Every morning when they spoke on the phone, she'd pull a card from her tarot deck. For nearly two straight weeks, she drew the Hanged Man: sacrifice, suspension, waiting. This was a thin version of living, with all the pleasure trimmed out. A worried friend asked Damien to intervene. "First of all—I am not depressed—and secondly, I have no desire to go out and 'do more' in this place," she wrote back testily. "The thought of going to a cafe or sitting somewhere 'drinking coffee' or something like that sickens me. Yes, I know I used to do that in NY— but I was searching for something and I am not searching anymore."

In 2004, she tallied up the cost of all their phone calls to date: $75,000. (They would ultimately end up spending about $150,000 on calls alone.) But that was nothing next to the cost of attorneys, court fees, forensic testing. More and more celebrities were signing on to support the cause: Margaret Cho, Patti Smith, Johnny Depp, Henry Rollins, the guy from Slipknot, the guy from *South Park*. On the season five finale of *Dawson's Creek*, Pacey shouted "Free the West Memphis Three!" over an airport intercom system. There were benefit albums, benefit art shows, benefit concerts. Yet somehow there was never enough money. At low moments, Lorri would try to remember that Damien was one of the lucky ones. If you started to think about how many other wrongfully convicted prisoners were out there, thousands of people who didn't have their faces on T-shirts and celebrities contributing to their legal funds, and what *their* chances were for ever getting out alive—it was enough to make you want to curl up and go to sleep for a long, long time.

Not that Lorri could afford to do that. Damien wrote in January 2005:

> It's time to start doing something, Lorri. You are withering up. All those things in you that are so magickal and that make my heart explode are drying up. Everything is going out and nothing is coming in. It's scaring me, Lorri. Very much so. Every day it becomes harder and harder to write these letters because there's not even anything to write about. I can't bring new life in, Lorri. It's impossible for me, I'm helpless. It's up to you.

Practically every case that passed through the West Texas public defender's office during the second term of the Obama administration involved immigration. The vast majority of Liz's clients were young men who had been apprehended crossing the border too many times—illegal entry was a misdemeanor, but illegal *re*entry was a felony, and the charges compounded from there. Sometimes drugs were involved, but not in the way that fearmongering cable news programs would lead you to believe. Most of the stories were heartbreaking in their mildness. A young guy would be working at a car wash in a border town and he'd start to get friendly with some older man who was always bringing his flashy cars in to get cleaned. Eventually, the older guy would offer to do his car-wash buddy a favor. Instead of paying someone to take him across the border, the kid could cross for free if he just brought this backpack along with him. If the young guy had the bad luck to be apprehended, he entered the legal system as one of those fearsome specters, a drug smuggler. One day I met a high school student who gave his girlfriend's undocumented brother a ride across town and faced human-trafficking charges for the favor. When I studied their faces as they sat with Liz in the cluttered conference room, they mostly just looked like nervous kids.

Each of these individual stories was translated into bland legal prose, and I filed away the paperwork like a diligent volunteer. On Monday mornings, six or ten or two dozen of the defender office's clients would appear at the federal courthouse wearing the baggy orange-striped uniform of the Brewster County Jail, shackled at the wrists, waists, and ankles. Since the implementation of a zero-tolerance immigration policy called Operation Streamline (instituted by the Bush administration in 2005 and continued under Obama), immigration cases were batch-processed to more efficiently handle the exponential rise in prosecutions. A dozen people would stand en masse, listen to the judge read their rights, affirm that they understood, accept their charges, and be processed for deportation, all within minutes. In the United States, the vast majority of criminal charges result in plea bargains, but the rate was even higher in the Western District of Texas—more than 99 percent.

It hadn't always been like this, Liz told me. Thirty years ago, when she'd begun her career as a public defender, there had been far fewer federal immigration prosecutions; back then, they were typically reserved for people with serious records. These days, though, her clients were more often people with no criminal history, and she saw more and more of them every week. The Western District had the second-highest caseload in the country; the four lawyers in Liz's office handled more than twelve hundred cases annually, nearly double the number recommended by national standards. Budget cuts meant there was hardly any money for transcripts or expert testimony. Every now and then, Liz won a minor victory—a pretrial diversion instead of a felony charge, say—but by and large, the law was an unstoppable machine moving in a single direction.

I had hoped that my days at the defender's office would provide me with purpose; instead, I started to dread them. Whatever I had thought I'd find—truth? justice? some other virtuous, abstract noun?— wasn't there. Instead, there were just people doing their best to be decent despite trying circumstances. I knew that wasn't nothing. But I also knew that it took a particular constitution to spend all day doing small work that only occasionally made bad situations incrementally better. To lose often. To spend most of your days enmeshed in a system you couldn't change. To my shame, I was realizing I wasn't cut out for it. I had wanted to belong to something bigger than my small, disappointing self. I had loved the idea of being the kind of person who would give herself up to a fight until nothing was left of her. I knew now that I wasn't. Nevertheless, I was also left with a nagging question: Even if I had been, would it have done any good?

A few months after I started volunteering at the public defender's office, Liz announced that she was retiring. The program was facing further budget cuts; as the senior lawyer, she had the highest salary, and she could free up some funding by stepping away now. She had heard it was possible get a cheap berth on a container ship, so she'd decided to spend a few months sailing around the world. After Liz's departure, I stopped coming by the office. But even as I settled back into the slow daily labor of writing, I thought often of the work that was happening back there, invisible to many, and of how in the courthouse every Monday a dozen men and women stood up and repeated their lines, players in a performance we'd somehow agreed to call justice.

* * *

In 2005, two new celebrities became interested in the West Memphis Three: New Zealand film directors and screenwriters Peter Jackson and Fran Walsh. Together, Jackson and Walsh had brought the *Lord of the Rings* franchise into being, which meant that they were flush with hobbit money and willing to spend a good chunk of it to try to get Damien off death row. The terms they gave Lorri were clear: they wouldn't provide any funding for additional lawyers, only for further investigation and forensic testing.

The financial support was key, but Fran Walsh's enthusiasm may have been even more important, in that it provided the shot of adrenaline that Lorri desperately needed. The emails that Walsh wrote her "kind of gave me a reason to live for a while," Lorri said later. Walsh, whom the *New York Times* once called "one of Hollywood's biggest living mysteries," rarely granted interviews and avoided making public appearances. She was also a serious true crime buff and something of a self-trained forensics expert. Thanks to the new influx of money, a private detective firm was now reviewing the case, but "Fran was definitely the one leading the investigation," said Rachael Geiser, one of the PIs assigned to the case. "She's brilliant." At the end of every day, Geiser sent Walsh her reports: interview transcripts, notes, ideas for where to go next; every day, Walsh would reply with pages of detailed notes and commentary.

It wasn't lost on Lorri that most of the investigatory team—as well as many of the West Memphis Three's most dogged supporters—were women. The wm3.org founders noticed the same thing: While two of the site's devoted founders were men, "the longest-term, most loyal and fervent supporters were women," Lisa Fancher told me. "Men did a lot of peacocking and really needed validation for doing something with possibly no upside."

We all know that men are the strongest runners, racking up the fastest times at dashes and marathons alike. But in races over a hundred miles, when psychological staying power is more important than muscle mass, women often cross the finish line first. Women are more likely to live through dire survival situations, such as the Irish potato famine or the desperate winter the Donner Party spent stranded in the eastern Sierras. That's partly because women have more subcutaneous fat, but anthropologists also chalk some of the survival-rate disparity up to socialized, gender-based personality differences. When a situation requires grim determination, a willingness to settle in and fight the long fight, women seem to have the advantage. For better or worse, we're adept at slogging.

And nearly a decade after the convictions, the fight to free the West Memphis Three was definitely feeling like a slog. Supporting the cause was less about making splashy speeches than staying committed year after year, showing up for dull proceedings where nothing of consequence happened, reviewing hours of courtroom footage, sending letters to politicians who couldn't be bothered to care, filling out piles of paperwork—in short, doing all the unrewarding, unglamorous work of advocacy.

Walsh and Jackson paid Lorri a salary to work on the case full-time—*work* being the operative word. Lorri would wake up every morning to lengthy emails from Walsh listing the dozen tasks she was supposed to accomplish that day: call these forensic pathologists, find these possible witnesses, look for this piece of evidence. "It was exhausting, it was amazing," Lorri told me. She had spent years hoping that some official mechanism would right the injustice of the convictions. But now she understood the justice system well enough to know that it was not likely to remedy an error of its own making. Instead it seemed as though it might largely be up to her. It felt like an awesome responsibility, in the old sense of the word: both terrifying and inspiring. Lorri had never been particularly comfortable advocating on her own behalf, but when Damien's life was at stake, she discovered new facets of her personality. She could be aggressive and hard-nosed when she needed to be. She could make demands. She could insist.

The new investigative team tracked down people who had been children at the time of the murders and interviewed them, and spent weeks locating a car that one of their suspects had sold back in 1993. They uncovered evidence that jurors had been compromised. Three girls who'd testified against Damien recanted their stories. A tantalizing partial DNA sample from the crime scene had never been matched to anyone, so one trash pickup day, Lorri and Geiser cruised through West Memphis in a pickup truck, waiting for a potential suspect to put his garbage out by the curb. After he went inside, they tossed the bags in the bed of the pickup and took them back to the office, where they sorted through them, looking for cigarette butts and soda cans—possible sources of DNA to compare to the unknown sample. "For a long time, the main focus was what can we learn about John Mark Byers," Geiser said. "We did a *lot* of investigation into John Mark Byers. Until the DNA came out with it looking like it might be someone else."

The law is like a huge ship: it changes course slowly, and with much grinding of gears. This is, in large part, by design. The criminal justice system is tasked with providing answers and finality. Objections are sustained or overruled. Evidence is admissible or not admissible. Someone is adjudicated guilty or not guilty. The result is supposed to serve as closure—though it rarely feels so satisfying, or final, or neat.

In the 1990s, DNA analysis improved significantly, and new tests of old evidence began calling hundreds of verdicts into question. The Innocence Project, founded in 1992 by Barry Scheck and Peter Neufeld, brought attention to the "staggering number" of wrongfully convicted people in US prisons. Law schools around the country began opening clinics focusing on wrongful-conviction cases; district attorney's offices launched special units to review questionable verdicts. Since 1989, the year of the first DNA exoneration, more than 2,300 people have been found to be wrongfully convicted, most of them black men; collectively, they'd served nearly twenty-one thousand years for crimes for which they were later exonerated. Though every case was different, themes recurred: 70 percent of DNA-based exonerations involved eyewitness misidentification; three in ten included a false confession; nearly half relied on erroneous forensic evidence.

Some prosecutors (and others) insisted that the attention devoted to exonerees presented a distorted view of reality, that there certainly were not tens of thousands—or even thousands—of innocent people languishing in prison. While popular culture may lead people to believe "that our prisons are chock-full of doe-eyed innocents who have been framed by venal prosecutors and corrupt police officers with the help of grossly incompetent public defenders," in reality "the hordes of Americans wrongfully convicted exist primarily on Planet Hollywood," the vice president of the National District Attorneys Association argued in a 2006 *New York Times* editorial. Supreme Court justice Antonin Scalia derided press coverage of exonerations as an "attack on the American criminal justice system." It's no wonder that some people felt compelled to pretend that innocent people behind bars didn't exist or were vanishingly rare, the hallucinations of bleeding-heart fools. The growing number of exoneration stories undermined the authority of the justice system, making it manifestly clear that the powers that be sometimes got it very, very wrong. Exonerations could be extremely expensive, too—in some cases, exonerees were awarded millions of dollars in payouts from the state—and when forensic evidence was called into question, that opened up more cases for costly appeals.

The DNA results on the West Memphis Three case finally came back in 2007. Absolutely no physical evidence from the crime site, not one stray skin cell or strand of hair, was matched to the three convicted men. The evidence wasn't matched to Mark Byers, either. (DNA found at the site was matched to one of the boys' stepfathers, Terry Hobbs, leading to much public speculation about Hobbs's role in the boys' deaths. Hobbs has repeatedly and unequivocally denied any knowledge of the murders and said that his DNA was present at the scene because he and his son shared a home.) That wasn't all. A new team of seven forensic pathologists, high-profile experts in their fields, reviewed the original autopsy findings and found much to quibble with. According to them, the state medical examiner had it all wrong: Christopher Byers hadn't been sexually mutilated, and the wounds to the boys' faces were not human bite marks; rather, most of the injuries were likely caused by postmortem animal predation, probably by the turtles or possums that lived in the ditch where the bodies were found. (The local nickname for the area was Turtle Hill.) "This was not *anything* like what the prosecution said," Kathy Bakken told me. "It wasn't torture, it wasn't a demonic ritual. These kids were knocked out, tied up, thrown into water, and then animals came along."

There had long been a split, with the West Memphis Three's supporters coming from California or New York or just generally *elsewhere*, and locals tending to believe the Three were guilty. With the new revelations, though, the tide began to turn, Bakken says: "When we first went to Arkansas, everyone hated us. They didn't want us to be there, they thought we were horrible for supporting these murderers. Slowly but surely, you'd get people saying, 'I always thought there was something funny about that case. . . .'" Even the prison guards whom Jason Baldwin knew over in general population started to come around. *We hope you get out, man,* they'd tell him.

The experts' findings caused a reckoning in the wm3.org community. Many people had been attached to Brent Turvey's profile, the one that focused attention on Mark Byers and that said that possible bite marks on one of the boys' bodies could help identify the killer. It had ratified all their theories about the case—theories that now seemed to be wrong. The West Memphis Three may have been innocent, but that didn't mean that Byers was guilty. "We really hard-core believed that the profile was real," Lisa Fancher told me. " *'Look, they're human bite marks!'* And . . . nope. When you get real people who cost a whole lot of money, they're like, 'No, those are turtle marks.'"

Damien wrote Byers a letter of apology, and the next time the wm3 .org founders were in West Memphis, they stopped by his trailer to tell him they, too, were sorry. Byers was gracious—beyond gracious; he'd had his own change of heart and now loudly proclaimed his belief that the West Memphis Three were innocent.

In April 2008 the three men's legal teams filed a motion for a new trial during which the new evidence could be presented. Five months later, the original trial judge, David Burnett, denied the request. The new evidence was, he wrote, "not compelling." The supporters knew they should've expected this; over and over, Burnett had ruled that evidence couldn't be heard, that new testimony wasn't warranted, that there hadn't been any problem with the original trial. Every time, though, it was heartbreaking. With Burnett as the gatekeeper, it seemed unlikely that anything would ever change.

The marathon of paperwork and court filings and legal maneuvering began anew, with more anxiety than ever, since Damien's pathways to appeal were running out. Meanwhile, Lorri fretted about him. When Damien had first entered prison, he and his fellow death row inmates had some small freedoms within their confined world. "They had barred doors so they could talk to each other and see one another," Lorri said. "They could see the guards and talk to them, for better or worse. They were able to have relationships. They had all these ingenious ways of passing things back and forth." But in 2003, that changed. Many states, including Arkansas, had built massive new supermax facilities during the crime panic of the 1990s. The prisons were intended for "the worst of the worst," and even then were supposed to be for brief, punitive stints of less than a year. But after the pricey supermaxes were built, many states had trouble filling them, even as their regular prisons were overcrowded. A number of states opted to relocate their death row prisoners to the supermax facilities, perhaps so the costly new prisons would seem like less of a boondoggle to voters.

For Damien, the move meant that his interactions with the world outside his cell were even more radically curtailed. He was in his cell alone, unable to see or speak to anyone else, for twenty-three hours a day. His one hour of "recreation" was also spent alone, in a small pen dotted with the corpses of dead pigeons. Soon, he stopped taking those recreation periods; they were just too depressing. Damien was only outside his cell three hours a week, for his visits with Lorri. The extreme isolation was hard on his body. He'd been a teenager when he was arrested, and now his joints ached with arthritis and his eyesight was deteriorating—it was as though prison had put a reverse Rip Van Winkle spell on him, making him age twice as fast as everyone else. After a multiyear immersion in Buddhism, Damien had wound his way back around to the occult practices that had caused such alarm in West Memphis. Back then, he'd been a dabbler; now, he was spending hours a day invoking the names of angels and casting circles of protection. He meditated on the seasons, conjuring up sensory memories of the taste of cheap chocolate at Halloween, or the way his skin had burned when he held a snowball in his bare hands.

Magick, as he understood it, was a way to conserve energy and use it mindfully. Thoughts shaped reality, he believed, so every day at the same time, both he and Lorri would spend an hour focused on their shared goal. *May I be home, free from prison, living happily with my Lorri,* Damien would intone. *May it come about in a way that brings harm to none and is for the good of all, and in no way let this reverse or bring upon me or my loved ones any curse.*

Less than a year after he and Lorri began performing this daily invocation, the case finally worked its way to the Arkansas Supreme Court. In September 2010, the state's highest court held a hearing to decide whether the new evidence merited the reopening of Damien's case. Hundreds of supporters filled the courtroom, the overflow room, and the steps outside. Inside, for the first time in the long history of the case, the panel of judges seemed sympathetic to the defense team's arguments. "Counsel, what harm is there in allowing him to present evidence from the last seventeen years?" one of the judges asked. The prosecutor looked startled. "Well, the harm is the finality of a criminal judgment. The harm is—is to the criminal justice system's interest in *finality*," he said.

That evening, back at the hotel, the West Memphis Three supporters allowed themselves to be cautiously hopeful. "I remember thinking, 'This is really going to happen,'" Lisa Fancher said. Sure enough: two months later, the state supreme court agreed to grant all three convicted men a hearing to present the new evidence. It wasn't freedom, but it was the first big judicial break they'd gotten in more than sixteen years. If all went well, the new hearing would result in a new trial, and the new trial would result in not-guilty verdicts. The process would likely take years, but at least it seemed to be moving in an encouraging direction. The legal teams hunkered down and began preparing for what everyone knew would be an extremely high-profile court case. Lorri allowed herself to dream that a couple of years down the road, Damien might finally be free.

Then, on an otherwise uneventful Friday in August 2011, Lorri got a phone call from one of Damien's attorneys. He admitted to her that he'd been having secret meetings with the prosecutors. He hadn't mentioned it before in case they came to nothing. But now there was the possibility of a deal. *Damien might be out as soon as Tuesday,* he told her. *But you can't tell anyone.* You would think the news would've come as a relief, but it provoked a more violent feeling than that, as if the whole world had been picked up, flipped over, and dropped back down, hard.

There was a catch. The prosecutors were offering to let the West Memphis Three go, but not to exonerate them. The convicted men would be released only if they made an Alford plea—that is, they'd plead guilty while still proclaiming their innocence. The deal made sense for the DA's office; they'd avoid the publicity of another trial, during which all their previous mistakes would be put under a microscope. But for the three convicted men, it was a cruel bargain: *We'll let you out of prison, but first you have to say you're guilty of the murders you've spent the last two decades vehemently denying you committed.* After their release, Damien, Jason, and Jessie wouldn't be able to sue the state or get wrongful-conviction compensation. They couldn't even technically call themselves wrongfully convicted because they would have to plead guilty.

Lorri knew that it would be tricky to get Jason, in particular, on board with the agreement. He'd entered prison as a thin-shouldered, overwhelmed teenager and had grown up to be a steadfast and principled man. It was hard to imagine him pleading guilty to a crime he didn't commit. The three men had separate legal teams and hadn't been in touch. Lorri didn't have a way to contact Jason directly, so she reached out to Eddie Vedder, who called Jason and let him know about the offer. Just as she'd feared, Jason was opposed to the plea offer. If they didn't take the deal, sure, they'd have to remain in prison for another couple of years, or however long the new trial took, but he was firmly convinced that they'd all be vindicated and set free with no strings attached. Even better, the West Memphis police and the State of Arkansas would have to publicly own up to everything they'd done wrong.

Through Vedder, Lorri made the case to Jason: Damien was not well, and his health might decline even further if he remained in prison for several more years. Besides, the trial might not go their way. Yes, the amount of new evidence was impressive, but in Arkansas there was no such thing as a sure bet. If Damien was found guilty again, his death sentence might well get carried out. Finally, Jason agreed: he'd plead guilty to help save his old friend's life.

On August 19, the West Memphis Three were released from prison straight to a press conference. They all looked shell-shocked, as if they half believed some uniformed man was about to say, "Just kidding!"— and hustle them back into their cells. Damien had a cold sore on his lip, and Jason's hair was thinning. Lorri was there in the courtroom, sitting next to Vedder. The district attorney held his mouth in a thin line and, against all evidence, insisted that this was a victory for his team. Mark Byers called the release of his former enemies "a gift from God." "I'm just tired," Damien told the cameras. And just like that, it was over. Jessie's dad whisked him away to a welcome-home party in West Memphis as Damien and Jason headed to a hotel downtown where hundreds of elated supporters awaited. "Just seeing them in *clothes*," Fancher said, "I cried all day."

For Lorri that party was more or less miserable. She was so grateful to so many of the people gathered in Memphis that day, but she was also attuned to Damien, who was practically vibrating with tension. He was thirty-six years old and hadn't ever been around this big a crowd, all of them clamoring for a piece of him. Neither he nor Lorri had been sleeping, and during these past few days of frantic negotiation, they'd barely had any time to plan for the future; all they knew was that they wanted to get out of the South as quickly as possible.

After a brief visit to Seattle, they flew to New York, where they took up temporary residence in Jackson and Walsh's two-story penthouse in Tribeca. The transition was surreal, from death row to an apartment so big you could get lost in it. (A few years later, Taylor Swift bought the place, reportedly for $20 million.) It sounded almost too good to be true, a sweet karmic gift from the universe. But in that beautiful apartment, Damien and Lorri were floundering. "It was just a free-fall situation for two years," she said.

I asked Lorri if there was anything she didn't know about Damien, after all those years of phone calls and letters and visits in which they constantly shared their inner worlds with each other. She took a long time to answer. "I didn't know what he was like in the world," she said eventually. Damien didn't know what he was like, either. He'd spent nearly his entire adult life in prison; leaving it was just as destabilizing as going in had been. Even just a quick walk down the street left him out of breath; he was physically and mentally overcome by the sensory stimulation of the world. He'd try to chill out by watching television, but even that old trick didn't work—all the actors looked the same to him. When he sat down to watch a movie, he'd pass out within the first five minutes, as if his brain, unaccustomed to so much visual content, just powered itself down. A neuroscientist recruited him to participate in a study of the effects of long-term imprisonment. If the research showed that protracted solitary confinement, particularly starting at a young age, resulted in long-lasting cognitive damage, it would be further evidence that such practices were cruel and unusual and therefore potentially unconstitutional. But the study also underlined Damien's fear that his brain would be forever broken.

In that first year or so after Damien's release, he couldn't stand to be alone. Lorri, who had lived by herself for so long, now rarely had time to herself. She had put all her energy toward getting Damien out of prison. The great dramatic story of her life had reached its crescendo— and then life went on, and now what were they supposed to do all day?

Despite Damien's precarious state, they almost immediately began a whirlwind world tour to promote various books and films about the case. Damien was eager to leave that part of his past behind him, but that past was also his and Lorri's primary source of income. (Damien's memoir, *Life After Death*, was a *New York Times* bestseller; he and Lorri also published a volume of their prison correspondence, *Yours for Eternity*, and coproduced Amy Berg's documentary *West of Memphis*.) Lorri and Damien presented a positive face to the world, but in truth they were just barely holding it together.

This is one of the risks of taking on the role of the defender: if the dream is to lose yourself in a cause, you might wake up one day and realize that you've succeeded, and that there's hardly anything left of *you*. Women, who are socially conditioned to be selfless, can be particularly susceptible to a version of heroism that sucks them dry.

I first met Lorri at a French café in the West Village, six and a half years after Damien's release from prison. We drank cappuccinos and ate salads as she tried to set me up with a handsome magician who had just moved to town. In person, Lorri radiated such a thorough and abiding sincerity that it never felt like the right time to start in on my list of cynical questions: Why did you give your life over to fight for this man's freedom? What parts of yourself did you have to hide away to do so? Isn't having a huge and tragic love the oldest and most limiting path to female glory? Do you at all regret that the great story of your life is fundamentally about someone else?

But it wasn't as dire as all that, from what Lorri told me. Things were calmer now, and it finally felt as if she and Damien were walking on solid ground. You could credit therapy, or Damien's spiritual beliefs—he was practicing magick again, up to several hours a day. Or maybe it was just the generosity of time smoothing everything over, making even the most difficult ordeals seem tolerable. Without the case dominating Lorri's days, at last she had time to be herself again.

She was reading lots of nineteenth-century novels and working on a screenplay about a woman who lives with a ghost.

The next evening, I stopped by Lorri and Damien's apartment in Harlem, a third-floor walk-up that they share with three suspicious, spoiled cats. (Jason Baldwin moved to Austin, Texas, with his wife, Holly, whom he met while he was in prison. He has continued to advocate for the rights of the wrongfully convicted through his organization, Proclaim Justice. Jessie Misskelley Jr. is back in West Memphis, taking care of his father.) I laughed when I saw that the two of them had on practically the same outfit—black gothy pants with excessive zippers, black shirts, stompy black boots. They professed to be embarrassed about it, but I could tell they weren't really. "We're so codependent," Lorri said fondly.

We headed to a taco place around the corner. Damien walked quickly, something slightly edgy in his energy. Lorri was such an easy person to be with that Damien's intensity startled me at first. At dinner he explained that his life since his release has largely been devoted to magick. As a kid in Arkansas, he'd daydreamed of becoming a great magician, and being in prison had given him plenty of time to study. His practice derives from the Hermetic Order of the Golden Dawn, the nineteenth-century mystery cult that counted W. B. Yeats and Bram Stoker as members. Every day, Damien spends several hours performing protective rituals, doing energy work, and invoking the names of angels. He told me that the most adept magicians can transcend time, space, and the rules of physics—not in a metaphorical way, or a karmic-progression-toward-enlightenment-over-many-lifetimes way, but literally: they can travel back to the eleventh century, find a pilgrim dying of thirst in the desert, and become an oasis for him.

All this lofty energy worried me; I could imagine being swamped by it, feeling as though there was no space for me and my small human concerns. Damien knew he wasn't a simple person to live with. The adaptive strategies he'd developed in prison—his incredible capacity to re-create the universe in his head; his complete immersion in the present moment—made it challenging to negotiate the outside world. He couldn't remember what he'd done even just the day before—where he'd eaten, what he and Lorri had talked about. More and more, his mind was elsewhere, operating on some other plane.

Lorri watched him carefully as he explained all this. But then the conversation shifted and Damien was silly again, telling me stories about the cats, about a creepy masseuse in El Paso, about getting lost in the penthouse that now belonged to Taylor Swift. Lorri laughed in a wide-open way, and I tried to just bask in the rare pleasure of hanging out with a long-married couple who still seemed to find each other delightful.

After we finished our tacos we walked down Lenox Avenue. It was one of those aspirational early-spring evenings that could be considered ice cream weather, if you were feeling generous. I was full but I ordered two scoops anyway, with hot fudge—why not? More than twenty years after they'd first exchanged letters, here were Lorri and Damien, free and alive in New York City, scarfing down sundaes. I grasped at the moment; it felt like a flicker of the small and flawed and rare thing we call justice. Then it flitted away.

On the subway home that evening, the clatter of the city surrounded me. Somewhere out in the wide world, innocent people sat in prison cells and immigration lawyers stayed up late, poring over paperwork. In Hollywood, a television executive plotted the return of Court TV. On an online forum, a woman argued that the satanist conspiracy had been real all along, that it had infiltrated the highest echelons of political power, that immediate action needed to be taken to protect the innocent children of America. Someone else watched a documentary about a miscarriage of justice and briefly forgot the injustices in her own life. And deep under the city I sat and let myself be overwhelmed with the thought of all the work that remained to be done.

THE KILLER

Who has not asked himself at some time or other: am
I a monster or is this what it means to be a person?

—Clarice Lispector

It was an extremely online romance, as many were in 2014: they
followed each other on Tumblr, then they became Facebook friends,
then they started chatting. Lindsay sent the first message, "Huzzah,"
and then a little poker-faced emoticon: ('-'). It was four days before
Christmas, and she was bored in her room. She could hear her parents
downstairs, talking to the dogs, laughing at some inane sitcom. James
wrote back right away: "hey!" They messaged back and forth for a few
hours that first night, tentatively at first, trying to suss each other out.

Lindsay did most of the talking. She apologized for being hyper;
she was all hopped up on coffee and half an energy drink. In person
she hardly spoke, but online she could just go and go. "Feel free to
tell me to shut up if I'm getting too boring/weird here," she wrote.

"I don't mind," James replied.

It wasn't obvious at first that they would be a match. Lindsay
casually mentioned her trips around the world, her family's horse.
She lived in the suburbs of Chicago and was working on a novel; in
her spare time, she painted ("mostly pale dudes with weapons") and
read Nietzsche. James was a stoner who lived in Nova Scotia and hung
out at metal shows. "I don't read much," he admitted, and "I can't

write for shit." He couldn't draw, either. He was basically terrible at anything that involved a pen and paper. "Plus I have roughly zero motivation." He was nineteen, aimless and unemployed. She was twenty-two, with a newly minted degree from a small liberal arts school in Iowa and vague plans to join the Peace Corps.

Over the next seven weeks, Lindsay and James would come to feel that their meeting was part of some great cosmic plan. They were in similar places in their lives: young adults still living with their parents, socially awkward, virgins. They didn't spend much time talking about the mundane building blocks of adulthood—school, family, work—in part because those parts of life had felt hostile to both of them for a long time. Instead they discussed the other things they had in common—how they both walked stiffly and too fast, how as soon as they entered a room, other people could sense that something about them didn't quite fit. How they could tell that strangers were afraid of them. How they had grown to like it, in a way, the perverse kind of power that came from being the kind of person everyone else wanted to stay away from.

In 1928, a twenty-three-year-old aspiring writer began taking notes for a novel she hoped to write. It would be called *The Little Street*, she decided, and it would center on a man a few years younger than her, a bright and misunderstood striver born into poverty. "A perfectly straight being, unbending and uncompromising," the woman wrote in her journal. "He cannot be a hypocrite."

The young writer had recently immigrated to the United States from Russia and was having a hard time getting her footing. She felt sure that she was destined for great things—she intended to be famous by age thirty—but the world was not yet cooperating. Her family was back in Russia, making meager birthday cakes out of potato peels, carrot greens, coffee grounds, and acorns; she was fortunate not to be *there*, particularly given the political situation, but *here* wasn't much better. After her arrival in Chicago, the young writer slept on a cot in her aunt's kitchen and struggled to learn English. She had no friends; for companionship, she lost herself in the movies, obsessively ranking hundreds of films in her journal. Her alienation had something to do with anti-Semitism and anti-immigrant prejudice, but her awkwardness and rigidity certainly didn't help. She thought things would be different when she moved to Hollywood to make it big in the movie business, but that didn't work out as she'd hoped, either. One of her roommates in a women's boardinghouse later remembered her as "grim and remote." She made ends meet by working as a waitress and a door-to-door saleswoman. She felt, she recalled later, like "an intruder with all the world laughing at me and rejecting me at every step."

During this bleak period, the young writer became increasingly invested in the fantasy worlds she created in her notebook. She decided that the main character of *The Little Street*, Danny Renahan, would be lonely and misunderstood, just like her: "Very unpopular in school . . . no love-affairs or drinks . . . he doesn't take part in any sports, that is, any *teamwork*." But his alienation wouldn't bother him; it would be a point of pride. He would, innately and from birth, know "that to be loved by the mob is an insult and that to be hated is the highest compliment it can pay you."

The lonely writer devoted many pages in her journal to Danny. Her description of him reads like fan fiction written eighty years too early. She decided that Danny would have "a man's psychology" and "a genuinely beautiful soul." He would be slender, not too tall, with "strong, rather irregular features, as though cut by quick, sharp blows." Dark, piercing eyes that made people uneasy. A large mouth. A brilliant, cruel sense of humor. "Straight, severe eye-brows." "More passionate than strong." "Tense, exalted, *active*." "Born with the spirit of Argon and the nature of a medieval feudal lord." You get the idea.

A girl would be in the novel, too, the writer decided—a kind of authorial analogue named Hetty. She would also be lonely and poor; in the manner of romantic heroines throughout time, she would be gray eyed and slim and "not beautiful but exquisite in her own way." Hetty was more frail and sensitive and confused than Danny. Sometimes he frightened her, delicate flower that she was, but she also instinctively sensed his worth. Danny didn't love Hetty back—he was too vital for love!—but that only made him more appealing. The writer based Hetty on herself, particularly the parts of herself she saw as weak: "the idealistic, longing side of me."

These journal entries are embarrassingly transparent; the plan for *The Little Street* reads less like a plot summary and more like a map of the gaps and longings in their author's life: "to be hated is the highest compliment." It's as if she were saying, "It's fine that I don't have any friends. Actually, it's *great*. You're all just threatened by me, probably."

I found it disconcerting to feel this upwelling of pity while reading the journal because the author was Ayn Rand. (At least I got some satisfaction from knowing that nothing would infuriate her more than my psychoanalyzing and then feeling sorry for her.) Within a few decades, she would write the famous novels—*The Fountainhead*, *Atlas Shrugged*—that would sell millions of copies and become what one of her biographers called "the ultimate gateway drug" to conservative politics. But in her early twenties, Rand was still underemployed and misunderstood, filling her journal with exhortations to just get herself together and *write*: "From now on—no thought whatever about yourself, only about your work. You don't exist. You are only a writing engine. . . . *Do you live for action or for rest? Stop admiring yourself—you are nothing yet.*"

Given Rand's already-rigid worldview, the plot of *The Little Street* proceeded as you might expect. Danny's strength and superiority threatened the fat and complacent fools in his hometown. (Also, he murders a pastor.) He ends up on trial and is sentenced to death. Just before his execution, he makes a speech: "It must be the essence, the very heart of the book: his wild, ferocious cry," Rand instructed herself. "It must be the strongest speech ever uttered in condemnation of the world. It must strike people like a whip slapping them in the face. It must be scalding in its bloody suffering, like the yell of an animal with an open, torn wound."

With the stakes that high, it's not surprising that Rand never wrote that speech or finished this book or even started it—instead, she just wrote pages about what kind of book it would be, how bracingly it would show the world the errors of its ways. I imagine her up late and alone in her boardinghouse room, smoking and furiously typing notes to herself, bitterly planning the novel that would establish her superiority once and for all, the novel that would bring the world to its knees. A novel that would never exist.

Lindsay Souvannarath hadn't always been so committed to being scary. She spent most of her childhood in Geneva, Illinois, an upscale community in Chicago's western suburbs, a place of groomed lawns and quaint architecture. The Chamber of Commerce slogan was "A Picture Postcard," and in 2013, *Businessweek* named it the best place in the state to raise kids. Lindsay took horseback-riding lessons and went on summer enrichment trips. Her mother, who is white, worked as a dog trainer; her father, who was from Laos and fled Southeast Asia during the Vietnam War, was a computer programmer. "We all loved each other very much," Lindsay told an interviewer later. In Geneva, a notably homogeneous town where more than 95 percent of the population was white, Lindsay's mixed-race family stood out. When she was eight, Lindsay was asked to pose for a local mural celebrating diversity. (My account of Lindsay's life is drawn from her prolific internet posts, court filings, interviews with people who knew her, the twelve-hundred-page record of her chats with James, and a few brief letters she wrote me; her parents did not respond to my interview requests.)

Lindsay was a dreamy kid who lived in her head, and on the computer. She learned to type before she learned to write by hand. She gobbled up fantasy books—*Harry Potter*, *The Chronicles of Narnia*—and filled her journals with long, inventive stories set in these worlds, accompanied by drawings of fantastical creatures. Her imagination was so vivid that she sometimes scared herself. She was in first grade when the Columbine massacre took place, and her teacher described the shooting in such detail, including the suicide of the two perpetrators, that Lindsay was too frightened to sleep alone for a week.

Lindsay's family moved from Chicago to Geneva when she was around eight years old, and she had a difficult time with the transition. In Chicago she'd been popular at school, but she grew more isolated in her new home. When she entered middle school, Lindsay kept writing obsessively, but the tone of her work shifted; there was less magic and more horror. She dressed in black and started fights with her classmates. Other kids called her "criminal," and "serial killer." She'd always been drawn to online fandoms, but now the *Harry Potter* universe seemed like kid stuff. Instead, she gravitated to edgier internet forums, Deviant Art, Cracked.com, Creepy Pasta, message boards where the tone was dark, nihilistic, and often emphatically non-PC. In this universe, serial killers were hilarious, and people who got self-righteously upset about serial killer jokes were even more hilarious.

Lindsay's art became more elaborate, stranger. She drew creatures she called Zoosapiens, "human in form, beast in spirit." She repeatedly sketched a guy wearing a hooded cloak, clutching two sickles. She named him Jimmy and decided he was a serial killer. Some people get all dewy-eyed about being a tween, those last years of childhood before the hormonal tsunami sweeps in, but for Lindsay it was an awful time. She was so angry, and so lonely. She loved the idea of love, but found every boy her age totally repulsive. A friend suggested she start "dating" Jimmy instead. At first it felt like a joke, then somehow it didn't anymore. Lindsay's relationship with Jimmy "was completely chaste," she wrote a few years later, "as I still thought sex was totally gross." (Also, he was a made-up character.) But she would talk about how she loved him and planned to marry him one day. She daydreamed about his becoming real, kidnapping her, and making her his accomplice.

As she grew older, Lindsay's creative output got even darker. She wrote at length about an imaginary realm that was at war. There was a Dark Lord and a vigilante named The Butcher. These stories were violent and atmospheric, full of portentous speeches. Her characters said such things as "Brothers in arms, I come bearing a message from the emperor!" and "I will not join the herd, for it so badly needs culling. No, I am The Butcher, and I will make this planet my slaughterhouse." Sometimes she posted her stories online, where she developed a minor following. A talented writer, she could be funny, but she was particularly good at doom and gore. Her fans appreciated how relentless her stories were, how she refused to offer any hint of redemption or hope or human warmth. In person, she'd learned to control her explosive temper. According to her high school friend Sabrina Szigeti, her classmates thought of her as shy, cute, and quiet, if they thought of her at all. "She was definitely on the 'fringe' and not really known at the school," Szigeti wrote later. "We were geeks in a very affluent, preppy, 97% white town." She and Szigeti ate lunch with the members of the anime club and the drama club and the writing club—"the outcast kids," Szigeti told me. "She had a dark sense of humor. It was nice to have someone who was as edgy as you. But then she would keep going."

Lindsay's parents later said she was subject to merciless bullying from middle school on, in part for being biracial. (Lindsay disputes this.) Online, though, she could manage her image. She put on makeup and took hundreds of pictures of herself, edited and filtered to make her eyes look anime-huge, her skin smooth and pale as a doll's. She "was obsessed with trying to make herself as beautiful (and as white) as possible," one online friend wrote later. Growing up in white neighborhoods among white family members meant that Lindsay "always identified more strongly with being white," she told an interviewer.

After graduation she attended a small liberal arts school a few hours away from home, where she majored in creative writing and English. She enjoyed her classes but made no friends. She was assigned a roommate freshman year, but that girl moved out after one semester. Lindsay became increasingly withdrawn, into her own world and into the world of her writing. She wrote a funny little flash-fiction story called "My Pet Skeleton," about a girl whose pet skeleton freaks everyone out:

Sometimes I wonder if he wishes he had skeleton friends to play with. A frolic of skeletons. They'd all run off to a graveyard and dance to xylophone music, because that's how skeletons frolic. I think. But I'd never know, because my skeleton's the only one I know, and he doesn't talk.

Everyone else's skeletons are locked up in closets. Most people think they should stay there. Maybe you do too. But I wouldn't say anything bad about skeletons. There's one inside you.

Lindsay also started working on a novel about a boy who falls in love with death. She sometimes sounded as though she half believed the stories she was creating weren't fictional, and that the characters were her friends. Perhaps that's because there was never a bright line between what was real and what was make-believe for Lindsay. The vast majority of her social life took place online; most of her boyfriends were guys halfway across the world whom she never met IRL.

During college, her most serious online boyfriend broke up with her, and she tried to kill herself. The hospital bills from that stressed her out, as did her student loans. She spent most of her time alone in her dorm room, drinking absinthe and dreaming up fictional realms. Her worried mother read psychology books and floated possible diagnoses—ADHD? clinical depression? social anxiety?—that made Lindsay roll her eyes. After one bout of alcohol poisoning, she was sent to a school counselor. The woman pressed Lindsay on her lack of social contact: Was she perhaps avoiding people because she was afraid that they wouldn't like her? "I just started shouting, *'No. Fuck no. Fuck that. Fuck you,'*" Lindsay later wrote.

The external world increasingly felt like a difficulty, an irritation. She hated how bland, saccharine girls could get boyfriends, but she apparently "wasn't the relationship type." One afternoon, not long after her breakup, she saw a happy couple hugging in the school cafeteria. Something bubbled up in her—she wanted to *punch* them. The feeling was sudden and startling, like a panic attack. And it didn't go away. For the rest of the semester, she'd see a couple and think, *What if I just walked up to them, shot her in the head, and walked away?*

The idea took root. During the fall of 2014, her final semester of college, Lindsay decided that her novel should have a mass-murder subplot. The future was bearing down on her, and she should probably have been prepping for the Peace Corps—she was applying to teach English in Asia—but suddenly she was spending all her time researching school shooters. She immersed herself in the school shooter / serial killer subculture that flourished on Tumblr. "It was all just academic at first, but I found myself identifying more and more with the shooters," she said later. "I made so many friends there that I felt I had a lot in common with. It just became very significant to me." That fall, she began reblogging mass-killer memes and various celebrations of gore, alongside images of cool-looking shoes from fashion week.

One meme she made, a satirical riff on girly BFF culture, featured a grisly photograph of the two Columbine shooters postsuicide, captioned NOT BEING ABLE TO LIVE WITHOUT YOUR BEST FRIEND. James Gamble liked it, and the two of them began following each other's blogs. Their aesthetics were a match from the start. James's Tumblr, created under the username Shallow Existences, featured a brief looping surveillance video from Columbine. There were Eric Harris and Dylan Klebold, the two shooters, stalking through the empty cafeteria, with toppled chairs and signs of chaos all around them. You could see them fling cups across the room and fire their guns at nobody, then the GIF restarted and they flung and shot all over again. As if they'd always be there, trapped in that cafeteria, causing mayhem forever.

Ayn Rand based the character of Danny—the manly, passionate, strong-browed hero of *The Little Street*—on nineteen-year-old William Hickman, a man she'd never met but whom she'd read about in the newspapers. Rand devoted dozens of pages in her journal to Hickman, whom she saw as "a brilliant, unusual, exceptional boy." Few people agreed.

Hickman, like Rand, had dreamed of making it big in Hollywood.

When that didn't work out, he turned to check forging and armed robbery. On December 15, 1927, he walked into an elementary school in Los Angeles and told the woman at the front desk that he was a family friend of Perry Parker's, whose twin daughters attended the school. Hickman claimed that Parker had been in an accident, and that he had been sent to pick up one of the girls. Hickman was calm and confident, the kind of man who instinctively inspired obedience. The administrator called twelve-year-old Marion Parker out of her classroom and delivered her to Hickman. The man and the girl walked together to his waiting car.

Perry Parker—Hickman's former boss—got the first ransom letter the next day, followed by several others. They were signed "Fate," "Death," and "The Fox," as if the kidnapper couldn't settle on a sinister pseudonym. He was clearer in his instructions: At nightfall on the appointed day, Perry Parker should drive alone to a particular intersection and deliver the $1,500 ransom. Then his daughter would be returned.

Parker did as he was told. On the isolated road, the kidnapper's car pulled up alongside him. A masked man sat behind the wheel— Hickman—and a smaller, blanket-wrapped figure was next to him in the passenger seat—Marion. Her eyes were open, but she didn't turn to look at her father; she just sat there, staring straight ahead, unnaturally still. After Parker handed over the ransom, Hickman began to speed away. Before he turned the corner, he opened the door and Marion's body tumbled onto the pavement. She'd been dead for hours.

The nation (and, presumably, Ayn Rand) followed along as the newspapers covered the unfolding case in all its horrifying detail: how Hickman had killed the girl, cut off her limbs, then realized that he would probably need a body to collect the ransom; how he'd stuffed rags in the dead girl's torso to keep her corpse upright, then sewn her eyes open so she looked more or less alive. How he managed to avoid arrest for a week after the murder, despite the thousands of police officers across the nation looking for him. How roadblocks were set up at the Mexican border in case he tried to sneak across. How Clara Bow contributed to the reward for his arrest, and Charlie Chaplin followed the case closely. How Hickman had finally been caught in Oregon and put on trial in Los Angeles.

For a few weeks, Hickman was perhaps the most loathed man in America. That made him appealing to Rand. That's not to say that she celebrated his murder of Marion Parker; she just preferred not to think about it. "There is a lot that is purposelessly, senselessly horrible about [Hickman]," she granted. "But that does not interest me." She would rather enumerate all the things she *did* appreciate: how daring he was, how calmly insouciant with the police, how defiant at trial. She liked "the fact that he looks like 'a bad boy with a very winning grin,' that he makes you like him the whole time you are in his presence." He refused to snivel and apologize, and he wasn't afraid to put himself first—qualities she found admirable. If Hickman inspired so much hatred and fear in the masses, she reasoned, he must have been doing something right.

I can understand why Rand abandoned her plans for a Hickman-inspired novel. It's clear from her notes that *The Little Street* would've been cruder and angrier than the books that made her famous. Perhaps she also had some qualms about her murderous protagonist. It's easier to romanticize a heroically selfish industrial titan than a child killer; the blood on his hands isn't quite so *visible*. But Rand had touched on something there, found a template that would prove to have some staying power well beyond her own work: a bad boy with a grin; a lonely girl with a crush on a killer.

*   *   *

Before the late 1990s, plenty of kids were furious and suicidal, but few of them dealt with their feelings by bringing a gun to school. In 1977, Stephen King (writing under his pseudonym Richard Bachman) published a novel called *Rage*, which told the story of an angry kid who shot his algebra teacher and took his classmates hostage. Throughout the 1980s and into the '90s, a handful of school shootings roughly followed this formula—violence directed at teachers and classrooms taken hostage by teenagers, who were later discovered to be fans of the novel. After a 1997 school shooting in Paducah, Kentucky (whose perpetrator had a copy of *Rage* in his locker), King asked his publisher "to take the damn thing out of print." Intermittent eruptions of school violence merited somber coverage on nightly newscasts for the next couple of years. A kid named Kip Kinkel murdered his parents, listened to a Wagner aria on repeat, then drove to Thurston High School with two pistols; a thirteen-year-old and his eleven-year-old sidekick killed four classmates and one teacher in Jonesboro, Arkansas. These were isolated incidents, but there were enough of them to see the outline of a trend forming. In 1998, after three shootings in less than a year, President Clinton devoted his weekly radio address to the topic. The public at large was horrified—and fascinated. The Jonesboro and Thurston High shootings—largely forgotten now—were the two most closely followed news events of that year, beating out the Clinton-Lewinsky investigation and the midterm elections.

In Littleton, Colorado, a high school junior named Eric Harris wrote about the spate of school shooters for an English-class project: "Every day news broadcasts stories of students shooting students or going on killing sprees," he wrote. "It is just as easy to bring a loaded handgun to school as it is to bring a calculator." *Ouch!* his teacher commented in the margin. A year and a half later, on April 20, 1999, Harris and his friend Dylan Klebold would kill twelve students, one teacher, and themselves at Columbine High School. Two decades after that, they'd both be unlikely internet heartthrobs.

Columbine, instead of Paducah or Jonesboro, became the archetypal school shooting for a number of reasons—most obviously because there were many more casualties: thirteen dead (fifteen, if you included the shooters themselves), twenty-one injured. Previous school shootings had been quick eruptions of violence that ended just as quickly. While the murders at Columbine elapsed over just seventeen minutes, the television coverage made the tragedy seem more protracted. Viewers watched live as SWAT teams charged the building, as students sprinted out with their hands on their heads, as a bloody boy scrambled out a shattered window. Cell phones were a relatively new phenomenon, but the Denver suburbs were full of well-off early adopters, which meant that kids trapped in the school could call news stations and be interviewed live on air. Class also played a role. This wasn't an eruption of violence in some distressed rural town; this was a middle-class, suburban shooting. The unspoken—or sometimes spoken—refrain went *This kind of thing doesn't happen in places like* this. *Not with kids like* ours.

Harris and Klebold had no intention of being ciphers; their murders were a *message*, and they provided ample documentation to ensure that everyone heard it. In their final days, they debated which director would film the story of their lives, Quentin Tarantino or Steven Spielberg. Both boys kept journals, and Eric had a website. Most notoriously, they had spent the weeks before the massacre filming themselves with a camcorder they'd borrowed from school. They'd intended to disseminate their videos to local television stations, but they'd run out of time. Before Harris left the house on the morning of the attack, he placed a microcassette on the kitchen counter with a message for his parents, and for posterity: "People will die because of me. It will be a day that will be remembered forever."

Columbine wasn't just a massacre; it was also a media spectacle, one that both unspooled as breaking news and was analyzed for months afterward. The school shooting was the second-most-covered news event of the 1990s (after the O. J. Simpson trial); 68 percent of the American public said they followed the story "very closely"—more than double those who closely watched the Clinton impeachment trial.

In the immediate aftermath of the attack, the media was flooded with misinformation. It was erroneously reported that the boys had been members of something called the Trenchcoat Mafia; that they had hit lists; that they targeted jocks. On 20/20 the day after the attack, Diane Sawyer warned "that the boys may have been part of a dark, underground national phenomenon known as the gothic movement, and that some of these goths may have killed before."

The most egregious errors were eventually corrected as the coverage continued into the subsequent months. Stories about Columbine and its aftermath lingered on the front page of the *New York Times* for nearly two weeks. Schools across the country were on high alert; the ACLU reported that students were punished or suspended for making jokes about Columbine, expressing sympathy for the shooters, or even discussing the massacre. Reporters obsessed over the details: the T-shirts the shooters were wearing, the types of weapons they carried, their kill count, their motivations. Media critics have since pointed out that this kind of close reading, heavy on the lurid details and emotionally inflected language, was the worst possible way to respond to mass violence. Just as detailed and dramatic stories about suicide can inspire more suicides, highly emotional accounts of school shootings that emphasize the specificities of a plot may also result in contagion. Columbine did indeed help reshape the idea of what a school shooting was supposed to look like—the methodology, the motivation, the aesthetic, even the sound track. The weapons should be semiautomatic. The look was paramilitary. The targets should be chosen at random and maximized. No one was taking hostages anymore.

In the years after the attack, victims' parents sued the sheriff's office and the high school, demanding the release of investigatory material. By 2006, huge amounts of information had been made public, including videos the boys had made, their journals, and some of their writing for school (including Klebold's essay "The Mind and Motives of Charles Manson"). The more than twenty thousand documents and videos painted a picture of two very different young men. Eric Harris, clever and arrogant and skilled at fooling adults, was generally accepted to be the mastermind behind the plan. He had been the overtly angry one, the builder of bombs, the gun fetishist. On his website, he tracked "the various things in the world that annoy the SHIT outa me," which ranged from people who pronounced espresso as "expresso" to *Star Wars* fans ("GET A FRIKIN LIFE YOU BOR- ING DICKHEADS!") to slow mall-walkers. Dylan Klebold, gangly and self-conscious and sad, was the more socially awkward of the two. His journal was full of self-loathing, awkward poetry, and existential and romantic despair. He drew huge piles of dead bodies, but also pages and pages of hearts. The prevailing theory was that Klebold was a suicidal kid who had the bad luck (or bad taste) to become best friends with Harris, a manipulative psychopath who convinced him to turn his self-hate against the world. This simple split is hard to square with some of Klebold's writing, though, which at times is just as cruel as Harris's: as early as 1997, Klebold was musing about a friend who could get him a gun so he could go on "my killing spree against anyone I want."

Sometime in their junior year, the two boys had begun planning an epic assault on their school designed to kill as many people as possible. They hoped for a hundred victims, maybe hundreds, maybe even a thousand. Harris tinkered with bombs, studied *The Anarchist*

Cookbook, tried (and failed) to DIY some napalm. They referred to the massacre with the code word NBK (an allusion to the film *Natural Born Killers*) and made joking and overt references to it for months: "God I can't wait till they die," Harris wrote in Klebold's 1998 yearbook. "I can taste the blood now - NBK."

Victims' families had hoped that reading through the killers' personal papers would help make sense of the tragedy. Harris and Klebold did offer one repeated explanation. They killed because they felt hate. Hate at what? The world. But it turned out that didn't clarify anything at all.

Making all that information public had another, unintended consequence: it helped make the Columbine shooters into icons of rebellion. Teenagers who didn't trust the oversimplified media narrative about Harris and Klebold now had lots of highly charged, intimate material to stoke their fascination, and they used it to build a counternarrative. In this version of events, Harris and Klebold were martyred revolutionaries who dared to rebel against the repressive, jock-centric culture of their school. The most ardent fans started uploading tribute videos to YouTube. They featured flattering images of the two boys set to Marilyn Manson songs, or strident social Darwinist poetry overlaid on news footage of sobbing Columbine High students. In-group references to the massacre began to emerge: NBK, Natural Selection, Reb (Harris's nickname), VoDKa (Klebold's). "RIP Eric & Dylan," read a typical comment. "They were the true victims."

Lindsay and James's dynamic solidified early on. She was chatty, arrogant, unapologetic. He was gloomy, self-hating, stoned most of the time. She tried to cheer him up by reminding him that he was a superior being, just like her.

LINDSAY: you're better than most people. . . .

JAMES: well thank you

LINDSAY: Also, because I like you when I do not like most people

JAMES: I'm glad aha

LINDSAY: You've earned the approval of a surly asocial narcissist! Congratulations!

JAMES: :D!!

LINDSAY: And now do you feel more confident? ('-')

JAMES: yeah I suppose

LINDSAY: Excellent. It's a good start.

During the first week of their online relationship, Lindsay asked James where he liked to hang out. She knew he lived nearly two thousand miles away and on the other side of an international border, but it was still fun to fantasize about what it would be like if she showed up there one day, the two of them both wearing trench coats, exchanging sly conspiratorial glances: "people would be like OH GOD THERE'S TWO OF THEM NOW," she wrote. "What a great way to spend a day, just terrorizing normal/inferior people."

"I hope to do that on a major scale someday," James replied.

"Same."

As the conversation continued, Lindsay sounded as if she was just riffing, but James seemed to mean it. He had everything he needed already, he said: guns, ammunition, a knife, a scary outfit. It was the most talkative he'd been during the short course of their friendship.

Lindsay didn't seem to notice; she chattered on about other things: Japanese candy and house music and Nordic liquor and stupid family Christmas parties and how cold it was outside. James kept bringing the conversation back to mass shootings: "I just wish I had a partner, that could take the shotgun while I take the hunting rifle. Way less chance of getting attacked/jumped if I had a partner."

"I could be your Eric," Lindsay wrote. "How's about that?"

"That'd be nice :p."

The next day was Christmas, and Lindsay was still pretty drunk when she and James started chatting that night. Alcohol seemed to make her bolder. She told him that her mom had given her a nice pair of black pants and a T-shirt that said TERROR in big black letters. The perfect outfit to wear for something like, oh, murdering strangers. "NBK could be only a plane ride away," she wrote.

The two of them circled around the idea for a while, at first jokingly and then with more seriousness. James admitted that he'd daydreamed about committing a mass shooting for years—since middle school. He figured he could steal his father's guns pretty easily. Recently, the idea had been on his mind nonstop. Sometimes it was hard to think about anything else. Halifax was so placid; the last time anything had shaken the place up was a maritime explosion a hundred years ago. The town could use a dose of random violence. He'd tried to convince his best friend, Randy, to join him, but Randy "[wasn't] down for the whole 'mass murder' thing," James said. He'd even tested out the idea on some online friends, rage posters who reblogged lots of Kill Mankind memes. But at the prospect of an *actual* mankind-killing opportunity, they had gotten all shocked and offended: *Oh, I could never do something like that!* So many people online were pretending to be edgy, but when it came down to it, they just craved attention. It pissed him off. He couldn't see himself going NBK without a partner. But now, maybe, he'd found one.

Or maybe not. Neither of them had nearly enough of their own money for a plane ticket, for starters. James was pessimistic by nature and quick to embrace defeat. "Ugh I wish it could happen," he sighed.

But Lindsay was more confident: "Anything can happen when we put our minds to it. Besides, you're working with me. I've already done a lot in my life, this should be easy."

*   *   *

In some ways, YouTube was an ideal platform for a Columbine subculture. Harris and Klebold had obsessively documented themselves on video; the video-sharing site allowed their followers to do the same. On YouTube, the Columbine-curious included those who celebrated the shootings as well as more circumspect viewers who described themselves merely as "researchers." But after a spate of copycat shootings in 2007 and 2008, YouTube began removing Columbine videos. By 2011, the Columbine community on YouTube was effectively gone, according to one researcher who'd been tracking the subculture for years.

Columbine content soon showed up elsewhere online, and in a more unexpected form. By 2012, it was decidedly a Tumblr phenomenon, and this time the devotees were mostly young girls. While YouTube lent itself to macho posturing and video manifestos, Tumblr's image-centric reblog format encouraged those interested in Columbine to see themselves as members of a distinct fandom, one with the same fanatical insularity as the cliques devoted to actors or fictional wizards. Because no fan community was complete without a cute name, they began self-identifying as Columbiners.

The emerging Columbiner scene got a boost when the first season of *American Horror Story* featured a broody heartthrob who was also a school shooter (and a rapist, and a ghost—it was complicated). Viewers tuned in, swooned, googled, learned about Columbine, and, improbably, swooned some more. Girls who'd been toddlers at the time of the massacre in Colorado had an easier time metabolizing the tragedy as an aesthetic: trench coats, violent video games, industrial techno, semiautomatic weapons, security-camera footage—and cute, misunderstood boys. From one angle, the Columbiners were just like any other online fandom: infighty and intense and full of arcane insider references. But their love objects weren't famous and unattainable because they were pop stars; they were famous because they were murderers, and unattainable because they were dead.

Some of the Columbiners seemed to have a crush not so much on the boys but on the pathos of the whole, horrible situation. They imagined themselves hiding under a desk in the school library, weeping. Most, though, were fixated on the shooters. They related to them or wanted to understand them or wished they could've saved them with the pure power of their love. The Columbiners drew fan art dedicated to Reb and VoDKa. They posted the same pictures of the killers over and over, sometimes transformed into memes of their own making: Klebold looking broodily handsome, followed by a GIF of an explosion, captioned "MY OVARIES"; Harris smirking in the cafeteria, accompanied by song lyrics: "You are my sunshine / my only sunshine / you make me happy / when skies are grey / You'll never know, dear / how much I love you / because you're dead." One recirculated image was just simple blocky letters superimposed over a Lisa Frank–style background of pink clouds, ice cream cones, and candy: "I LOVE YOU EVEN THOUGH YOU KILLED ALL THOSE PEOPLE."

The endless scroll of Tumblr seemed to suit the bottomless appetite of a girl in the full fever of a crush. Columbiners reblogged everything related to either of the two killers, no matter how dull or gruesome: a photograph of his parents' house, a doodle in the margin of his math homework, his middle school yearbook photo, a stock photo of the gun he preferred, his autopsy report. They made collages and baked the boys birthday cakes. Most didn't condone the murders—the unspoken rule seemed to be that you had to put that right up in your profile's header, "I Don't Condone"—but the Columbiners also got competitive when other mass shooters made the headlines. "Columbine will forever hold a place inside my heart no matter what other massacre happens," one wrote. They declared an allegiance, Reb or VoDKa. The Reb/Harris girls tended to be angry and rebellious, ready to write off the world. The VoDKa/Klebold fans were softer, prone to rescue fantasies and close reads of Klebold's bad love poems. One meme I saw summed it up nicely:

DYLAN COLUMBINERS:

crying at night
"dylan protects me I swear"
"for dylan" *chugs something with .02 alcohol* *rETCHES*

ERIC COLUMBINERS:

its not a phase mom
Sideblog full of guns with captions like "aaaaahhhh yeah
   mmhm"
literally anything happens fucker should be shot

One image kept coming up, a grainy crime scene photo of the two boys' bodies in the library postsuicide, their gory head wounds blatant and difficult to look at. Someone had superimposed glittery hearts all over it.

The Columbiner world was creepy, but it was also unexpectedly familiar—all the giddy emotion of adolescence channeled into shrines to distant boys. In eighth grade, my friends and I defined ourselves by our crush objects. If you knew whom a girl professed to love—and you would know as soon as you walked into her bedroom—you understood something about her. Emily loved Paul McCartney, not in his current old-man form, but some impossible time-travel version of him from her mother's girlhood. Mary loved Leonardo DiCaprio as he was in

Titanic. I loved Gavin Rossdale, the lead singer of Bush, who had recently appeared shirtless and disheveled on the cover of *Rolling Stone*. It was an expensive infatuation. I bought every magazine he appeared in, even the European ones. I hoarded trivia about him—his mother's name, his dog's birthday. The facts weren't the point; they were just a container for the vastness of my feelings. Of course they were inadequate; nothing would ever be adequate. It didn't matter much that Emily's crush was a haggard guy in his midfifties, or that Mary's was dying as the *Titanic* sank, or that my romantic rival was Gwen Stefani. Our crushes weren't about anything as simple as attainability, or kissing. You couldn't take Paul McCartney to the homecoming dance; the idea was absurd because the homecoming dance was an absurd nothing, especially when compared with the immensity and violence of our feelings.

In the years since, whenever I've been brought low by the sudden fever of a crush, I feel distinctly adolescent: that is, at once abject and powerful. Chris Kraus, in *I Love Dick*, describes crushing as plummeting back into "the psychosis of adolescence": "Living so intensely in your head that boundaries disappear. It's a warped omnipotence, a negative psychic power, as if what happens in your head really drives the world outside."

Lovestruck girls have long been both condescended to and feared. In the popular imagination, a girl in the thrall of a crush embodies every cliché about femininity taken to its most insulting extremes. She is brainless and unhinged, a body driven hysterical by hormones. She squeals and squeaks; what comes out of her mouth is something before words, or beyond them. She is dumb, but she's also *scary*. She grabs and won't let go. Contemporary culture is perfectly happy to objectify teenage girls, but when those same girls act as the subjects of desire rather than its object, they're seen as beastly and threatening. "A Beatle who ventures out unguarded into the streets runs the very real peril of being dismembered or crushed to death by his fans," *Life* reported in January 1964. A girl with a crush is also capable of *crushing*.

So while I knew I was supposed to be shocked and offended by the Columbiners and their Gen-Y amorality, I wasn't. These girls with their killer crushes weren't enacting some perverted counterpoint to sweet, innocent teen love, but crush logic made monstrous through amplification. They deployed the ditzy vernacular of internet teens ("*fangirling*"; "UGH every time i look at him i just flail around for a minute"), but the language had a different valence when applied to mass murderers. The cuteness was tinged with menace. The Columbiners had weaponized their girliness.

People often make the mistake of thinking a crush is about the crush object, but as someone who was able to generate colossal feelings toward a pretty mediocre rock star, I can attest it is *not* about the crush object. Rather, a crush is a way to take up space, and to make something about yourself known to the world. And it seemed that being a Columbiner was, more than anything else, about having enormous emotions. Adolescence is overwhelming for everyone, but girls are permitted a narrower range of expression. It's the time when many of us learn to be on guard against our *too much*-ness. Columbiners felt their crushes hugely; many also blogged about their depression and anxiety in the same grandiose terms. Experiencing bullying or social rejection made them want to die, or to kill; it was difficult to tell the difference sometimes. They wallowed in their empathy for Klebold, staying up late weeping into their pillows about how sad he'd been, how much they wanted to save him—or was it about how they hoped someone would save them? For some girls with their own deep wells of pain, this famous crime was a useful metaphor—operatic in its intensity, flattened by media overrepresentation into something not precisely real. It provided a language, and a set of shared reference points, to talk about end-of-the-world feelings: apocalyptic despair, unacceptable rage.

Maybe that's what was truly frightening about the Columbiners—not their veneration of Harris and Klebold, but what they articulated about themselves through their very public devotion. What did they want the world to know about their own fury and despair? About the ugly things they couldn't quite own?

Once they'd talked openly about murder, the conversations between Lindsay and James had a new intensity, and also an unexpected sweetness. Gloomy, human-hating Lindsay couldn't stop smiling. She told other online friends that she was no longer depressed. "It feels like I've been dead for years and then I suddenly came back to life and I can actually feel things and it's like WHOA," she wrote to James.

"It's such a special feeling isn't it?" he said. "Knowing that there's somebody else out there who feels just like you do."

She sent him some pictures, first of her face, a selfie shot from above using a filter that made her eyes look enormous. Then she sent more, ones of her dressed up in strappy leather underwear, pouting seductively. One thing led to another. Technically speaking, they were both virgins, but their virtual sex was soon pretty out there, with lots of talk of knives and blood and restraints.

In the final days of 2014, they chatted for hours every day. For years they'd both felt as if no one understood them, so it was intoxicating to finally have found someone who did. "You feel like you don't belong with society, right?" Lindsay asked. That was exactly it, James said—"like I was never born with the mindset/ability to interact with people properly, function properly on my own, or get into a relationship/have kids/get married." Lindsay told him about her suicide attempt, and how she'd almost died from alcohol poisoning.

He told her how his mom fed him vitamins that were supposed to help with his depression and told him he'd feel better if he found a career he enjoyed and was challenged by—as if his problems were so minor they could be fixed by some pills and a job. As if she had mistaken him for a person who was meant to live in this world.

Many Columbine experts posit that neither Harris nor Klebold would've murdered their classmates on their own; rather, there was something fatal in their dynamic. They provided each other with a permission, or an instigation. Together they created the shared reality they called NBK, and together they inflicted it on the world.

Something similar seemed to be happening with Lindsay and James. He said he'd fantasized about committing a mass shooting since middle school, but it had always remained a fantasy. His depression sank him into inaction. Lindsay was attracted to the aesthetic of spectacular violence, even as she seemed not at all interested in the practicalities of planning such an act. She didn't have a gun, had never shot a gun, had no idea how to get a gun, had never tried to get a gun. But in her bedroom, drunk on fruity vodka, she could imagine herself capable of anything.

"And you feel like when the moment actually calls for it, you could actually shoot people?" James asked.

"Yes sir," she said.

Lindsay thought she'd have enough money for a plane ticket by June—six months away. It was going to be so amazing, they told each other. "I'll feel more alive that day than I did my entire fucking life," James said.

The Columbiners' crushes were also, of course, about sex. A half century ago, screaming and fainting in George Harrison's presence was a way to assert desire at a time when girlhood ostensibly meant bobby socks and virginal purity, Barbara Ehrenreich has argued. "For girls, fandom offered a way not only to sublimate romantic and sexual yearnings but to carve out subversive versions of heterosexuality," Ehrenreich and her coauthors wrote in 1992. Beatlemania was a harbinger of the sexual revolution to come; no wonder the grown-ups were all so simultaneously freaked out by and dismissive of it.

A half century later, the Columbiners were much more self-aware and fluid in their sexuality. Girls who had grown up online had thorough knowledge of fetish categories; they were sexually sophisticated in ways that didn't always seem to align with their embodied experience. In the Columbiner world, desire was omnivorous and strange. The girls wanted to fuck their crush objects, but it wasn't just about that—they also wanted to save them, to be killed by them, to kill alongside them, to share lunch with them, to spoon with them, to eat them, to be them. One Columbiner drew Harris and Klebold as wet-eyed anime girls; another sketched them sitting on an unmade bed, holding each other's erect cocks. Girls posted pictures of themselves dressed up like Reb or VoDKa in cargo pants, NATURAL SELECTION T-shirts, and black trench coats. "You look so cute," other Columbiners commented. "I want to cuddle with you." They unabashedly admitted that guns turned them on. Girlishness and sophistication coexisted in ways that were sometimes disconcerting. "I want to touch Dylan's pee pee," a girl confessed in a Columbiner video. "I don't, like, label my sexuality," another teenage Columbiner wrote, "but if I did I would be pansexual. :)" The Columbiners, most of whom were more than a decade younger than me, taught me a new sexual preference: *hybristophilia*, the attraction to someone who has committed murder.

Hybristophilia predates the internet. When the Columbiners reblogged photos of slinky Richard Ramirez, Ted Bundy and his vacant prep school smile, or wild-haired Charlie Manson making freak-out-the-squares faces, they were telling an old story in a new medium. Our icons of depravity—the baddest of the bad boys—have long attracted groupies: the woman with long hippie hair who started writing letters to Manson when she was a teenager and announced her engagement to him when she was in her twenties; the journalist who saw Ramirez on television, was moved by his "vulnerability," and married him in 1996.

When I told people I was writing a book about women, crime, and obsession, this was always what they thought I meant: serial killer groupies, prison weddings, Manson pen pals. It got on my nerves. As I saw it, these women were just playing out the most reductive and depressing tropes of heterosexuality: in a world where masculinity meant power and power meant violence, some women would always opt to align themselves with that violence, and exert their own perverse power through love. It was a story as old as Beauty and the Beast: being the exception, the woman that a violent man doesn't kill, was a way to feel special, *chosen*. But it was an ugly kind of special, tainted with other people's pain.

Women who flirt with—or marry—notorious murderers are widely condemned. Yet behind that condemnation may be a form of complicity, even understanding. Our culture is obsessed with men who kill, and what else are these groupies doing but taking that obsession to its natural conclusion? In *Natural Born Celebrities: Serial Killers in American Culture*, David Schmid argues that the serial murderer is "the exemplary modern celebrity, widely known and famous for being himself." An alien landing on Earth might assume that we esteem these men, based on the number of books and movies and television shows and podcasts devoted to delving into their childhoods and musing about their motivations. Hybristophiliacs hold a mirror up to contemporary culture; what we don't like in them is what we don't like in ourselves.

And then there was Lindsay. To her, the Columbiners' romantic obsession with Klebold and Harris seemed a little ridiculous. As she wrote to James, "I'm over here like 'why be in love with them when I can BE them?'"

If some corners of the Columbiner world were darkly empowering, some parts were just dark. A community based on transgression and flirting with violence can easily slide into fetishization, particularly when algorithms ensure that the most extreme posts get the most attention.

Jesse Osborne, an eighth grader in Townville, South Carolina, became involved in the Columbine fandom via Instagram. One day in September 2016 he told his private chat group to look for him on the news soon. He shot his father in the back of his head, kissed his rabbit Floppy goodbye, and went to his former elementary school. Shouting "I hate my life," he injured three students and a teacher before his gun jammed and he was tackled by a volunteer firefighter. The most grievously wounded victim, six-year-old Jacob Hall, died at the hospital and was buried in a Batman costume. Osborne seemed to see the shooting as a form of asserting his existence. "Now I have a life," Osborne told police in his confession. "Probably won't get a job but I'll—I'll at least have a life." According to one expert, he was the thirty-third school shooter to have cited Harris and Klebold as his inspiration.

Osborne seemed to have absorbed an alarming lesson from Columbine: if you were an average maladjusted young person, no one would care much about you, but as soon as you magnified your awkwardness into monstrousness—as soon as you started shooting—then you'd have people poring over your diaries and trying to understand your innermost thoughts. "I felt like I wasn't taken seriously and I wasn't here and I was a joke to everyone," explained a sixteen-year-old girl who was charged with conspiracy to commit murder after police found her troubling Tumblr and her Google searches for *how to make a bomb*. "I wanted to be heard."

Over the past two decades, Columbine itself has become a kind of meme, an idea that self-replicates through the actions of troubled teenagers. School shootings are still rare, statistically speaking, although they are more common now than in the pre-Columbine era. (In the two decades since the massacre there have been about ten school shootings per year, according to the *Washington Post*.) There aren't many commonalities among those who plan campus massacres, other than that the vast majority of them are young white men. Their ranks have included kids who are psychotic, kids who want revenge on a particular enemy, and kids who are suicidally depressed. It's a mistake to assume that every school shooter is a meticulous plotter with a long-standing desire to kill, such as Eric Harris. After Columbine, it became easier for other disaffected or mentally ill young men to mold their fury or despair into the now-familiar shape of a shooting. On their own, they may not have come up with the idea of a school massacre—few before 1999 did—but they didn't have to. The template was at hand; that narrative was already implanted in the collective consciousness, buzzing with latent energy. "The problem is not that there is an endless supply of deeply disturbed young men who are willing to contemplate horrific acts," Malcolm Gladwell wrote in his 2015 *New Yorker* article about a putative school shooter. "It's worse. It's that young men no longer need to be deeply disturbed to contemplate horrific acts."

The bleak irony is that Jesse Osborne's Columbiner friends probably didn't see him on the news; his attack didn't merit much coverage outside South Carolina. Mass shootings had become common enough that they didn't usually make the national news unless they were spectacularly horrific. There were plenty of those, unfortunately, and they inspired their own fandoms. At Sandy Hook Elementary School, Adam Lanza killed twenty children and six staff members. The Tumblr girls who stanned for him called themselves Stanzas. After avowed white supremacist Dylann Roof killed nine worshippers at the Emanuel African Methodist Episcopal Church in Charleston, I was afraid to check Tumblr. Surely this pale, hateful worm wouldn't merit groupies—but he did, and they proclaimed themselves Roofies. (One recent mass murderer without much of a Tumblr following is Virginia Tech shooter Seung-Hui Cho. Cho has all the markers of a hybristophilic icon—including both a high body count and plenty of creepy writing available for analysis—so it's hard to chalk this up to anything but racism.)

I understood that part of the pleasure of professing love for a mass murderer was knowing that it would gross out people like me—but still, I was grossed out. So were many of the Columbiners. Tumblr was uncomfortable in those days after the Charleston massacre, full of girls contorting themselves to explain how *their* mass shooters were different, better.

I wasn't convinced. I'd always defended the Columbiners to those who saw them as merely shocking and shameful; it seemed to me that through their misguided idolatry they were saying something that needed to be heard. But by 2016 I had started to notice other, less defensible strains of thought within that world and in the #tcc, Tumblr's True Crime Community. For instance, Nazi imagery popping up next to Columbiner content. Suddenly, the community's tone seemed less puppyish and more straightforwardly angry. Or had this level of contempt been there all along, but I had just been better at turning a blind eye to it before, not wanting to give the posters the satisfaction of my outrage? In any case, it was growing harder to maintain any kind of critical distance from the Columbiners. I wasn't the only one that year who was wondering how you could tell the difference between ironic Nazis and teen-shock Nazis and actual Nazis. And whether there was even a difference at all.

Before Lindsay adopted "school shooter chic" as her aesthetic, she had tried on another identity that inspired hatred and disgust: she was a self-proclaimed National Socialist. "As a Nazi, I rather like being seen as a threat," she wrote in a comic she drew in high school. By the time she was in college, she was spending most of her online hours with fascists. Her internet boyfriend, Slavros, was the founder of Iron March, an influential forum for internet Nazis. Slavros lived in Russia, so it was unlikely that he and Lindsay would ever meet in real life. Still, she was obsessively devoted to him and skyped with him whenever she could.

The few hundred members of Iron March made fun of social-justice warriors, got in heated debates about the differences between white nationalists and Bolshevik Socialists and neo-Nazis, and attempted to uncover fascist themes in children's movies such as *The Brave Little Toaster*. One member wrote a long post praising Elliot Rodger, the incel who murdered six people in Isla Vista, California, as a "beta ubermensch." The layers of irony and meme culture and in-jokes made it hard for me to get a handle on Iron Marchers' actual ideology, beyond their generic, racially inflected hatefulness, when I looked through their archive. "Most of what is posted is not meant to be taken serious, it should be obvious that a large portion of it is not remotely serious," one member wrote. Reading through old posts, I felt unsettled in a way that I associate with being on the internet in the mid-2010s, which too often felt like navigating slippery ground. It was impossible to tell whether everyone else was joking or not. Every reaction to offensive content seemed like a trap: if you took the poster seriously, you were a fool and a dupe; if you didn't, you risked complicity—because it was increasingly clear that underneath the internet's ironic racism was a firm bedrock of actual racism.

(Predictably, things ended badly for Iron March. In 2017, one prolific poster named Devon Arthurs began writing about his conversion to Islam. Some of his fellow fascists thought he was just "memeing and pranking"; others dismissed it as "some autistic phase." That May, Arthurs took hostages at a Tampa vape shop. After police arrested him, he sent them to his apartment, where they discovered the bodies of two of his friends and fellow neo-Nazis; Arthurs had allegedly killed them because they disrespected his new religion. A fourth neo-Nazi who called himself Odin was also discovered outside Arthurs's apartment, dressed in camo, sobbing. He subsequently pled guilty to explosives charges. Six months after the arrests and murders, the Iron March website shut down under mysterious circumstances.)

At the time, internet cynics lumped the online Nazis together with the serial killer fetishists and the dumbest goths and dismissed them all as edgelords: kids who tried to be scary online. I thought of most of these edgelords as basement-dwellers, pale faces lit by the glow of their computer screens, puffing themselves up with nihilism. An edgelord was a scrawny guy with a LARP-y vibe, possibly wearing a cloak, dreaming of omnipotence. Or a girl with excessive eyeliner and lots of Tumblr posts about self-harm. The disturbing content posted by edgelords was undermined by its predictability: "The image as shock and the image as cliché are two aspects of the same presence," as Susan Sontag said. It was easy to dismiss them, these kids who thought they were frightening but who were actually pathetic—though, as the 2010s wore on, and as more and more alienated, internet-obsessed young men shot up yoga studios and drove their cars into crowds, it was increasingly unclear whether "pathetic" and "frightening" were such distinct categories after all.

Lindsay also seemed to take pleasure in being difficult to categorize. Her online presence was a confounding mix of cute, taboo, nerdy, fascist, and homicidal. She described herself as "the George Costanza of online neofascists" and as "a post-ironic neo-nazi edgelord who worships school shooters." She posted images of a swastika made of cute cat faces, and of a gaggle of My Little Ponies embracing Hitler. She wasn't secretive about her political beliefs; the short stories she wrote for her English classes included characters with such names as Svastikron, and one of her favorite hats was a replica of an old SS cap. Her Tumblr username was cockswastika. While the other members of her school's role-playing game club chose to portray such characters as "gentle giants and elves," according to Szigeti, Lindsay was busy doodling pictures of a Nazi ghost.

Lindsay told James her mom knew that she was a Nazi, but kept trying to dismiss it as a phase or a joke. When Lindsay wrote Nazi-themed creative-writing assignments, her teachers occasionally made her rewrite them; other times, they attempted positive reinforcement, praising her creativity and ignoring the fascist themes. After turning in one particularly genocidal story in college, Lindsay was called in to meet with the dean. Reconciling this painfully shy, acne-plagued half-Asian girl with her rhetoric about godlike supremacy and racial purity enacted through violence must have been difficult. Should the college be scared of her? Feel sorry for her? Once in class she pulled her phone out of her pocket and her professor laughed nervously: *For a second, I thought that was a gun!*

In 2013, the year before she met James, Slavros broke up with Lindsay and began dating a woman in Moscow. Lindsay tried and failed to kill herself, then began harassing him and his new girlfriend so intensely that she was banned from Iron March. By the time she found the Columbiners, Lindsay had been exiled from the fascist Web for trolling too hard, had no real-life friends to speak of, and was staring down a future that didn't have much meaning for her. She thought she might lose followers when she started sharing Columbine content, but the opposite happened—school-shooting posts were quite popular, and her Tumblr soon had more followers than ever.

Murder wasn't the only thing that motivated Harris and Klebold; they were also out for glory. They planned to make copies of the Basement Tapes, their videotaped manifesto, and mail them to local television stations. They never got around to it, and in the aftermath of the massacre the police declined to release the tapes, worried that they'd inspire copycats. (The Basement Tapes are the Holy Grail of the Columbiner world; Tumblr is full of posts aching for their release.) More recent mass shooters used social media to circulate their writings or YouTube confessions. Before the far-right shooter Anders Breivik murdered seventy-seven people in Norway in 2011, he issued a media kit of sorts, mass-distributing copies of his fifteen-hundred-page, heavily plagiarized manifesto, which included a dozen publicity photos of him playing dress-up in various military costumes. Some mass shooters seemed less motivated by murder than by the attention that was given to mass murderers. Killing people had become a public relations strategy; some shooters seemed to see themselves as macabre versions of social media influencers, imagining a public eager for details of the music they listened to, the clothes they wore, the poetry they wrote.

From their seven weeks of Facebook-chat conversations, it's clear that Lindsay and James were driven less by the desire to kill than to be seen as killers. They spent more time daydreaming about how people would react to their massacre than they did planning it, and the prospect of becoming celebrities in their own fandom excited both of them. They imagined the Columbiner community flying into a tizzy when the news broke: "OMG GUYS I THINK SHALLOW EXISTENCES AND COCKSWASTIKA JUST KILLED PEOPLE." Maybe everyone would first assume it was a joke, Lindsay predicted, "but then NOPE."

If it all went well—and how could it not?—they'd inspire a fandom of their own. Lindsay predicted that Tumblrs would be devoted to the two of them, featuring the requisite disclaimer: *I don't condone their actions but they're still kinda hot.* Maybe someone would hack into Lindsay's Google account and release her novel. Maybe it would become a collector's item. Maybe these very conversations would be released, complete with all the racy images from their sex chats. Certainly they would inspire fan fiction. "No one would care about us if for whatever unholy reason we ended up living 'normal' lives," Lindsay wrote—but they wouldn't be normal; they would be in the pantheon of mass murderers. Picturing what it would be like to be on the other side of fascination, to be the person obsessed about rather than the person obsessing, was intoxicating. "Imagine the people in the #columbine tag reposting all of the shit that we've been saying over these past few days," Lindsay wrote. "Kind of surreal."

"They'll be reblogging literally everything of ours," James replied. "Every picture of you will be viewed by so many of these people."

James liked to think about all the celebrities who would soon know his name. Lindsay wanted Lana Del Rey to write a song about them. James hoped he and Lindsay would inspire a wave of copycat killers. They dwelled on the aftermath of their massacre—not so much the carnage itself, but the *coverage* of the carnage. The public reaction to shootings was so rote by now that they could predict how it would play out, beat by beat: the exhausted recitation of thoughts and prayers, strangers' saccharine tribute videos for the victims, solemn-faced news anchors opining about mental health. "The story will go like this," Lindsay wrote. "One of us was manipulating the other and telling them what they wanted to hear so they'd carry out the massacre. . . . Who was the clinical sociopath??? Who was the promising young person whose life was thrown away???"

If the spectacle of killing was more a means to notoriety than an end in itself, they had one big problem—they expected they wouldn't be around to enjoy any of it, because they planned to kill themselves before they got arrested. "We could go on the internet with our phones once we're done but before we die," James suggested. "We could get a glimpse of the early news reports. Plus check Tumblr one last time, see what people are saying about our posts."

"Maybe there'll already be a post about the massacre circulating," Lindsay suggested. She could reblog it before she shot herself.

When James prodded her about logistics—fundamental stuff, such as where the shooting should happen and whom they should kill—Lindsay said she didn't much care. (Although when he suggested a nearby elementary school as a target, she did voice an objection: "I'd rather not.") Instead, she obsessed over aesthetics. Should she wear her green jacket, which had more of a military vibe? Or her black jacket, and go for a starker, monochromatic look? Which would photograph better? And what color lipstick should she wear? James tried to talk her out of wearing high heels during the attack—he imagined that she might have to run, to tackle people—but she insisted that they were crucial to her outfit, and that she was used to wearing them.

During the next few weeks, the details of the plan slowly came together over Facebook chat. Lindsay would use her Christmas money and whatever other funds she could scrounge up to buy a one-way plane ticket to Halifax. While she was in transit, James would shoot his mother in her bed, then kill his father when he came home from work. Meanwhile, Lindsay would get a ride from the airport with James's best friend, Randy. Sometime that evening, James would shoot Randy, who didn't want to live but had never been able to finish the job himself. Then James and Lindsay would lose their virginity to each other. The next day, they'd head to the mall, where they'd open fire on the mindless, unsuspecting Saturday-morning shoppers. James said he planned to target middle-aged women, his least favorite demographic: "fucking wrinkly, fat, short hair, probably believes in god. and is just the sweetest person you could ever know. I want to see them all bleed." Lindsay would target "basic bitches" and people who looked genetically inferior.

Their massacre would be optimized for virality. James would make one of his victims hold the camera so they'd be filming their own murder. If someone had a phone out and was documenting the shooting, he'd spare the person so there'd be more footage. He gallantly offered to die second so he could upload video of Lindsay's suicide before he finished himself off.

On New Year's Eve, James almost cried with exhaustion and relief. Soon, he'd be dead, which meant he'd never have to go through this miserable, "festive" ritual again. He was ragged, close to the edge, thinking about suicide every day. He began taking forty-five-minute showers so he could sob without his parents hearing. The more he and Lindsay talked about the massacre, the more James insisted that it happen soon—spring was too far away, he couldn't stand the idea of living that long. February 1, they decided.

As James unraveled, he took comfort in his online relationship with Lindsay.

JAMES: I wish I could be hugging you right now. I need it bad.
LINDSAY: I'd hug you, and I'd hold you

JAMES: Thank you for not finding me weak

JAMES: Even though I cry constantly

At his worst moments, she told him to imagine his head resting on her lap. Or on her chest so he could listen to her heartbeat. The sweetness was undercut by the context:

LINDSAY: I wonder if people are going to be reading these chatlogs thinking about how cute we are before accidentally remembering that we're killers who are both incapable of relating to other human beings in any meaningful way?

JAMES: I hope we'll fuck with their emotions.

JAMES: 'Do I hate them or not!!???'

Though she acted confident online, in her day-to-day life Lindsay wasn't doing much better than James. She would chat with him until six in the morning and then sleep until midafternoon. With no job or friends or future—she'd been rejected by the Peace Corps—her life was increasingly confined to the computer. One night she dreamed that her mother threatened to take away her laptop, so she killed her with her bare hands. In other dreams she had superstrength and could fling people across the room with the smallest flick of her wrist.

She grew increasingly detached from any reality apart from the plan—and her novel, which she was still diligently working on. "It's really weird, I can't separate my characters from Eric from myself any more," she told James. Her thoughts grew increasingly bizarre; she became preoccupied with the idea that she and James were literally possessed by the spirits of Harris and Klebold: "Maybe Eric and Dylan have somehow become us, become part of our minds," she theorized. "We both feel like we 'died' a long time ago, maybe it's because we've taken on the minds of these actual dead people, and that marks the time we both died. You want to die so badly because you know this isn't the body you actually belong in. . . . When Eric and Dylan both died, their mission on Earth wasn't really finished yet, so they had to take us over at some point." This theory would also explain why people told Lindsay that she was emotionally stunted, and why James could never get it together enough to keep a job—they were both homicidal high school boys trapped in the wrong bodies.

January 9 was Lindsay's birthday. Dinner with her mother felt surreal, as if she were there and not there at the same time. Her mother thought she was talking to Lindsay Souvannarath, age twenty-three, but was in fact talking to mass murderer Eric Harris, who'd been dead since 1999. Over the next few weeks, Lindsay's theories grew even more complex: maybe the world was a simulation, and she and James—that is, Harris and Klebold—were the only ones with real consciousness. "The people we're going to kill could very well not even be people," she told James. "Another realization: If it turns out that no one else is real, then the whole 'lack of empathy' thing makes a hell of a lot of sense."

Suddenly February 1 was just ten days away, and Lindsay didn't have a plane ticket. She and James decided to push the massacre back to Valentine's Day. The two of them were so keyed up that they were barely eating or sleeping. James figured out where his dad hid his ammunition and sent Lindsay pictures of neat rows of bullets. He'd only found thirteen for the rifle and twenty-three shells for the shotgun, but that would have to do. He began carrying around in his pocket the bullet he planned to kill himself with. Sometimes he ran his thumb over it, just to feel its secret weight. He kept it with him even when he was sleeping. It was a comfort to remember that soon he'd be done with the miserable work of living.

But then the first week of February passed, and there was still no plane ticket. On the ninth, five days before the massacre was supposed to go down, Lindsay sent James a message: "So I have some bad news." She had procrastinated long enough that the only tickets left were too expensive. There was a cheap flight on the sixteenth, although that would mean a weekday massacre, which was obviously not ideal. There was an even cheaper one on March 2, if he was willing to wait that long.

James didn't reply as he normally would. He thought he'd found the perfect partner, but then she turned out to be just as useless as everyone else. He was terse with Lindsay and then gave her the silent treatment for an entire day—an eternity in their relationship. The idea of living another few weeks, even another few days, was physically painful to him—how could she not understand that? "What's the point of choosing a later date if you're not going to buy the ticket then either?" he typed eventually.

Lindsay scrambled to reassure him: "I'm sure Eric and Dylan experienced setbacks as well. You have every right to be upset with me but please let's not lose hope. . . . I know how much this meant to you and I'm just a complete idiot sometimes." She told James that she'd got enough money together to buy the more expensive ticket after all. The Valentine's Day plan would proceed as they'd envisioned. Basically nothing was left in her bank account, but what did that matter? She told James that she would arrive in Halifax a little before midnight on Friday: "We are the dead living."

Lindsay wrote another online friend that day, "I'm leaving for Canada tomorrow, and the only way I'm coming back is in a body bag. This is what I was meant to do my whole life. . . . I've had so many revelations this past month and a half. . . . I don't expect it to make much sense right now. But it goes like this: I want to kill, he wants to die. Just like Eric and Dylan."

On her last day in her parents' house, Lindsay packed a small suitcase. She wasn't bringing much along with her to Canada: a change of clothes, the skeleton mask she planned to wear during the shooting, her makeup, her laptop, a couple of comics, and *Thus Spoke Zarathustra*, her favorite book. It was eerie to think that these were the last hours she'd spend inside this house where she'd grown up. She painted her nails to pass the time. She also worked on a manifesto of sorts, a strident Nietzsche pastiche with Ayn Rand overtones. It talked about battles and hate and strength, about being beyond good and evil, about how being free from empathy means that "the isolated man sees the world for what it truly is." She scheduled it to go up on Tumblr after the attacks, when she presumed she'd be dead and millions of people would be searching for answers.

In Halifax, James took the shotgun out from under his bed and loaded it. He'd reserved three of the meager stash of bullets to kill his parents with, in case either of their murders required more than one shot. James's best friend, Randy, sent a message apologizing for not being able to participate in the massacre: "I don't know what I am james. I've been through so much shit in my life and yet still I could not raise my hand to another. . . . I'm sorry I couldn't be your dylan Klebold." Randy also made a video he intended his parents to see after his death. "I was never a good son," he told the camera.

Lindsay and James exchanged a few final messages before she snuck out of the house early on the morning of the thirteenth. She was about to make the three-mile walk to the train station before she'd board a series of flights that would eventually take her to Halifax. "How are you feeling?" James asked.

"Eager," she said.

Lindsay and James's plan began to fall apart almost immediately. The first obstacle: James's dad didn't go to work as usual that day. "So yeah, I'm going to have to wait until tomorrow to kill them," James messaged Lindsay. That meant she would have to spend the night at Randy's. And *that* meant they couldn't fuck all night as planned. James sounded dispirited; it was still afternoon, but he told Lindsay he was going back to sleep. She was about to board her final flight. Within a few hours, she'd be in Halifax.

Sometime earlier that day, the Halifax police's Crime Stoppers tip line received information about a local teenager, his online girl-friend, and their Valentine's Day plans. A quick internet search turned up some troubling pictures of James dressed in fatigues, fondling weapons—enough confirmation of the tip to justify an arrest. That afternoon, plainclothes officers placed James's parents' house under surveillance. Because James had access to weapons, they decided that an outright confrontation was too dangerous.

Early that evening, James's parents left the house to run errands. Police officers stopped them and told them that there was an issue with their son, and that violent threats had been made online. *Someone is threatening Jamie?* his mother, Patti, asked, confused. No, the officer explained gently. Her son was the *source* of the threats. Patti admitted that her son had been acting secretive, but said that she had never known him to be violent. Yes, there were guns in the house, but she didn't think he had access to them. She was sure he'd cooperate with whatever the police asked him to do. He was a good kid. Both of James's parents begged to go back into the house to speak with their son, to sort out this whole mess, but police refused—it wasn't safe, they insisted.

At 8:59 p.m., a Halifax police officer called James's cell phone. During their five-minute conversation, James was cooperative and unemotional, the officer said later. He told James that police had seen his social media posts and wanted him to come in for questioning. Officers were outside his home in unmarked cars; there didn't need to be any fuss. James agreed to meet the police outside. He was heading downstairs right now, he said. He'd be out in just a minute. But the officer watching the front door didn't see any signs of movement. "Are you outside?" the cop asked. "Yes," James lied. Moments later, the officers heard the sharp blast of a hunting rifle. James had shot himself in the head.

Lindsay's flight landed in Halifax just before midnight. Although the border agents had been alerted to look out for her, thanks to the Crime Stoppers tip, Lindsay somehow passed through the first customs screening. But the next agent she spoke to thought she seemed strange. She had bad teeth, bad skin, and an odd affect, he said later. She also had a one-way ticket bought at the last minute, little cash, and a small suitcase. He wondered if she was on drugs or was transporting drugs. She told the agent she was in town to spend a "memorable" Valentine's weekend with her boyfriend, but that she didn't know what his address was. Officials soon connected her to the Crime Stoppers tip and arrested her. Randy, who was waiting for her at the international-arrivals area, was also taken into custody. At first, Lindsay wasn't too worried. "What had I really done, other than have some conversations on Facebook and get on a plane? I didn't think I would be in that much trouble," she said later. The day after her arrest, she bragged to another prisoner about the failed plan: "I had a skull mask I was going to wear, and he had his scream mask. We would've looked perfect." The prisoner was an undercover officer, and a transcript of the conversation was added to the growing trove of evidence against her.

As news of the arrests and the planned massacre broke, the Columbiner community reacted with shock, though not in the way that Lindsay had hoped. James had been a popular poster, and many of his online friends refused to believe he was capable of murder. Rumors began to circulate that he was the one who'd phoned in the Crime Stoppers tip. (He was not.) Randy, too, inspired sympathy; a petition was even circling: "Halifax Police Department: Give Randall Shepherd the help he deserves!"

Spooked by the rush of publicity, some Columbiners who'd known James, Randy, or Lindsay deleted their Tumblrs. Otherwise, though, the fandom proceeded without much disruption. With so much turnover within the community, in a few months plenty of people on the scene didn't even know what had happened. Every so often, someone would post a hot picture of James, or some sad musings about him: "imagine if there was an afterlife and James has met Eric and Dylan in it and they've become friends." Apart from one irritating and edgelordish white supremacist from New Mexico, hardly anyone posted online about Lindsay. When her manifesto was entered into evidence, though, someone did put that on Tumblr. The comments were dismissive: "Lol this is annoying af."

In November 2016, Randy Shepherd, James's friend who helped keep the massacre plan a secret, was sentenced to ten years in prison for conspiracy to commit murder; six months later, when it became clear that her chat logs would be admissible as evidence, Lindsay switched her plea from not guilty to guilty. That meant that she would forgo her right to a trial, and that her sentence—which could range anywhere from ten years to life in prison—would be determined by a judge. No one had any idea how it would go for her since Canada had never seen a comparable case; unlike in the United States, there weren't an abundance of mass-shooting (and prospective mass-shooting) precedents to draw from.

In April 2018, I flew to Canada to attend Lindsay's sentencing hearing. My flight landed close to midnight, around the same time that Lindsay had arrived in Halifax three years earlier. I watched my fellow passengers hoisting suitcases for strangers and stepping aside to let others go ahead and was caught off guard by an ugly twinge of suspicion. Who could say whether any of them had murder on their minds? My Airbnb hosts had left the front door to their downtown apartment unlocked and a handwritten note on the table: "Welcome to our city. Please make yourself at home. It is very safe here."

The Nova Scotia license plates informed me that the province was "Canada's ocean playground," but all the taffy shops on the seaside boardwalk were closed for the season, and the offshore wind was biting and punitive. I had packed inadequate sweaters and was stuck with a shiver I couldn't get rid of. Wandering through town, I found some gloomy graveyards and a pretty little park where a miniature replica of the *Titanic* drifted along, serene and intact. I felt inexplicably nervous, as if I were the one who was about to be on trial.

Perhaps part of me felt as though I should have been. I couldn't stop thinking about how I, like Lindsay, had internalized the idea that murderers were fascinating. Over the years, I've read thousands of pages about various varieties of Killer (Zodiac, Green River, BTK, Lonely Hearts) and Strangler (Hillside, Boston); don't even get me started on the time I've devoted to goofy little Charlie Manson. My brothers can have entire conversations where they're just tossing sports statistics back and forth; certain friends and I can do the same thing with serial murderers.

Most of the killer-centric media I consume at least ostensibly condemns its subject. But a clear ambivalence is at work, too. Would any of us linger so long if there weren't? The killer, or at least the version of the killer who hogs most of the airtime, is set apart from the rest of humanity because of his bad deeds, but that apartness also marks him as *special*. Something of the animal is in him, and also something of the artist. He's a mastermind, someone who doesn't play by the same rules as the rest of us. (This celebrity killer is almost always a "he," both because the vast majority of all murderers are male, and because the stereotypical roles allotted to female killers—the bad mom, the jealous ex, the gender-nonconforming monster—are less easy to glamorize.)

If anyone should've known better than to fall for this trope, it was me. I'm a reporter; I've met murderers. In my experience, they tend to be dull, damaged people, nothing like the cultural construction of the evil genius. I've underlined the appropriate Simone Weil quotation: "Imaginary evil is romantic and varied; real evil is gloomy, monotonous, barren, boring." Yet if I'm flipping through the channels on a motel TV and a teaser promises to give me a peek inside the mind of a murderer, I'll always stay tuned—as if something incredibly complex were going on in those minds, something deserving of my time and scrutiny. As any toddler can tell you, negative attention is still attention. I couldn't shake the sense that those hours I spent zoning out to *Dateline* contributed, even if in the smallest way, to the mystique that swirled around people such as Harris and Klebold.

Lindsay's sentencing hearing began the next morning, in a third-floor courtroom paneled in warm wood. A dozen Canadian journalists, James's parents, and a handful of spectators clustered on the smooth benches. Eventually Lindsay was led in and sat facing away from me. She had narrow shoulders and wore her hair loose. After I'd spent so much virtual time with her, seeing her physical form was startling—she seemed so slight next to the bailiffs.

The prosecutors read aloud from the chat transcripts, focusing on the places where Lindsay fantasized at length, and in detail, about killing people. They noted that she had not expressed any remorse, except for regret that James had died. Her case, they argued, was most comparable to those involving terrorist plotters: "When it becomes unsafe to engage in ordinary activities—watching a soccer match, going to the mall—deterrence takes on a different dimension." Canada didn't yet have regular eruptions of mass violence like the United

States, which was all the more reason to make an example of Lindsay; it was crucial to illustrate that such threats were taken seriously here. They asked for a sentence of at least twenty years.

I tried to divine whether the judge—an older white man, dignified and enrobed—was sympathetic to their arguments. At times he seemed not to be. "Was there perhaps a certain limit on realistically how much carnage could've been created here?" he asked, frowning. It was true that there was a virtual feel to Lindsay and James's murder plot. Neither of them had experience with firearms; instead of going to a gun range to learn how to shoot, they watched YouTube videos. Their weapons were far from ideal massacre equipment, at least by the standards of US spree killers; the single-action shotgun would've needed to be reloaded after every shot, and the shells were birdshot—unlikely to be lethal, except at close range. James had never gotten around to making the Molotov cocktails he had talked about so confidently. Other than buying the plane ticket, picking out an outfit, and making some foreboding Tumblr posts, Lindsay had done little to physically prepare for the attack. Steps one and two of the plan—James killing his parents; Lindsay and James losing their virginity to each other—had fizzled even before the police got word of the attack.

Lindsay's court-appointed attorney made similar points, enunciating his words with debate-class precision. He argued that Lindsay was a good writer with an active imagination, but that she should not be punished because she used "colorful language." On the phone and in person, Lindsay was meek and polite, the opposite of frightening; only in writing did her words come alive. The chat logs showed that Lindsay and James "loved the idea of being notorious mass murderers but did virtually nothing to make it happen," the attorney said. He noted that a prison psychiatrist had given Lindsay preliminary diagnoses of Asperger's and severe depression. She was now receiving psychiatric treatment for the first time. The attorney thought a twelve-to-fifteen-year sentence would be fair.

The judge announced that he would give his verdict on Friday, which meant I had three gray days left to my own devices in Halifax. It should've felt like a reprieve, a vacation within a reporting trip. But Halifax seemed to have sunk me into a gloom I couldn't claw my way out of. Making pleasant small talk with strangers was an unexpected struggle. At first I blamed the storms—day two was worse than day one, rain-lashed and howling, umbrella-wrestling weather. Then I wondered whether the Haligonians were at fault—sure, they seemed friendly enough on the surface, but maybe they were actually sending out subtle cues warning me to keep away. That night I stayed in and ordered takeout, which I ate while reading Reddit threads about unsolved murders. I don't remember what I read, but I remember how it made me feel: full and empty at the same time.

Only the following day, when I was holed up in the city's spiffy new library, did I begin to understand what was happening to me. In the lobby, a youth chorus was singing something innocent and unabashed as I read through Lindsay and James's massive, multivolume chat transcripts. Then I came up short. In early February—on page 1179—James suggested that rather than shooting up the mall, they should target this library instead: "I'm telling you, that place gets packed since it's a new building, especially on weekends. Plus if we have molotov cocktails, we could throw them at all the books and the whole fucking place would go up in flames. . . . We could start on the first floor and work our way up, it's a huge open space, and people on the upper floors would be trapped. There are elevators but there's no way they'd all fit." James was right; the place was packed. I looked over at the books, the elevators, the upper floors, and then around at the other library patrons. A guy at a corner table was talking too loud, as if he imagined himself onstage. A woman was patiently helping a toddler walk up some stairs. The girl working the coffee-kiosk cash register stared out the window, a pensive look on her face. They were everywhere—just, you know, people. Irritating, generous, bored, boring, frivolous, sleepy normal people. Living their lives.

An image flashed across my brain—all of us screaming, stamping. This had been happening to me since I started working on this book, and this part of this book in particular—mental intrusions, brief, vivid visions of random violence. Like what if that three-year-old on the stairs was screaming. Like what if we were all barricading ourselves behind the coffee kiosk.

I closed my eyes and tried to breathe deep and re-center myself in my body. I hated when my mind went to these places. I had done the research, parsed the numbers; I knew how vanishingly small the odds of being a victim of a mass shooting were. I was a white woman in a library in Canada; statistically speaking, I was astronomically safe. Even so, some more lizardy part of my brain kept creating these personalized horror movies and playing them on the screen of my mind, against my will. Because what if. Because you never know. When I walked into buildings, I had started reflexively taking note of where the exits were. This low-key, ambient paranoia—this conviction that no place was secure and that any moment could tip into cataclysm—was a new feature of my consciousness, but it was lodged so firmly that I worried it was here to stay.

Obviously I had spent too much time mind-melding with Lindsay and James. But they weren't the only ones warping my sense of reality—it was also the many flavors of online Nazi, the school shooters and the girls who longed to love them, the edgelords and their aggressive brooding, cranky old Ayn Rand—all these various manifestations of a worldview that insisted what mattered most was power, and that getting attention gave you power, and that the quickest way to get attention was through violence. I had never bought into that narrative; survival-of-the-fittest stories seemed to me like a lazy way to justify structural advantages. But I had been steeping in Lindsay's flawed logic for so long, I had accidentally begun to absorb some of its ugly lessons.

In the library lobby, the children were still singing. No one had a gun; I was perfectly safe. The flash of internal horror passed as quickly as it had descended. But it left a residue behind, and all afternoon I felt as if something unpleasant and difficult to name was gumming up my thinking. I had been worried that paying close attention to killers lent them some sinister glamour, and that the natural end point of that fascination was someone such as Lindsay, who believed that the only way for her to matter was by murdering people. But what I hadn't thought about was what all that time spent in dark places might do to me.

"Mean world syndrome" was a theory developed in the 1970s by a professor of communications named George Gerbner. Gerbner argued that the more media people consumed, the more likely they were to believe that the world was a dangerous place; in the decades since, a number of studies have borne out Gerbner's conclusions. Mean world syndrome is one explanation, perhaps, for why even though crime has declined precipitously since the early 1990s, pretty much every year a majority of people, particularly women, instead believe that it's rising.

A distorted sense of danger isn't just psychologically taxing; it also encourages us to perceive risk where there isn't any. Steeping in ominous stories can make people into threats themselves. The news is full of examples of how ambient anxiety gets turned against people of color going about their daily lives—taking a nap in the student lounge; walking down the street; selling lemonade. I thought of the woman who called the cops on two Native American brothers who were on a college tour at Colorado State. The teenagers made the woman "nervous," she told the 911 operator. "If it's nothing, I'm sorry. But it actually made me like feel sick and I've never felt like that."

Many people are feeling sick these days, for many reasons. But we should all be careful about the stories we tell ourselves to explain why.

Schools have changed in the wake of Columbine—which is to say, schools have become increasingly surveilled and policed. The idea that another Columbine could happen anywhere at any time has been used to justify a number of interventions aimed at keeping kids safe. Certain kinds of interventions, that is. Attempts to enact significant firearm regulations—making it harder to get them, or keeping better track of them, or limiting the sale of the most lethal kinds of them— have largely been legislative failures. Instead, the focus has been elsewhere, such as on buying more surveillance cameras and hiring more cops. In 1999, 19 percent of schools had security cameras; by 2015, more than 80 percent did. Many more armed resource officers are in school hallways today than twenty years ago. Metal detectors, zero-tolerance policies, and systematic locker searches are now a normal part of the school day in many parts of the country. School safety has become its own industry: Security consultants with military or law enforcement backgrounds hire themselves out to conduct vulnerability assessments and create "threat management solutions" for school districts. "There are no safe zones," one such firm warns. "There is no room for error." Over 70 percent of schools have run active-shooter drills. (Perhaps another reason school shootings loom so large in our collective imagination is that we force students to enact them every year.)

The imperative to *keep the children safe*—with its rhetorical echoes of the Satanic Panic—is used to justify any number of alarming developments. "There is something disconcerting about needing security cameras, panic buttons, and armed officers at schools," an August 2018 article in *Popular Mechanics* noted. "But if they're used to guard banks and stadiums and museums and subways and movie theaters, experts say, shouldn't they also be used to protect our children?"

But those "experts"—some of them the very same consultants who sell threat-management solutions—have a narrow understanding of protection, one steeped in militarized language and oriented toward security (that is, policing). Efforts focused on improving school climate, increasing counseling, and providing support to struggling students and families have not gotten anywhere near as much funding or attention. When researchers in Colorado surveyed counselors at public high schools throughout the state to learn how policies and procedures had changed since Columbine, they learned that 63 percent of schools had imposed tighter security procedures, 40 percent had instituted stricter discipline, and 32 percent had boosted their security presence on school grounds; in contrast, a mere 13 percent had increased their mental health staff, and only 5 to 7 percent had increased interventions for at-risk students or funded more programs to help students deal with emotions.

Whether these various actions keep kids safe depends, in part, on what "safe" means, and also on which kids you're talking about. Zero-tolerance policies, which have expanded in the wake of Columbine, have had a disproportionate effect on students of color, who are more likely to get suspended or expelled and who are also more likely to be punished for minor infractions, despite that black students "did not generally misbehave or endorse deviant attitudes" more than white students, one study found. Zero-tolerance enforcement in schools is about far more than just Columbine—it echoes broader broken-windows policing trends, for one—but the shooting and its successors have provided a cover for such policies.

The outcomes of the school-shooter era include more cops in schools, a more punitive stance toward rule breaking, and a collapse in distinction between minor (dress code) and major (bringing a gun to school) violations, all of which contribute to the school-to-prison pipeline. Considering that black and Latino students witness gun violence at school at much greater rates, this means that students of color are doubly burdened by school violence: both through the trauma of witnessing it and through the racialized enforcement that ensues.

How big a threat are school shootings, really? At least one hundred forty-three students, teachers, staff, and family members were killed during assaults on schools between 1998 and early 2018, according to an exhaustive analysis by the *Washington Post*, and another 254 were injured. (The study only considered incidents at primary and secondary schools.) Three incidents—Columbine, Sandy Hook, and Parkland—accounted for 43 percent of those fatalities. Each of those deaths was an unimaginable tragedy for a family and a community— but the raw numbers are quite small.

American children *are* exposed to gun violence at alarming rates— it's the third-leading cause of death for kids in the United States—but rarely at the hands of a sociopath in a ski mask stalking through the school cafeteria. American children are vastly more likely to die by suicide using a gun or to be accidentally shot by a firearm. In recent years, toddlers in the United States have accidentally shot people, and sometimes themselves, at a rate of almost one per week—which is to say that, logically speaking, you should be more afraid of a kindergartner in a house with unsecured firearms than a teenager in a trench coat.

But counting the number of victims doesn't come close to painting a full picture of the damage done by a school shooting. Exposure to violence is physically and psychologically taxing—and more than 187,000 students have experienced a shooting on campus during school hours over that twenty-year period, according to the *Post*. Random violence casts a long shadow; it worms its way into our nightmares, gets held up as justification for stricter policies. And the idea furthered by each high-profile shooting—that one way to air your grievances is to bring a gun to a public place and point it at strangers—is persistently infectious. *School shooting* is starting to seem like an obsolete phrase—similar to *going postal*, which fell out of favor once workplace shootings expanded beyond post offices in the 1990s—now that massacres have taken place at churches and country music festivals and nightclubs.

Amid all this darkness, it's possible to see the faintest glimmer of a silver lining. The proliferation of random violence means that killing strangers is no longer a surefire path to becoming famous; off the top of my head, I couldn't tell you the name of the man who shot hundreds of people in Las Vegas in 2017, or the man who murdered twenty-six in a church in Sutherland Springs, Texas, one month later. Both were among the deadliest shootings in modern US history, knocking Columbine out of the macabre top-ten list, but their perpetrators have not become celebrities. In part that's because the media has made a concerted, collective effort to avoid mentioning the names of those who commit mass murder whenever possible, and to instead focus their coverage on victims. Perhaps we're also suffering from shooter fatigue. After scores of massacres, after the exhausting manifestos and YouTube confessions, after all the trials and press conferences, maybe we've finally realized that we won't get any satisfying answers from those who pulled the trigger. You could read all this as some form of victory—at least we're no longer granting cultural-icon status to spree killers. Or maybe it's just that we've accommodated intermittent mass violence as our new normal.

* * *

On the morning that Lindsay would receive her sentence, I woke up with a swimmy feeling in my stomach. I still hadn't figured out how to think about her, and I had no idea what the judge would do. In her online presence and in her conversations with James, Lindsay was a god of sex and violence, someone to be desired and feared in equal measure. At times, the chat transcripts sounded like a role-playing game in which Lindsay was adopting the voice of a character in one of her (or Ayn Rand's) novels, confident and commanding and in control. If you took that version of her at face value, she was a serious threat deserving serious punishment.

But another Lindsay seemed meek and intimidated by the world. Her mother and grandparents wrote letters to the judge assuring him that Lindsay was bright and imaginative but "emotionally immature" and had been socially ostracized for being biracial. ("Everything my mother said in her letter to the judge was a complete lie," Lindsay told me. "Not once in my life was I ever bullied for being biracial.") She would never have followed through on the plot, her family believed; she was "incapable of violence." (James's mother told me the same thing—if he hadn't died by suicide that day, she is convinced he would never have murdered anyone at the mall.) Though the distance between Lindsay's online persona and her IRL presentation was vast, parents don't always know their kids as well as they think they do. And if most of Lindsay's life was spent online, then who was to say which version of her was more real?

It was April 20, 2018, the nineteenth anniversary of the day that Harris and Klebold shot up Columbine High School, a coincidence of scheduling that no one seemed to notice except me—and, I presumed, Lindsay. The judge spoke slowly, as if considering the case caused him physical pain. From his high seat, he spoke about Lindsay, James, and Randy—how they were each socially isolated and despondent, and how they had each come to be fixated on Columbine. "As with dripping water on a stone, the repeated internet messages and imagery justifying and glorifying extreme violence left an indelible mark on each of them," he said. He turned to Lindsay and told her that she bore moral responsibility for James's suicide. "Ms. Souvannarath's prospects for rehabilitation are very questionable. She is an ongoing danger to public safety, which danger will persist for an indefinite period of time." And then he sentenced her to life in prison.

A few weeks after my return home to Texas, I was still obsessing about Lindsay's punishment. Court proceedings are supposed to provide some sense of closure, but this situation felt unfinished. I kept getting stuck on this one thing: how in imposing the strictest sentence possible, one usually reserved for the most violent criminals—over 90 percent of people serving life terms in Canadian prisons have been convicted of murder—the judge was validating Lindsay's virtual self, giving too much credence to the part of her that loudly proclaimed how frightening she was, how unlike other people. A Canadian firearms expert was claiming publicly that the massacre she had helped mastermind was practically impossible, given her and James's weaponry and lack of experience. Meanwhile, in prison she seemed to be retreating even further into her internal world, someone who knew her had told me. That didn't seem right to me.

But then again, it wasn't accurate to say that she hadn't actually done anything. She'd unsettled a whole city, and worse. In 2017, Lindsay's one outspoken fan, the white nationalist who wouldn't stop posting about her on message boards, returned to his former high school in rural New Mexico, where he shot and killed two student-athletes, then himself. That wasn't her fault, but it wasn't unrelated. Who's to say what she would have done at the mall that afternoon? I couldn't sort any of it out.

It's too bad there was no way to sentence her in the virtual realm, a friend of mine said one day. It was a funny idea, and it appealed to me. I liked imagining what a Tumblr tribunal would look like. If that was the world that Lindsay cared about the most, maybe that was the world where she needed to face consequences.

In August 2018, Tumblr announced updates to its terms of service, announcing that it was going to take a harder stance against hate speech, pornographic images, and violent content. "The glorification of mass murders like Columbine, Sandy Hook, and Parkland could inspire copycat violence," the company said in a statement. The new guidelines warned users not to "post violent content or gore just to be shocking" and banned "content that encourages or incites violence, or glorifies acts of violence or the perpetrators." Meanwhile, Nikolas Cruz, who committed the deadliest school shooting (to date, at least) at Marjory Stoneman Douglas High School in Parkland, Florida, was getting record amounts of mail, even as some of his classmates were gaining notoriety in another way—by spearheading a youth movement for gun control.

I checked in on some of the Columbiners I had followed back in 2012 to see how they were reacting to the changes in Tumblr's rules, but most had deleted their blogs long ago. One was still active on the site, but she now mostly seemed to reblog posts supporting abortion rights and punching Nazis. "This isn't a community I would like to align myself to anymore," she told me. It seemed that she had found another way to be furious, and I can't say I was sorry to see it.

SCARY STORIES
TO TELL IN THE DARK

My whole life, I've been sharing scary stories with other women. Sometimes we talk about things that happened to us, or to our friends; sometimes we talk about strangers we heard about on a podcast. They might be accounts of near misses, or ones with awful, bloody endings. Their beginnings, though, are almost always innocuous: She went to a party. I was riding my bike home. My sister met the sweetest guy.

There's a perverse comfort in pooling this dark knowledge. Part of the curriculum of growing up as a girl is to learn lessons about your vulnerability—if not from your parents, then from a culture that's fascinated by wounded women. From an early age, women are primed to notice potential danger. For better or worse, this can make us more attuned to catastrophe, to how quickly daily life can slip into something terrifying.

At its best, true crime is a recognition of this subterranean knowledge; it brings it up and out into the open. Through crime stories, we can talk about the violence that's been done to us, or to people we love; we can tell difficult truths and work through our anxieties. These accounts of the worst parts of human experience open up conversations about subjects that might otherwise be taboo: fear, abuse, exploitation, injustice, rage.

The four women in this book were encouraged to lead small lives or to keep parts of themselves hidden; becoming entwined with a famous crime enlarged their worlds and allowed them to express things they couldn't otherwise voice. Building tiny homicidal puzzles enabled Frances Glessner Lee to briefly access the respect, authority, and control that was otherwise denied her. Lisa Statman's relationship with a famously tragic family transformed her into a spokeswoman for blameless victimhood. Lorri Davis, the "kite without a string," fell in love and became part of a grand redemptive story. Lindsay Souvannarath hoped to assert her superiority by committing mass murder.

Everyone else, even those of us prone to falling into crime funks, likely won't take things as far as these women did. Still, we may be similarly seduced by the outsize characters who populate true crime stories, the brilliant detectives and sinister criminal masterminds; the tragic victims and heroic defenders. These archetypes are compelling in part because they are so reductive. Narratives of virtue and vice populated by good guys and bad guys assure us of our own righteousness, even as they often eliminate nuance and ambiguity in the process.

Detective stories satisfy our desire for tidy solutions. They make the seductive promise that we can tame the chaos of crime by breaking it down into small, comprehensible pieces. They allow us to inhabit the role of the objective observer, someone who exists outside and above the scene of the crime, scrutinizing the horror as if it were a dollhouse. That objectivity is a fantasy; the forensic scandals that have sent so many innocent people to prison are an example of what can happen when we overestimate our capacity to understand. Stories that invite us to identify with victims let us in on the secret universe of someone else's pain. For those of us with our own wounds—which is perhaps all of us—these accounts can feel reparative, a way to feel less alone. But empathy has its blind spots. When only certain kinds of people—the "innocent"—are allowed to claim victimhood, we're all diminished. Stories of staunch defenders are appealing for their acknowledgment of justice's flaws; they stoke our sense of outrage while offering a way to be of use, through exposing and correcting past errors. But when that sense of purpose is taken too far, it can slide into vigilantism; it can also subsume the self. Stories that ask us to identify with killers can be the most unsettling. In trying to understand the perpetrators of violence, we're put in touch with our own unacceptable urges. But when we make killers into objects of fascination—when we can't stop looking at them, even as we claim to revile them—we risk contributing to their mystique.

Sensational crime stories can have an anesthetizing effect—think of those TV binge-fests, or late nights spent tumbling down a Wikipedia rabbit hole—but we don't have to use them to turn our brains off. Instead, we can use them as opportunities to be more honest about our appetites—and curious about them, too. I want us to wonder what stories we're most hungry for, and why; to consider what forms our fears take; and to ask ourselves whose pain we still look away from.

Perhaps true crime stories are contemporary fairy tales—not the Disney versions but the dimmer, Grimm-er ones, where the parents are sometimes homicidal, where the young girls don't always make it out of the forest intact. We keep following them into the dark woods anyway. Parts of ourselves long for these shadowy places; we'll discover things there that we can't learn anywhere else.

By my final night at CrimeCon, I had amassed an enviable cache of snacks, which I spread out before me on the hotel bed. After a long day of reporting I usually craved the moment when I opened a bag of chips, flipped on the TV, and turned off my overactive brain via some trusty channel such as, well, Oxygen. But this time it seemed as though the trick had lost its magic. There they were again, on the screen, the usual characters: another victim, another detective, another defender, another killer. This time, though, their familiarity didn't feel comforting; it felt claustrophobic, like a mirrored hallway where the same faces repeated over and over into infinity. Catch one monster and another would pop up right behind him.

I slept fitfully that night, waking up periodically in between tense, tangled dreams. In the morning, I was scheduled to attend one final CrimeCon event, the mysteriously named "Sensory Experience." Intriguingly, it was the only event with an age restriction: twenty-one and up only. When I arrived at the conference room fifteen minutes early, the line to get in was already long. An assistant walked down the hallway, handing everyone a blindfold and a looped cord that I assumed was a key chain. "Actually they're wrist restraints," the assistant chirped.

Women kept pouring into the room; soon all the seats were full, and the latecomers had to stand in the wings. The presenter, whose logo (a blood-splattered magnifying glass) was on the blindfold and restraints, was a good-humored criminologist named Kimberlie Massnick. Her presentation was about a serial killer who she felt had not gotten enough attention. As a Florida sheriff's deputy in the 1970s, G. J. Schaefer had kidnapped two teenage hitchhikers; a few months after they managed to escape, he abducted and killed two others.

Massnick's tone veered between the morbid and the gossipy. "Schaefer loved pain and torture," she explained. "Like if I could get ahold of you and just *squeeze* you a little bit—that would be fun for him." His victims, she took pains to tell us, were "one hundred percent innocent." After his arrest, he claimed he'd killed as many as thirty women, but that was most likely because he wanted to rank higher on the most-prolific-killers lists. Still, Massnick had a hunch that other victims were out there. It was likely we'd never know the truth; Schaefer had been stabbed to death in prison decades ago, allegedly for being an informant.

So far none of this—even Massnick's PowerPoint presentation, with its images of bound women and the occasional jarring, horrifying phrase ("pieces of the heads were found later")—seemed particularly adults-only, at least by CrimeCon standards. But then Massnick announced that it was time for us to put on the blindfolds and bind our hands.

"I never want you to experience *real* fear," she told us. "But you learn things by feeling. You like roller coasters that go really fast. You like haunted houses. You like to feel fear. And I want you to understand what it is for somebody else. I want you to hear and feel what these women were going through." The two women seated next to me gamely helped each other into the wrist restraints, then assisted me. "We would be great torture buddies," one said. "Like, if we got kidnapped together?" Then we used our bound hands to awkwardly slip the blindfolds on.

We all settled down into an anticipatory silence. Massnick turned on some background sounds meant to evoke the swamps where Schaefer had killed his victims, a thick sound track of chirps and insectoid chittering. She explained that Schaefer had written a novel, *Killer Fiction*, in prison. It was an exceedingly graphic account of the murders he'd committed and the murders he wished he'd had a chance to commit, a muddled mix of memory and fantasy. (*Killer Fiction* was compiled and published by Schaefer's ex-girlfriend, Sondra London, who stayed friendly with him in prison until she became engaged to another serial killer, whom she was also helping write a book.) *Killer Fiction* was out of print and used copies sell for $100, but Massnick had got her hands on one. Her voice solemn, she told us that Schaefer's victims had been found blindfolded, with their hands bound above their heads. Now that we had our blindfolds on, she wanted us to hold our hands in the air as a male volunteer read Schaefer's words aloud.

What do you imagine a serial murderer thinks about? It was exactly that, a detailed, sadistic dream of degradation that just went on and on. A slow ache built in my arms. We had decided to honor the victims by amplifying that one, worst moment of their lives until the room vibrated with their terror, everyone's mirror neurons in panic mode. Now the man playing the killer was talking about how he'd rape his victims. Now he was talking about how he'd make them shit themselves. The women sitting next to me occasionally let out little gasps of horror. I did feel anxious and alone, but not in the way Massnick seemed to intend. Actually I felt angry—no, I felt *furious*—that I was being forced to listen to this man's sick fantasies. The reading went on and on, proceeding with painful slowness from humiliation to torture, from torture to murder. I couldn't stop thinking about how much it would've thrilled Schaefer to have a room of several hundred women, blindfolded and bound, listening raptly to his torture daydreams. To have his thoughts live on beyond him, inside all our heads.

My hands were still in the air, my arms burning. How long was I going to be trapped inside this terrible narrative? But I wasn't trapped; I was just pretending that I was. Then, even though the torture story wasn't over, I lowered my hands and pulled my blindfold off.

Acknowledgments

I am brimming with thanks. Many of them go to my delight of an agent, PJ Mark, and my sharp and insightful editor, Sally Howe. Thanks also to the rest of the great team at Scribner: Rosie Mahorter, Ashley Gilliam, Steven Boldt, Laura Wise, Jaya Miceli, Zoe Norvell, Kyle Kabel, Roz Lippel, Colin Harrison, and Nan Graham. Thanks to Nick Pachelli for facts, Elisa Rivlin for legal guidance, and Sasha Von Oldershausen for research.

For providing information, clarifying context, suggesting readings, and/or sparking insights, thanks to John Aes-Nihil, Jordan Bonaparte, Emma Eisenberg, Bruce Goldfarb, Jason Majick, Susan Marks, Sarah Marshall, Lily Kay Ross, and Jenifer Smith. Thanks to the archivists at the Rockefeller Archives and Harvard's Countway Library of Medicine, Jennifer Stairs and the other helpful people at the federal courthouse in Halifax, and to Jerry D. at the Maryland Medical Examiner's Office.

Thanks to everyone who took the time to share their stories with me: Kathy Bakken, Damien Echols, Lisa Fancher, Susan Fisher, Rachel Geiser, Deborah Glanville, Robin Olson, Kelly Rudiger, Lindsay Souvannarath, Sherry Spivey, Lisa Statman, Sabrina Szigeti, and Debra Tate. Thanks particularly to Lorri Davis for her warmth and generosity. Thanks to Liz Rogers and everyone at the Federal Public Defender's Office in Alpine, Texas, for their crucial work and for allowing me to lurk around. Thanks to the people who preferred not to be thanked by name.

ACKNOWLEDGMENTS

Thanks to the wonderful editors—Carrie Frye, Choire Sicha, and Evan Kindley—who shaped and improved pieces that made their way into this book in some form. And buckets of thanks to all the other editors who have helped make me a better writer over the years. Thanks to the MacDowell Colony and the Headlands Center for the Arts for the time and space and support, and thanks to the friends encountered at both spots. Thanks to all my teachers, official and un-.

Thanks to Tim, Caitlin, Ash, Laura, Logan, Colt, Elise, Yoseff, Ian, Erin, Jana, Liz, Sarah, Mary, Kate, Hesper, Cricket, and Lola. Thanks Eric.

Thanks to my parents, to my brothers, my brilliant aunts and uncles and cousins, to Herm and Rengo. Thanks to my rude cats, Musa and Ghost. Thanks to the entire town of Marfa. Thanks to everyone else who talked to me about creepy things or distracted me from thinking about creepy things, went on walks with me, or otherwise bolstered me over the past few years.

Writing a book like this could easily leave a person with very dark feelings about humanity; I'm grateful for all of you for making me feel the opposite.

Notes

ALL CRIME ALL THE TIME

1 *According to network executives*: Gina Hall, "Oxygen network wants to be breath of fresh air for millennials," *Business Journal*, May 6, 2014.

1 *When the struggling network*: Frances Berwick, "Oxygen Officially Rebranding as Crime-Focused Network," *Hollywood Reporter*, February 1, 2017.

1 *Viewership skyrocketed*: Michael Malone, "A Year In, Cold-Blooded Oxygen Rebrand Is Hot," *Broadcasting & Cable*, July 23, 2018.

1 *The vast majority of violent crimes*: US Department of Justice, Uniform Crime Reporting Program, "Crime in the United States, 2017"; United Nations Office on Drugs and Crime, "Global Study of Homicide, 2013"; Stephanie A. Scharf and Robert D. Liebenberg, "First Chairs at Trial: More Women Need Seats at the Table," American Bar Foundation, 2015.

4 *More than seven in ten students*: Dena Potter, "More women examine a career in forensic science," Associated Press, August 15, 2008.

4 *A few years ago, two undergraduates*: Marin Cogan, "The Girl Detectives," Topic. Accessed at https://www.topic.com/the-girl-detectives.

THE DETECTIVE

12 *"as sweet as a peach"*: Frances Macbeth Glessner, "Journals (1879–1921)," November 28, 1897, Glessner House Museum.

12 *"a sweet and lovely bride"*: Ibid.

14 *It will simplify*: Frances Glessner Lee, "The Nutshell Studies of Unexplained Death, Notes and comments, circa 1946," Harvard Medical School, Department of Legal Medicine Records 1877–1967 (inclusive). Francis A. Countway Library of Medicine.

15 *"It is the accuracy"*: Alice Gregory, "Little Things," *Harper's*, February 2017.

15 *To create the paper*: My description of the Nutshells here and elsewhere is indebted to Corinne May Botz, *The Nutshell Studies of Unexplained Death* (New York: Monacelli Press, 2004).

16 *"It must not be overlooked"*: Lee, "Nutshell Studies of Unexplained Death, Notes and comments."

18 *"everything in the world"*: Louise Fitzhugh, *Harriet the Spy* (New York: Delacorte, 2002), p. 24.

19 *"Pathologically private"*: Botz, *Nutshell Studies of Unexplained Death*, p. 18.

19 *"Fanny called me"*: Glessner, "Journals," March 29, 1881.

21 *"The marriage, instead of being"*: Botz, *Nutshell Studies of Unexplained Death*, p. 23.

21 *"Also, she was probably spoiled"*: Ibid.

23 *"It is certainly"*: Sally Sexton Kalmbach, *Mrs. Throne's World of Miniatures* (Chicago: Ampersand, Inc., 2014), p. 112.

25 *"a bony, muscular, masculine person"*: Chloe Owings, *Women Police* (New York: Bureau of Social Hygiene, 1925), p. 103.

25 *"do not know what guns are"*: Erika Janik, *Pistols and Petticoats: 175 Years of Lady Detectives in Fact and Fiction* (Boston: Beacon Press, 2016), p. 114.

25 *"where a woman could seek"*: Ibid., p. 118.

26 *"all the modest sex appeal"*: "The Festive Murder Trial of Jessie Costello," New England Historical Society. Accessed at www.newenglandhistori calsociety.com/festive-murder-trial-jessie-costello.

27 *"Student Magrath took off his clothes"*: "Like a Lion Resting," *Boston Globe*, December 18, 1938.

27 *"shouldn't know anything"*: "How Murderers Beat the Law," *Saturday Evening Post*, December 10, 1949.

28 *"She impressed me"*: L. C. Schilder, "Memorandum for Mr. Edwards," May 16, 1935, U.S. Federal Bureau of Investigation.

28 *"If you want coroners condemned"*: Frances Glessner Lee to Alan Moritz, December 8, 1948, Harvard Medical School, Department of Legal Medicine Records 1877–1967 (inclusive). Francis A. Countway Library of Medicine.

29 *"The system we are using"*: *Southern Pathological Conference Reports*, Novem-

ber 1933, Rockefeller Foundation records, projects, Harvard Legal Medicine, Rockefeller Archives.

30 *"no one, including alas! my own self"*: Botz, *Nutshell Studies of Unexplained Death*, p. 27.

30 *"from contact, and distances"*: Frances Glessner Lee, "Skeleton Plan for Department of Legal Medicine," Rockefeller Foundation records, projects, Harvard Legal Medicine, Rockefeller Archives.

31 *"The interior world of forensic science"*: Marilyn Stasio, "Post-Postmortem," *New York Times*, Sunday Book Review, October 21, 2007.

31 *Scarpetta's "self-aggrandizement and interminable complaints"*: Review of Patricia D. Cornwall's *Postmortem*, Publishers Weekly, https://www.publishersweekly.com/978-0-684-19141-6; Robert Merritt, "Details Dominate Gruesome Thriller Set in Richmond," *Richmond Times-Dispatch*, December 10, 1989.

33 *"It is very heartening"*: Frances Glessner Lee to Alan Gregg, March 30, 1935, Rockefeller Foundation records, projects, Harvard Legal Medicine, Rockefeller Archives.

34 *"As you know . . ."*: Alan Moritz to Frances Glessner Lee, January 9, 1943, Harvard Medical School, Department of Legal Medicine Records 1877–1967 (inclusive). Francis A. Countway Library of Medicine; Alan Moritz to Frances Glessner Lee, November 10, 1943, Harvard Medical School, Department of Legal Medicine Records 1877–1967 (inclusive). Francis A. Countway Library of Medicine.

34 *"Dr. Magrath always said . . ."*: Mary Elizabeth Power, "Policewoman Wins Honors in Field of Legal Medicine," *Wilmington Journal*, June 16, 1955, p. 43.

34 *She told friends*: Alan Gregg Diary, April 16, 1947, Rockefeller Foundation officers' diaries, Rockefeller Archives.

35 *Her "household is still in somewhat of a turmoil"*: Frances Glessner Lee letter to Alan Gregg, January 5, 1944, Harvard Medical School, Department of Legal Medicine Records 1877–1967 (inclusive). Francis A. Countway Library of Medicine.

36 *Within a few months*: Frances Glessner Lee letter to Alan Gregg, August 10, 1944, Harvard Medical School, Department of Legal Medicine Records 1877–1967 (inclusive). Francis A. Countway Library of Medicine.

37 *Her mind "worked . . ."*: Erle Stanley Gardner, *The Case of the Dubious Bridegroom* (New York: Ballantine, 1983).

37 *"I found myself constantly tempted . . ."*: Frances Glessner Lee letter to Alan Moritz, August 21, 1945, Harvard Medical School, Department of Legal Medicine Records 1877–1967 (inclusive). Francis A. Countway Library of Medicine.

38 *"I wish you could see the latest model"*: Botz, *Nutshell Studies of Unexplained Death*, p. 36.

39 *"How pleasant to hear units 15 . . ."*: Frances Glessner Lee letter to Major Woodson, March 1943, Harvard Medical School, Department of Legal Medicine Records 1877–1967 (inclusive). Francis A. Countway Library of Medicine.

39 *the* Saturday Evening Post *printed a picture*: "How Murderers Beat the Law," *Saturday Evening Post*, December 10, 1949.

40 *"Some day, innocent Americans . . ."*: George Oswald, "Grandma Knows Her Murders," *Coronet*, December 1949.

41 *Lee commanded the Ritz's manager*: Joe Harrington, "Woman, 82, Gives Ritz Dinner for 40 Policemen," *Boston Globe*, November 6, 1960, p. 51.

41 *In 1949, Lee's ally Alan Moritz*: Alan Gregg Diary, July 12, 1949, Rockefeller Foundation officers' diaries, Rockefeller Archives.

42 *Eventually the FBI*: "Memorandum to Director, Subject Frances Glessner Lee," December 21, 1950, US Federal Bureau of Investigations.

43 *It's a hard letter*: Frances Glessner Lee letter to Alan Gregg, January 31, 1951, Rockefeller Foundation records, projects, Harvard Legal Medicine, Rockefeller Archives.

43 *In Gregg's reply*: Alan Gregg letter to Frances Glessner Lee, February 13, 1951, Rockefeller Foundation records, projects, Harvard Legal Medicine, Rockefeller Archives.

43 *"It has been difficult . . . "*: Rockefeller Foundation, internal report, March 29, 1955, Rockefeller Foundation records, projects, Harvard Legal Medicine, Rockefeller Archives.

44 *"This has been a lonely . . ."*: Botz, *Nutshell Studies of Unexplained Death*, p. 22.

44 *Though her various medical issues*: "Memorandum to Director, Subject Frances Glessner Lee," September 19, 1955, US Federal Bureau of Investigation.

44 *"Perhaps FGL should have been a man"*: Botz, *Nutshell Studies of Unexplained Death*, p. 22.

46 *That women are flocking*: Marina Kamenev, "Silent Witnesses: Why do females make up most of those investigating crime using science?," *Sydney Morning Herald*, November 10, 2017; Dena Potter, "Women dominate forensic science," *Washington Times*, August 18, 2008; Melissa Beattie-Moss, "Probing Question: Do women dominate the field of forensic science?," *Penn State News*, May 7, 2013.

46 *In 2012, the* Washington Post *spoke*: Michael Alison Chandler, "Women at forefront of booming forensic science field," *Washington Post Magazine*, August 2, 2012. Accessed at https://www.washingtonpost.com /lifestyle/magazine/women-at-forefront-of-booming-forensic-science -field/2012/07/27/gJQAkASRPX_story.html.

47 *The British sociologist*: Jim Fraser, *Forensic Science: A Very Short Introduction* (New York: Oxford University Press, 2010), p. 2.

47 *That fantasy of omniscience*: Steven Millhauser, "The Fascination of the Miniature," *Harper's*, May 1984.

49 *In 2009, the National Academy of Sciences*: National Research Council, National Academy of Sciences, "Strengthening Forensic Science in the United States: A Path Forward" (Washington, DC: National Academies Press, 2009), p. 14.

50 *The lack of gatekeeping*: Ibid., p. 6.

50 *"I don't think we should suggest . . ."*: Ari Shapiro, "Congress Probes Science Behind Convictions," *All Things Considered*, National Public Radio, September 9, 2009.

56 *"The case dragged me under quickly . . ."*: Michelle McNamara, *I'll Be Gone in the Dark: One Woman's Obsessive Search for the Golden State Killer* (New York: Harper 2018), p. 5.

58 *"Since you and I have perpetrated . . ."*: Frances Glessner Lee letter to Alan Moritz, August 21, 1945, Harvard Medical School, Department of Legal Medicine Records 1877–1967 (inclusive). Francis A. Countway Library of Medicine.

NOTES

THE VICTIM

61 *The victim is every victim:* "Victims of Crime in America," President's Task Force on Victims of Violent Crime, December 1982, p. 3. Accessed at https://www.ovc.gov/publications/presdntstskforcrprt/87299.pdf.

62 *"I can't begin to explain it . . ."*: Lisa Statman, Truth on Tate-LaBianca forum post, August 24, 2012. Accessed at web.archive.org/web/20131122160129 /http://truthontatelabianca.com/threads/could-you-live-at-cielo-drive -post-murders.5018/page-2.

63 *"What's the matter?"*: Vincent Bugliosi, *Helter Skelter: The True Story of the Manson Murders* (New York: Bantam Books, 1974), p. 10.

66 People *magazine reported*: Alex Tresniowski, "Who Killed Taylor?," *People*, October 24, 2005. Accessed at https://people.com/archive/who-killed -taylor-vol-64-no-17.

66 *The* Washington Post *fretted*: "Remains Found Are Missing Va. Student's," *Washington Post*, October 7, 2005.

66 *"Young Taylor did do a few things . . ."*: Janet Pelasara, *Love You More: The Taylor Behl Story* (New York: Regan Books, 2006), p. 136.

66 *"You know, she seems very dramatic"*: "Do Taylor Behl's online writings provide clues?," *Rita Cosby Live & Direct*, MSNBC, October 4, 2005.

68 *After years of trying*: Bill Nelson, *Manson Behind the Scenes* (Santa Fe, NM: Pen Power Publications, 1997), p. 153.

70 *Not long after his visit to Cielo Drive*: Ibid., p. 154.

74 *"The first time I ever met her"*: John Aes-Nihil, author interview, 2018.

75 *Even before Statman entered their lives*: Alisa Statman, *Restless Souls: The Sharon Tate Family's Account of Stardom, the Manson Murders, and a Crusade for Justice* (New York: HarperCollins, 2012), p. 350.

77 *On August 9, 2000*: Steve Stephens, "Conspiracy Buffs Have a Way to Go to Top This One on Sharon Tate," *Columbus Dispatch*, August 21, 2000, p. B1.

81 *"It began out of our personal need"*: Bill Robinson, "Her Daughter a Murder Victim, an Ohio Mother Reaches Out to Other Grieving Parents," *People*, March 16, 1981.

82 *"Trauma isolates"*: Judith Herman, *Trauma and Recovery* (New York: Basic Books, 1992).

82 *"The body reacts to the shock"*: Robinson, "Her Daughter a Murder Victim."

83 *"It was a time of excitement"*: Marlene Young and John Stein, "The History of the Crime Victims' Movement in the United States," Office for Victims of Crime, Office of Justice Programs, US Department of Justice, December 2004.

84 *"There's an emptiness"*: "Excerpts from victim impact statements," *Boston Globe*, June 25, 2015; "Here's the Powerful Letter the Stanford Victim Read to Her Attacker," BuzzFeed News, June 3, 2016.

84 *"People are in need"*: Laura Browder, "Dystopian Romance: True Crime and the Female Reader," *Journal of Popular Culture* 39, no. 6 (2006), p. 934.

85 *Another bestseller of the era*: Gavin de Becker, *The Gift of Fear* (New York: Dell, 1998).

85 *"Doris just steamrolled into a room"*: Kelly Rudiger, author interview, 2018.

85 *"What about my family?"*: Greg King, *Sharon Tate and the Manson Murders* (New York: Open Road Media, 2016).

86 *"If Suzan LaBerge were here"*: *A Current Affair*, 1990. Accessed at https://youtu.be/g2hosmU4l8o.

86 *"One thing is certain"*: Statman, *Restless Souls*, p. 186.

87 *Like Doris, Nelson*: Bill Nelson, *Tex Watson: The Man, the Madness, the Manipulation* (Santa Fe, NM: Pen Power Publications, 1991).

88 *"If this is the year"*: Nelson, "Manson: Behind the Scenes," pp. 91, 121.

88 *Nelson visited Atkins*: Ibid., p. 152.

88 *In 1990, Doris Tate agreed*: Bill Nelson, "Doris Tate: In Her Own Words." Accessed at https://youtu.be/xSgD-4b_y1g.

90 *I read about all this online*: Robb Crocker and Caine O'Rear, "Suspect: Behl's Death an Accident," *Richmond Times-Dispatch*, October 17, 2005.

92 *This enraged Bardo*: Aubrey Malone, *Hollywood's Second Sex: The Treatment of Women in the Film Industry, 1900–1999* (Jefferson, NC: McFarland, 2015), p. 188.

92 *Bardo got her home address*: Beth Johnson, "Six years ago Rebecca Schaeffer was fatally shot," *Entertainment Weekly*, July 14, 1995.

93 *When she answered the door*: Debra A. Pinals, ed., *Stalking: Psychiatric Perspectives and Practical Approaches* (New York: Oxford University Press, 2007), p. 231.

97 *"By 1993, Lisa had discontinued"*: Nelson, "Manson: Behind the Scenes," p. 158.

98 *"Things looked different"*: Statman, *Restless Souls*, p. 266.

99 *When Proposition 8 passed*: J. Clark Kelso and Brigitte A. Bass, "The Victims' Bill of Rights: Where Did It Come From and How Much Did It Do?" *Pacific Law Journal* 23 (1992): 843–79.

100 *"Sharon was sentenced to death"*: Susan Atkins 1985 parole hearing. Accessed at https://www.youtube.com/watch?v=e_-CL9jCeMg.

100 *"We quickly grow used"*: David Garland, *The Culture of Control: Crime and Social Order in Contemporary Society* (Chicago: University of Chicago Press, 2001), p. 1.

101 *As Ronald Reagan said*: Ronald Reagan, "State of the Union," February 2, 1985. Accessed at https://www.reaganlibrary.gov/research /speeches/20685e.

102 *"You are a 50-year-old woman"*: President's Task Force, "Victims of Crime in America," p. 3.

103 *they could invoke*: Garland, *The Culture of Control*, p. 136.

103 *"This struggle between victims"*: Markus Dirk Dubber, *Victims in the War on Crime: The Use and Abuse of Victims' Rights* (New York: NYU Press, 2006), p. 3.

103 *Nationwide, a new and distinctly populist*: Garland, *The Culture of Control*, p. 13.

105 *"She was a wonderful, genuine person"*: Kelly Rudiger, author interview, 2018.

105 *But some of Patti's old friends*: Deborah Glanville, author interview, 2018; Sherry Spivey, author interview, 2018.

108 *"In 1969 my sister"*: Debra Tate, *Sharon Tate: Recollection* (Philadelphia: Running Press, 2018), p. 8.

108 *"It's difficult to describe"*: Ibid., p. 223.

109 *Reagan's Task Force report focused*: President's Task Force, "Victims of Crime in America," pp. 25, 114.

110 *Meanwhile, violent crime rates*: Michelle Alexander, *The New Jim Crow: Mass Incarceration in the Age of Colorblindness* (New York: The New Press, 2012), p. 237.

114 *"I have a message for all of you"*: John Nichols, "If Trump's Speech Sounded Familiar, That's Because Nixon Gave It First," *The Nation*, July 21, 2016. Accessed at https://www.thenation.com/article/if-trumps-speech-sounded -familiar-thats-because-nixon-gave-it-first.

115 *In* Against Empathy: Paul Bloom, *Against Empathy: The Case for Rational Compassion* (New York: HarperCollins, 2016), p. 120.

116 *"Only a very small fraction"*: Emma Eisenberg, "'I Am a Girl Now,' Sage Smith Wrote. Then She Went Missing," Splinter News, July 24, 2017.

116 *It was the week that*: Mohamed Gad-el-Hak, *Large Scale Disasters: Prediction, Control, and Mitigation* (New York: Cambridge University Press, 2008), p. 45.

116 *"It makes visible the suffering"*: Bloom, *Against Empathy*, p. 123.

THE DEFENDER

122 *"I knew from when I was real small"*: Joe Berlinger and Bruce Sinofsky, *Paradise Lost: The Child Murders at Robin Hood Hills*, HBO, 1996.

123 *On the stand*: Damien Echols trial transcript. Accessed at http://callahan .mysite.com/wm3/damien1.html.

123 *That whole week*: Damien Echols and Lorri Davis, *Yours for Eternity: A Love Story on Death Row* (New York: Penguin, 2014).

124 *"conservative as all get-out"*: Ibid.

124 *"a kite without a string"*: Ibid.

124 *She didn't choose her strangers*: Ibid.

127 *It kicked off in 1973*: Richard Beck, *We Believe the Children: A Moral Panic in the 1980s* (New York: PublicAffairs, 2015).

128 *Stratford "was part of a group"*: Lona Manning, "Oprah and Fictitious Non-fiction," *American Thinker*, January 29, 2006.

129 *"There is no longer any doubt"*: "Devil Worship: Exposing Satan's Underground," *Geraldo Rivera Show*, NBC, October 22, 1988.

129 *"Not a single state is unaffected"*: "Why the Silence?," *20/20*, ABC, January 3, 1985.

130 *"We are seeing in the streets"*: Robert D. Hicks, *In Pursuit of Satan: The Police and the Occult* (Amherst, NY: Prometheus Books, 1991), p. 42.

130 *Eight percent of Richmond*: Ibid., p. 102.

131 *"We have kids being killed"*: "Why the Silence?"

131 *Griffis agreed*: Dale Griffis, "West Memphis Three Case Information," S.M.A.R.T. Accessed at https://ritualabuse.us/ritualabuse/articles/dale -griffis-west-memphis-three-case-information.

132 *Echols, many people in the small town agreed*: Damien Echols, *Life After Death: Eighteen Years on Death Row* (New York: Atlantic Books, 2013).

133 *Damien looked the part*: Mara Leveritt, *Devil's Knot* (New York: Atria, 2002), p. 108.

133 *The satanic situation*: Ibid., p. 112.

133 *"Looks like Damien"*: Greg Day, *Untying the Knot: John Mark Byers and the West Memphis Three* (Bloomington, IN: iUniverse 2012).

133 *The next day, detectives interviewed Damien Echols*: Leveritt, *Devil's Knot*, p. 148.

134 *"We thought it was a game"*: Ibid., p. 218.

135 *They were eight years old*: Dale Griffis testimony, *Damien Echols v. Arkansas*, March 8, 1994, transcript accessed at http://callahan.mysite.com/wm3 /ebtrial/dgriffis.html.

135 *In 1995, even Geraldo*: Beck, *We Believe the Children*.

136 *The letter she finally sent*: All quotations from letters are from Echols and Davis, *Yours for Eternity*.

141 *"It's natural drama"*: Kara Bloomgarden-Smoke, "Steve Brill Hands Down His Verdict on Serial and The New Republic," *New York Observer*, March 25, 2015.

141 *Even in the channel's early years*: Jess Cagle, "Confessions of a Court TV Addict," *Entertainment Weekly*, November 12, 1993.

142 *Travelers crossing from Buffalo*: Anita Susan Brenner and B. Metson, "Paul and Karla Hit the Net," *Wired*, April 1, 1994.

143 *"As the infosphere grows"*: Ibid.

145 *Within a year*: Leveritt, *Devil's Knot*.

146 *"I think their favorite letters"*: Burk Sauls, "Frequently Asked Questions," wm3.org, updated November 17, 2003. Accessed at https://web.archive .org/web/20030411092345/http://wm3.org/framesets/helpframe.html.

148 *"Bite marks can be as unique as fingerprints"*: Brent E. Turvey, "Equivocal Examination and Psychological Profile of Case Evidence." Accessed at http://www.midsouthjustice.com/turvey2.htm.

148 *Years later, Byers admitted*: Day, *Untying the Knot*.

149 *They lingered on his various arrests*: Joe Berlinger and Bruce Sinofsky, *Paradise Lost 2: Revelations*, HBO, 2000.

150 *Sure enough, the reviews*: Day, *Untying the Knot*.

152 *Lara Bazelon, who worked*: Lara Bazelon, "What It Takes to Be a Trial Lawyer If You're Not a Man," *The Atlantic*, September 2018.

152 *When male attorneys express impatience*: Ibid.

152 *As the Stanford law professor*: Deborah L. Rhode, "The Unfinished Agenda: Women and the Legal Profession," ABA Commission on Women in the Profession, 2001. Accessed at http://womenlaw.stanford.edu/pdf/aba.unfinished.agenda.pdf.

158 *The emails that Walsh wrote*: Andy Hunsaker, "West of Memphis: The Miscarriage of Justice Explained," Mandatory, January 22, 2012. Accessed at https://www.mandatory.com/fun/181661-west-of-memphis-the-miscarriage-of-justice-explained.

158 *Walsh, whom the* New York Times *once called*: Brooks Barnes, "Middle-Earth Wizard's Not-So-Silent Partner," *New York Times*, December 2, 2012, p. AR1.

161 *While popular culture may lead people*: Joshua Marquis, "The Innocent and the Shammed," *New York Times*, January 26, 2006, p. A23.

161 *Supreme Court justice Antonin Scalia derided press coverage*: Kansas v. Marsh, 548 U.S. 163, (2006) (A. Scalia, dissenting).

163 *The new evidence was*: "No New Trial in West Memphis Killings, Judge Rules," *Arkansas Democrat Gazette*, September 10, 2008.

164 *May I be home, free from prison*: Damien Echols, *High Magick: A Guide to the Spiritual Practices That Saved My Life on Death Row* (Louisville, CO: Sounds True, 2018), p. 2.

165 *"Counsel, what harm is there"*: Joe Berlinger and Bruce Sinofsky, *Paradise Lost 3: Purgatory*, HBO, 2011.

THE KILLER

173ff. All quotes from conversations between Lindsay Souvannarath and James Gamble were taken from their Facebook chat logs, which were entered into evidence as part of Lindsay's sentencing.

174 *"A perfectly straight being"*: Ayn Rand, *The Journals of Ayn Rand*, edited by David Harriman, Kindle edition (New York: NAL, 1999).

174 *The young writer had recently immigrated*: Anne C. Heller, *Ayn Rand and the World She Made* (New York: Anchor, 2010).

175 *"grim and remote"*: Ibid., p. 67.

175 *"an intruder with all the world laughing"*: Ibid., p. 63.

175 *She decided that the main character*: Rand, *Journals of Ayn Rand*.

177 *"We all loved each other very much"*: "The Story of Lindsay Souvannarath: Life Before Choosing Death," *The Night Time Podcast*, February 10, 2019. Accessed at https://www.nighttimepodcast.com/episodes/lindsay-sou vannarath-2.

179 *"human in form, beast in spirit"*: "The Creepy Pasta Fandom," Kiwi Farms post 230, November 8, 2014. Accessed at https://kiwifarms.net/threads /the-creepypasta-fandom.5635/page-12#post-397366.

179 *"She was definitely on the 'fringe'"*: "Lindsay Kantha Souvannarath / Heretics on Holiday / Failed Halifax Mass Shooter," Kiwi Farms post 331, February 15, 2015. Accessed at https://kiwifarms.net/threads/lind say-kantha-souvannarath-heretics-on-holiday.7744/page-16.

180 *Growing up in white neighborhoods*: "The Story of Lindsay Souvannarath: Life Before Choosing Death," *The Night Time Podcast*, February 10, 2019.

180 *She wrote a funny little flash-fiction story*: Lindsay Souvannarath, "My Pet Skeleton," *Coe Review* 43 (2013).

182 *"a brilliant, unusual, exceptional boy"*: Rand, *Journals of Ayn Rand*.

184 *"There is a lot that is purposelessly, senselessly horrible"*: Ibid.

184 *"the fact that he looks like"*: Ibid.

185 *"to take the damn thing out of print"*: Stephen Spignesi, *Stephen King, American Master: A Creepy Corpus of Facts About Stephen King & His Work* (Brentwood, TN: Permuted Press, 2018).

185 *"Every day news broadcasts stories"*: Dave Cullen, *Columbine* (New York: Grand Central Publishing, 2009), p. 199.

186 *"People will die because of me"*: Ibid., p. 337.

187 *On 20/20 the day after the attack*: Ibid., p. 156.

188 *On his website, he tracked*: Jeff Kass, *Columbine: A True Crime Story* (Golden, CO: Conundrum Press, 2014).

188 *"my killing spree against anyone I want"*: Cullen, *Columbine*, p. 198.

189 *"God I can't wait till they die"*: Ibid., p. 257.

192 *By 2011, the Columbine community on YouTube*: Nathalie Paton, "Media Participation of School Shooters and Their Fans: Navigating Between Self-Distinction and Imitation to Achieve Individuation," *Studies in Media and Communication* 7 (2012), pp. 205–234.

194 *One meme I saw*: Reb-thejuvey, Tumblr post. Accessed at https://reb-the juvey.tumblr.com/post/182148620485/cool-ranch-humans-dylan-col umbiners-crying-at.

195 *"the psychosis of adolescence"*: Chris Kraus, *I Love Dick* (Cambridge, MA: MIT Press, 2016), p. 65.

195 *"A Beatle who ventures out unguarded"*: Timothy Green, "They Crown Their Country with a Bowl-Shaped Hairdo," *Life*, January 31, 1964, p. 30.

199 *"For girls, fandom offered"*: Barbara Ehrenreich, Elizabeth Hess, and Gloria Jacobs, *Re-Making Love: The Feminization of Sex* (New York: Anchor, 1986), p. 32.

200 *David Schmid argues*: David Schmid, *Natural Born Celebrities: Serial Killers in American Culture* (Chicago: University of Chicago, 2006), p. 15.

201 *Jesse Osborne, an eighth grader*: John Woodrow Cox, "Inside an accused school shooter's mind: A plot to kill '50 or 60. If I get lucky maybe 150,'" *Washington Post*, March 3, 2018.

202 *"I felt like I wasn't taken seriously"*: Rob Low, "Evidence released in deadly school plot," KVDR Online, August 11, 2017. Accessed at https://kdvr .com/2017/08/11/evidence-released-in-deadly-school-plot.

202 *"The problem is not that there is an endless supply"*: Malcolm Gladwell, "Thresholds of Violence," *New Yorker*, October 19, 2015.

204 *"beta ubermensch"*: "Alexander 'Slavros' Mukhitdinov/Iron March/Iron march.org," Kiwi Farms post 13, February 15, 2015. Accessed at https:// kiwifarms.net/threads/alexander-slavros-mukhitdinov-iron-march-iron march-org.7747.

204 *"Most of what is posted"*: "Alexander 'Slavros' Mukhitdinov/Iron March /Ironmarch.org," Kiwi Farms post 110, December 18, 2015. Accessed at https://kiwifarms.net/threads/alexander-slavros-mukhitdinov-iron -march-ironmarch-org.7747/page-6#post-1155637.

205 *"Predictably, things ended badly"*: Michael Edison Hayden, "Visions of Chaos: Weighing the Violent Legacy of Iron March," *Hatewatch*, Southern Poverty Law Center, February 15, 2019.

205 *"memeing and pranking"*: "Alexander 'Slavros' Mukhitdinov/Iron March /Ironmarch.org," Kiwi Farms post 158, June 2, 2017. Accessed at https:// kiwifarms.net/threads/alexander-slavros-mukhitdinov-iron-march-iron march-org.7747/page-8#post-2314639.

205 *"The image as shock"*: Susan Sontag, *Regarding the Pain of Others* (New York: Picador 2004), p. 23.

206 *"gentle giants and elves"*: Brett Bundale, "High School friend says Halifax mall plotter had a 'creepy' interest in Nazism," CBC, April 16, 2018. Accessed at https://www.cbc.ca/news/canada/nova-scotia/halifax-mall -plot-valentines-day-shooting-shopping-centre-court-1.4621122.

213 *"I'm leaving for Canada tomorrow"*: R. v. Souvannarath, 2018, NSSC 96. Accessed at https://www.dailyherald.com/assets/PDF/R.%20v.%20 Souvannarath%20-%20Nova%20Scotia%20Courts.pdf.

214 *"the isolated man sees the world"*: Ibid.

214 *"I don't know what I am james"*: R. v. Gamble, 2016, NSSC 329.

214 *Randy also made a video*: Ibid.

215 *Early that evening, James's parents*: Kayla Hounsell, "Mother of teen behind mall plot speaks out about dangers of online underworld," CTV News Atlantic, March 13, 2017. Accessed at https://atlantic.ctvnews.ca /mother-of-teen-behind-mall-plot-speaks-out-about-dangers-of-online -underworld-1.3323049.

216 *"What had I really done"*: "The Story of Lindsay Souvannarath: Lindsay, James, and the Valentine's Day Massacre," *The Night Time Podcast*, February 19, 2019. Accessed at https://www.nighttimepodcast.com/episodes /lindsay-souvannarath-3.

216 *"I had a skull mask"*: R. v. Souvannarath, 2018, NSSC 96. Accessed at https:// www.dailyherald.com/assets/PDF/R.%20v.%20Souvannarath%20-%20 Nova%20Scotia%20Courts.pdf.

217 *"imagine if there was an afterlife"*: Inannibal, Tumblr post, February 15, 2015. Accessed at http://lnannibal.tumblr.com/post/111054559945.

219 *"Imaginary evil is romantic and varied"*: Simone Weil, *Gravity and Grace* (Abingdon-on-Thames: Routledge Classics, 2002), p. 70.

223 *"Mean world syndrome"*: George Gerbner, Larry Gross, Michael Morgan, and Nancy Signorielli, "The 'Mainstreaming' of America: Violence Profile No. 11," *Journal of Communication* 3 (1980), pp. 10–29.

224 *"If it's nothing, I'm sorry"*: Niraj Chokshi, "Native American Brothers Pulled From Campus Tour After Nervous Parent Calls Police," *New York Times*, May 5, 2018.

224 *"There are no safe zones"*: Layne Consultants International, accessed at www.layneconsultants.com/school-security.

225 *"There is something disconcerting"*: Lara Sorokanich, "What Littleton Learned," *Popular Mechanics*, August 1, 2018.

226 "At least one hundred forty-three students": John Woodrow Cox, Steven Rich, Allyson Chiu, John Muyskens, and Monica Ulmanu, "School Shooting Database," *Washington Post*, updated December 19, 2018. Accessed at https://www.washingtonpost.com/graphics/2018/local/school-shootings-database/?utm_term=.bfadacd6440b.

228 *"emotionally immature"*: R. v. Souvannarath, 2018, NSSC 96. Accessed at https://www.dailyherald.com/assets/PDF/R.%20v.%20Souvannarath%20-%20Nova%20Scotia%20Courts.pdf.

230 *"The glorification of mass murders"*: "Our Community Guidelines Are Changing," Tumblr, August 27, 2018. Accessed at https://staff.tumblr.com/post/177449083750/new-community-guidelines.

Bibliography

Alexander, Michelle. *The New Jim Crow: Mass Incarceration in the Age of Color-blindness.* New York: The New Press, 2012.

Balko, Radley, and Tucker Carrington. *The Cadaver King and the Country Dentist: A True Story of Injustice in the American South.* New York: PublicAffairs, 2018.

Bazelon, Lara. "What It Takes to Be a Trial Lawyer If You're Not a Man." *The Atlantic*, September 2018.

Berlinger, Joe, and Bruce Sinofsky. *Paradise Lost: The Child Murders at Robin Hood Hills.* HBO, 1996

———. *Paradise Lost 2: Revelations.* HBO, 2000.

———. *Paradise Lost 3: Purgatory.* HBO, 2011.

Birkland, Thomas A., and Regina Lawrence. "Media Framing and Policy Change After Columbine." *American Behavioral Scientist* 52 (2009).

Bloom, Paul. *Against Empathy: The Case for Rational Compassion.* New York: HarperCollins, 2016.

Botz, Corinne May. *The Nutshell Studies of Unexplained Death.* New York: The Monacelli Press, 2004.

Browder, Laura. "Dystopian Romance: True Crime and the Female Reader." *Journal of Popular Culture* 39, no. 6 (2006).

Bugliosi, Vincent. *Helter Skelter: The True Story of the Manson Murders.* New York: Bantam Books, 1974, p. 10.

Byers, Michele, and Val Marie Johnson, eds. *The CSI Effect: Television, Crime, and Governance.* Lanham, MD: Lexington Books, 2009.

Cornwell, Patricia. *Postmortem.* New York: Scribner, 2009.

Cullen, Dave. *Columbine.* New York: Grand Central Publishing, 2009, p. 199.

Day, Greg. *Untying the Knot: John Mark Byers and the West Memphis Three.* Bloomington, IN: iUniverse 2012.

Downing, Lisa. *The Subject of Murder: Gender, Exceptionality, and the Modern Killer.* Chicago: University of Chicago Press, 2013.

Dubber, Markus Dirk. *Victims in the War on Crime: The Use and Abuse of Victims' Rights.* New York: NYU Press, 2006.

Echols, Damien. *High Magick: A Guide to the Spiritual Practices That Saved My Life on Death Row.* Louisville, CO: Sounds True, 2018.

———. *Life After Death: Eighteen Years on Death Row.* New York: Atlantic Books, 2013.

Echols, Damien, and Lorri Davis. *Yours for Eternity: A Love Story on Death Row.* New York: Penguin, 2014.

Eisenberg, Emma. "'I Am a Girl Now,' Sage Smith Wrote. Then She Went Missing." Splinter News, July 24, 2017.

Erez, Edna. "Communication in Sentencing: Exploring the Expressive Function of Victim Impact Statements." *International Review of Victimology* 10 (2004), pp. 223–44.

Fitzhugh, Louise. *Harriet the Spy.* New York: Delacorte, 2002.

Garland, David. *The Culture of Control: Crime and Social Order in Contemporary Society.* Chicago: University of Chicago Press, 2001.

Gladwell, Malcolm. "Thresholds of Violence." *New Yorker,* October 19, 2015.

Hayden, Michael Edison. "Visions of Chaos: Weighing the Violent Legacy of Iron March." Hatewatch, Southern Poverty Law Center, February 15, 2019.

Heller, Anne C. *Ayn Rand and the World She Made.* New York: Anchor Books, 2010.

Herman, Judith. *Trauma and Recovery.* New York: Basic Books, 1992.

Hicks, Robert D. *In Pursuit of Satan: The Police and the Occult.* Amherst, NY: Prometheus Books, 1991.

Janik, Erika. *Pistols and Petticoats: 175 Years of Lady Detectives in Fact and Fiction.* Boston: Beacon Press, 2016.

Jentzen, Jeffrey M. *Death Investigation in America.* Cambridge: Harvard University Press, 2009.

Kalmbach, Sally Sexton. *Mrs. Throne's World of Miniatures.* Chicago: Ampersand, Inc., 2014.

Larkin, Ralph. *Comprehending Columbine.* Philadelphia: Temple University Press, 2007.

Leveritt, Mara. *Devil's Knot.* New York: Atria, 2002.

Nelson, Bill. *Manson Behind the Scenes*. Santa Fe, NM: Pen Power Publications, 1997.

——. *Tex Watson: The Man, The Madness, The Manipulation*. Santa Fe, NM: Pen Power Publications, 1991.

Nelson, Maggie. *The Art of Cruelty: A Reckoning*. New York: W.W. Norton & Company, 2012.

——. *The Red Parts: Autobiography of a Trial*. Minneapolis, MN: Graywolf Press, 2016.

Paton, Nathalie. "Media Participation of School Shooters and Their Fans: Navigating Between Self-Distinction and Imitation to Achieve Individuation." *Studies in Media and Communication* 7 (2012), pp. 205–234.

Pelasara, Janet. *Love You More: The Taylor Behl Story*. New York: Regan Books, 2006.

Rand, Ayn. *The Journals of Ayn Rand*, edited by David Harriman, Kindle ed. New York: NAL, 1999.

Robinson, Bill. "Her Daughter a Murder Victim, an Ohio Mother Reaches Out to Other Grieving Parents." *People*, March 16, 1981.

Smith, Michelle, and Lawrence Pazder, M.D. *Michelle Remembers*. New York: Pocket Books, 1980.

Sontag, Susan. *Regarding the Pain of Others*. New York: Picador, 2004.

Statman, Alisa. *Restless Souls: The Sharon Tate Family's Account of Stardom, the Manson Murders, and a Crusade for Justice*. New York: HarperCollins, 2012.

Tate, Debra. *Sharon Tate: Recollection*. Philadelphia: Running Press, 2018.

Van Dijk, Jan. "Free the Victim: A Critique of the Western Conception of Victimhood." *International Review of Victimology* 16 (2009), pp. 1–33.

"Victims of Crime in America." President's Task Force on Victims of Violent Crime, December 1982.

Young, Marlene, and John Stein. "The History of the Crime Victims' Movement in the United States." Office for Victims of Crime, Office of Justice Programs, US Department of Justice, December 2004.

An Interview with Rachel Monroe

The Women
with an
Appetite for Murder

In *Savage Appetites*, journalist Rachel Monroe delves into four very different women and their obsession with true crime.

Rachel Monroe has spent a great deal of time carefully considering aspects of American culture most would prefer to forget. In particular, she's focused a lot on murder.

In *Savage Appetites*, the Marfa, Texas–based journalist writes an exacting study of four different women and their unique relationships to crime: an early pioneer of forensic science from the 1940s, a Beverly Hills woman who enmeshes herself in Manson lore, a selfless advocate for a man wrongfully convicted of murder, and a Columbine-obsessed twentysomething who plots a mass shooting via Tumblr. It's equal parts engrossing and disturbing.

As Monroe delves into the dark world of true crime, her investigations include not only the people incorporated into the narratives but also the people who consume them. Accordingly, she examines herself, looking at her own predilection for a culturally ascendant genre comprising a unique set of myths and suppositions.

Andru Okun: You start your book writing about American women being enthralled by murder-related media, but you also point out how this fascination coincides with the U.S. murder rate nearing historic lows. What do you make of these contrasting realities?

Rachel Monroe: I think it speaks to how the stories, particularly those that are categorized as "true crime," have an element of fantasy or unreality. They almost feel like fables in some way in that they purport to be telling us about the world, but they're telling us more about our fears and our dreams. The fact that people who are statistically at a very low risk of being murdered are fascinated by murder is actually not that surprising to me. I was just reading a book about the Weimar Republic. During a period when crime rates were dropping around World War I, there was also this culture that was really obsessed with crime. There were obviously reasons that people might have felt that their world was spinning out of control or heading in a frightening direction, but when there's something else that you're afraid of—something that's more ineffable or huge and structural—then maybe crime stories reinforce that feeling of anxiety but with a narrower target.

AO: Why do you think so many women are fans of the true crime genre?

RM: I think there's a lot of aspects to it. That's why I wrote this book with four different sections, because every time I start to try and theorize about why, I feel a little stuck. There are so many reasons why somebody might find these stories fascinating. I think that women have a complex relationship with their own vulnerability, and the culture is obviously preoccupied with female vulnerability, particularly white female vulnerability. Not everybody gets to be vulnerable in the same way. I think growing up in a culture that's informing you about how at risk you are, about the dangerous things that can happen to you, you develop a really complicated relationship to those stories.

AO: Your book addresses how popular accounts of murder tend to exclude and ignore marginalized communities. What do you think is the cumulative effect of these more common narratives?

RM: I've been asking people what percentage of all U.S. murders they think are committed with a male perpetrator and a female victim. Seventy or 80 percent is the standard guess, but it's really 25 percent. Male violence against women is obviously a huge problem that needs to be addressed, but in fixating on these particular story lines, what others are we leaving out? Native women have the highest rate of sexual victimization, but you never hear about it. Thinking about watching Oxygen or going to CrimeCon, those stories are not the ones that get to be emblematic of true crime. I've been wondering about what gets to fit into the genre, and what gets excluded, and whether it has to do with the fact that stories about black people, brown people, or Native people are coded as political. True crime is something else—it's about psychodrama and relationships, and it's not political. Which is of course ridiculous. Everything's political, and these stories are *particularly* political because they're mobilized and politicized. But when someone says "a victim of crime," cultural conditioning would have it that the image that pops up in your mind would be a white woman, which is statistically not representative at all.

AO: This fits in with what you write about regarding the politics of empathy: "Pain that looks more like our own pain is easier to imagine as real."

RM: Totally. With the Quentin Tarantino movie [*Once Upon a Time in Hollywood*] coming out, I've been thinking a lot about Debra Tate and the conversation I had with her. To me, she was such a fascinating example of this. She was of course Sharon Tate's sister, and she's become an advocate of victims' rights and the way that she talks about crime and criminals... she's a charming lady, but we disagree on a lot of things politically. The way that she talks about crime is very hard-ass, lock-'em-up. For her, if people break the law they should be punished for it. But as soon as I started asking her about someone she knew, Roman Polanski, who broke the law and raped a young girl, there was all this nuance and there were excuses. "Oh, he didn't know," or, "Oh, this was fine in France," or, "The judge was crazy." It was such a stark contrast to me, how when we think of a criminal as an "other," we're willing to take all these extreme measures. When we flip that narrative and realize any of us could be in that position of victim or victimizer, we think about it in such a different way.

AO: Debra Tate was someone I was hoping to hear you talk more about. You write about being Manson obsessed at an early age, finding a copy of *Helter Skelter* on your parents' bookshelf. So you grow up, become a writer, and find yourself meeting up with Sharon Tate's sister for coffee. What was that like?

RM: That was a really fascinating and complicated moment. I had spent so much time, not just in this book but elsewhere, thinking about people who were obsessed with Manson. That's a world that I found really interesting. The Manson murders were such a huge cultural story that defined the way that people think about the era. In some ways I think that I too have come to think about the Manson murders in a slightly abstracted way, thinking about what they symbolize and how they function culturally. Then to actually talk to this person who was a teenager when her sister was murdered, and how that shaped the rest of her life . . . so much of the book is about people who identify with murders that didn't happen to them, but she was someone who was directly impacted. It was good to bring me up short and think of all these people who feel entitled to these stories in a way, to think of what impact that has on the people who actually lived through them. She was a really interesting lady.

AO: How so?

RM: I read a lot about her mom, Doris, who died a couple of decades ago, and was this famously fiery force. She had a great steely drawl and could boss around politicians. She was a badass, but also a badass who helped pass some laws that I feel uncomfortable with. You can see a lot of that in Debra—she has this kind of brassy, no-nonsense demeanor. Her life has been wild, she was still dealing with these health effects from when she was a mail carrier and there was a mad bomber at large. And she had some story about a horse that Ronald Reagan had given her that was stolen. She was just full of these wild stories and was super frank. I appreciated that I could tell her that I disagreed with her.

AO: I identified with the way you describe mass incarceration in America as a "bleak normality." I'm thirty-two. I think you have a few years on me?

RM: Yeah, I'm thirty-six.

AO: So we're both of this generation that's grown up in a world where prisons are part of the status quo, but the substitution of punishment for reform and rehabilitation is relatively new. How would you say that the victims' rights movement impacted criminal law and incarceration in the United States?

RM: The victims' rights movement has a fascinating history, arising out of the feminist movement in the '70s. It started out doing these really amazing things that needed to happen, like educating police officers about sexual assault and creating rape crisis centers. But then around the '80s it took this hard turn, as much of the country was doing, and it became all about being "tough on crime." These rare stories of the white woman victimized by a stranger were mobilized, used as something like a cover story that people could hold up when they say that they're afraid. These stories became the impetus for all of these scary, rigid, punitive laws that we're still dealing with now: three strike laws, parole denial, minimizing the use of the juvenile justice system. All of these things have led to mass incarceration, done on behalf of victims, even though victims as a group are obviously a wide and diverse one and what victims might want out of the justice system or what they think justice might look like is not one thing. But the "victim" as a political archetype became this wounded white woman who needed protection at all costs.

AO: Columbine is a long-standing fascination of yours. It's included in this book, and you've written about it previously. You once almost visited the school, only to be overwhelmed by an impulse to turn around instead. Can you talk about that?

RM: I think anybody that is interested in these crime stories, if they're self-aware at all, will run into these moments that edge up against a kind of voyeurism or exploitation, something that just feels unsavory. I didn't want to just shut it down, to say this is good and this bad. There's a policing of women's appetites that happens a lot. When things are deemed problematic, that seems like a good reason to look at them more closely, not necessarily as an endorsement but just to understand them rather than close it off to further inquiries. But it's hard and it shifts. When are you honoring something and when are you feeding off it? I've gone through phases where I was really fascinated and horrified by Columbine and I read a lot about it, similar to a lot of these girls on Tumblr, people who call themselves "researchers" because they don't want to identify as fans. It frames it as intellectual, but in practice it does look a lot like fandom. When I was visiting family in Denver I saw the highway exit and I thought, "I'll just go look at it." Thank god for all the traffic that slowed me down enough to ask myself, "What am I really doing here? What am I looking to get out of this? Am I trying to provoke a feeling in myself?" That just didn't seem like a good enough reason to turn somebody else's tragedy into a tourist stop.

AO: There's an interesting thread in your writing related to the Internet and crime—the discussion ranges from amateur sleuths in the dial-up days to serial-killer-obsessed teens on Tumblr. How important do you think the Internet is to the cultural obsession with crime?

RM: It's so important. I mean, I don't think it's necessary—people have been fascinated by crime and crime stories as long as there has been media, and probably even before that. But it is striking that the woman that I wrote about who came into this world before the Internet, Frances Glessner Lee, making her dollhouses in the '40s, she was wealthy enough that she could subscribe to all these journals and collect all these old books. She was influential enough that she could schmooze with the big players in early forensic science. Now the Internet allows more access to information, so it democratizes things and people can find what they want. And I think often what people want in these obsessive communities is primary source information. They sense that the official story from the newspaper, the prosecutor, or the police is incomplete. The internet allows you to access full documents directly, and that can really lead people to go deep with these stories. And it creates communities, that's the other thing that's interesting. A lot of these worlds are social worlds.

AO: Why do you think this online community of "Columbiners" is mostly teenage girls?

RM: That community has shifted so much and it's so hard to talk about what young people do on the internet because as soon as you look at it it has shifted and changed. When I first wrote about the Columbiners in 2012, it did seem to me that it was young girls, teens and tweens on Tumblr, overwhelmingly female. I sort of built up an idea in my head of what they were doing based on that. In the way that a lot of teen girls use their crushes to say something about themselves, a crush on a famous violent misfit is maybe telling us something, expressing feelings without owning it. But when I first heard about Lindsay [Souvannarath] and I'd heard that members of the Columbiner community had actually planned a shooting, it really did give me pause and made me want to go back to that community and question whether it was as harmless as I originally thought. I think in the vast majority of cases it really was, but Columbine fandom has a complex history. Before it was on Tumblr it was a big YouTube thing, and that was mostly boys who identified with the shooters rather than girls who wanted to love them. Checking back in with Tumblr, I realized that this world had shifted a little bit and that with some of these people there was more of an adulation of violence and proximity to Nazi imagery and racialized violence. There's a lot of different strains in that community that ebb and flow and it's become a very elastic myth that people apply in different ways.

AO: You write that television programs about violence can be soothing. Why?

RM: The one that gets talked about a lot is *Law & Order: SVU*. There's also the more formulaic crime programming on Investigation Discovery. A lot of people will leave that on all night. There's something about fear being stoked, but in this familiar shape with familiar characters. If you listen to the podcast "Running from *COPS*," it makes it really clear how some of the police officers in that show are acting how they've seen other police officers they've seen on TV act. It's this feedback loop the producers are helping achieve. I think the television programs are soothing when they fit into a known category and the beats are familiar. It's a contained fear.

AO: Would you say it also validates some of the overblown fears people might have?

RM: Yes, exactly. It gives them a face and a shape, validating what you already thought that you feared.